iPod

10th Edition

the missing manual®

The book that should have been in the box

J.D. Biersdorfer
with David Pogue

O'REILLY®

Beijing | Cambridge | Farnham | Köln | Sebastopol | Tokyo

iPod: The Missing Manual, Tenth Edition

BY J.D. Biersdorfer with David Pogue

Copyright © 2012 J.D. Biersdorfer. All rights reserved.
Printed in Canada.

Published by O'Reilly Media, Inc., 1005 Gravenstein Highway North, Sebastopol, CA 95472.

O'Reilly books may be purchased for educational, business, or sales promotional use. Online editions are also available for most titles (safari.oreilly.com). For more information, contact our corporate/institutional sales department: 800.998.9938 or corporate@oreilly.com.

Senior Editor: Brian Sawyer
Editor: Peter McKie
Production Editor: Kristen Borg
Copyeditor: Marcia Simmons
Illustrations: Rob Romano, Lesley Keegan, Nellie McKesson, and J.D. Biersdorfer
Indexer: Julie Hawks
Cover Designers: Randy Comer and Karen Montgomery
Interior Designer: Ron Bilodeau and J.D. Biersdorfer

Print History:
October 2010: Ninth Edition.
December 2011: Tenth Edition.

ISBN: 978-1-449-31285-5
[TI]

Contents

CHAPTER **3**

Touring the Touch **51**

CHAPTER **8**

It's Showtime: Video on the iPod **185**

CHAPTER **9**

Picture Your Photos On the iPod **199**

CHAPTER **10**

The iPod as Personal Assistant **215**

CHAPTER **11**

Surf the Web and More with the iPod Touch **233**

The Missing Credits

About the Authors

J.D. Biersdorfer (author) is the author of several O'Reilly books, including *iPad 2: The Missing Manual*, *Best iPhone Apps, Second Edition*, and *Netbooks: The Missing Manual*. She's been writing the weekly computer Q&A column for the *New York Times* since 1998 and has covered everything from 17th-century Indian art to the world of female hackers for the newspaper. She's also written articles for the *AIGA Journal of Graphic Design*, *Budget Travel*, the *New York Times Book Review*, and *Rolling Stone*. She studied in the Theater & Drama program at Indiana University and now spends her limited spare moments playing the banjo badly, drinking copious amounts of tea, and watching *BBC World News*. Email: *jd.biersdorfer@gmail.com*.

David Pogue (co-author) is the weekly tech columnist for the *New York Times*, an Emmy-winning correspondent for *CBS News Sunday Morning*, a weekly CNBC contributor, and the creator of the Missing Manual series. He's the author or co-author of more than 50 books, including 25 in this series, six in the *For Dummies* line (including *Macs*, *Magic*, *Opera*, and *Classical Music*), two novels, and *The World According to Twitter*. In his other life, David is a former Broadway show conductor, a piano player, and a magician. He lives in Connecticut with his three awesome children.

Links to his columns and weekly videos await at *www.davidpogue.com*. He welcomes feedback about his books by email at *david@pogueman.com*.

About the Creative Team

Peter McKie (editor) lives in New York City, where he traces the history of old buildings. He has a master's degree in journalism from Boston University. Email: *pmckie@oreilly.com*.

Kristen Borg (production editor) is a graduate of the publishing program at Emerson College. Now living in Boston, she originally hails from Arizona and considers New England winters a fair trade for no longer finding scorpions in her hairdryer. Email: *kristen@oreilly.com*.

Acknowledgements

I would like to thank David Pogue for suggesting this book to me way back in 2002, and for being a terrific editor through the mad scramble of the first two editions. Also thanks to editors Peter Meyers and Peter McKie for guiding me through the past eight updates. Thanks to Kristen Borg, Lesley Keegan, Ron Bilodeau, Rob Romano, Karen Ippoliti, Monica Kamsvaag, Sara Peyton, Betsy Waliszewski, Laurie Petrycki, and all the folks at O'Reilly. Thanks to Apple for courteously providing the iPod images and to the assorted iPod accessory companies who made their photos available. Thanks also to Hans White of the band Nacho Business for letting us use his album art on the cover.

I'd also to thank all my friends and family (especially and most importantly, Betsy Book) for putting up with me every year when Apple announces new iPods and I disappear into my computer for several weeks, muttering incoherently and cranking up the show tunes and bluegrass playlists to a hearty volume.

The Missing Manual Series

Missing Manuals are witty, superbly written guides to computer products that don't come with printed manuals (which is just about all of them). Each book features a handcrafted index and cross-references to specific pages (not just chapters). Recent and upcoming titles include:

Access 2010: The Missing Manual by Matthew MacDonald

CSS: The Missing Manual, Second Edition, by David Sawyer McFarland

Creating a Website: The Missing Manual, Third Edition, by Matthew MacDonald

David Pogue's Digital Photography: The Missing Manual by David Pogue

Dreamweaver CS5.5: The Missing Manual by David Sawyer McFarland

Droid 2: The Missing Manual by Preston Gralla

Droid X2: The Missing Manual by Preston Gralla

Excel 2010: The Missing Manual by Matthew MacDonald

FileMaker Pro 11: The Missing Manual by Susan Prosser and Stuart Gripman

Flash CS5.5: The Missing Manual by Chris Grover

Galaxy S II: The Missing Manual by Preston Gralla

Galaxy Tab: The Missing Manual by Preston Gralla

Google+: The Missing Manual by Kevin Purdy

Google Apps: The Missing Manual by Nancy Conner

Google SketchUp: The Missing Manual by Chris Grover

HTML5: The Missing Manual by Matthew MacDonald

iMovie '11 & iDVD: The Missing Manual by David Pogue and Aaron Miller

iPad 2: The Missing Manual, Third Edition by J.D. Biersdorfer

iPhone: The Missing Manual, Fifth Edition by David Pogue

iPhoto '11: The Missing Manual by David Pogue and Lesa Snider

JavaScript & jQuery: The Missing Manual, Second Edition by David Sawyer McFarland

Kindle Fire: The Missing Manual by Peter Meyers

Mac OS X Lion: The Missing Manual by David Pogue

Mac OS X Snow Leopard: The Missing Manual by David Pogue

Microsoft Project 2010: The Missing Manual by Bonnie Biafore

Motorola Xoom: The Missing Manual by Preston Gralla

NOOK Tablet: The Missing Manual by Preston Gralla

Office 2010: The Missing Manual by Nancy Connor, Chris Grover, and Matthew MacDonald

Office 2011 for Macintosh: The Missing Manual by Chris Grover

Personal Investing: The Missing Manual by Bonnie Biafore

Photoshop CS5: The Missing Manual by Lesa Snider

Photoshop Elements 10: The Missing Manual by Barbara Brundage

PHP & MySQL: The Missing Manual by Brett McLaughlin

QuickBooks 2012: The Missing Manual by Bonnie Biafore

Switching to the Mac: The Missing Manual, Lion Edition by David Pogue

Windows 7: The Missing Manual by David Pogue

For a full list of all Missing Manuals in print, go to *www.missingmanuals.com/library.html*.

Introduction

WHAT A DIFFERENCE A decade makes. When Apple introduced the very first iPod back in October 2001, it was a bulky chunk of white plastic, chrome, and glass that held a mere 5 gigabytes of music. But its concept was simple and enticing: you could carry 1,000 songs around in your pocket. And people did.

Fast-forward 10 years, and the iPod line has blossomed into a quartet of very different models: the Internet-friendly Touch; the fitness-minded Nano; the tiny, no-fuss Shuffle; and the versatile, old-school Classic. From that original ur-Pod, Apple has created a family of iPods with something for just about everybody—as long as you know what features they offer and where to find them.

That's where this book comes in. *iPod: The Missing Manual* shows you how to use all the impressive capabilities of the Touch, Nano, Shuffle, and Classic in one convenient volume.

Like that original 2001 model, all of today's iPods play music. But most of the gadgets in the line have evolved to become full-fledged *media* players, too. The Touch, Nano, and Classic all show off your photos. The Touch and the Classic let you watch Hollywood movies. The Nano offers an FM radio and a pedometer. The Shuffle, which doubles as a very entertaining lapel pin, can talk back to you with the push of a button. And the Touch, the most popular of all iPods, shoots video, surfs the Web, and can run half a million practical little mini-programs called apps, making it a real pocket computer.

Along with this guide to your device, you'll get a detailed look at iTunes, Apple's desktop media manager for all iPods, and learn about the Touch's new iOS 5 system software and iCloud syncing service.

As the iPod line moves into its second decade, some things hold true: You can still create your own inner world of music and have it right there in your pocket. But on the iPods of 2011 and beyond, you can now fit a big part of the *outside* world in your pocket, too. Like most 10-year-olds, the iPod keeps on growing.

How to Use This Book

THE TINY PAMPHLET THAT Apple includes with each iPod is enough to get your player up and running, charged, and ready to download music.

But if you want to know more about how your iPod works, all the great things it can do, and where to find its secret features, the official pamphlet is skimpy in the extreme. And the iTunes help files that you have to read on your computer aren't much better: You can't mark your place, there aren't any pictures or jokes, and, quite frankly, help files are a little dull. This book gives you more iPod info than that wee brochure, is available in both eBook and treeware editions, *and* it has lots of nice color pictures.

ABOUT→THESE→ARROWS

Throughout this book, and throughout the Missing Manual series, you'll find sentences like this: "Go to View→Column Browser→On Top." That's shorthand for a longer series of instructions that goes something like this: "Go to the menu bar in iTunes, click the View menu, select the Column Browser submenu, and then slide over to the On Top entry." Our shorthand system avoids lots of long, drawn-out instructions and helps keep the book snappy.

THE VERY BASICS

To use this book, and indeed to use a computer at all, you need to know a few basics. This book assumes that you're familiar with these terms and concepts:

Clicking. To *click* means to point the arrow cursor at something on your screen and then to press and release the clicker button on your mouse (or laptop trackpad). To *right-click* means the same thing, but you press the right mouse button instead (or the top-right corner of a Mac mouse). Often, right-clicking calls up a menu of commands you select from.

To *double-click* means to click twice in rapid succession without moving the cursor. To *drag* means to move the cursor *while* pressing the button.

When you're told to *Ctrl-click* something on a PC, or ⌘-*click* something on a Mac, you click while pressing the Ctrl or ⌘ key.

Menus. The *menus* are the words at the top of your screen or window: File, Edit, and so on. Click one to make a list of commands appear, as though they're written on a window shade you've just pulled down.

Keyboard shortcuts. Jumping up to menus in iTunes takes time. That's why you'll find keyboard workarounds that perform the same functions sprinkled throughout the book—Windows shortcuts first, followed by Mac shortcuts in parentheses, like this: "To quickly summon the Preferences box, press Ctrl+comma (⌘-comma)."

If you've mastered this much information, you have all the technical background you need to enjoy *iPod: The Missing Manual*.

ABOUT THE MISSING CD

As you read this book, you'll find references to websites that offer additional resources. To save yourself some typing, you'll find a clickable list of those sites on this book's Missing CD page at *www.missingmanuals.com/cds/ipodtmm10/*.

The Missing CD page also includes corrections and updates to this book. Click the View Errata link to see them. You can submit your own corrections by clicking "Submit your own errata" on the same page. To keep this book as accurate as possible, each time we print more copies, we'll make any confirmed corrections.

While you're online, you can register this book at *http://tinyurl.com/yo82k3*. Registering means we can send you updates about the book, and you'll be eligible for special offers like discounts on future editions of the iPod Missing Manual.

SAFARI BOOKS ONLINE

Safari® Books Online is an on-demand digital library that lets you search over 7,500 technology books and videos.

With a subscription, you can read any page and watch any video from our library online. Read books on your smartphone and mobile devices. Access new titles before they're available for print, get exclusive access to manuscripts in development, post feedback for the authors. Copy and paste code samples, organize your favorites, download chapters, bookmark key sections, create notes, print out pages, and benefit from tons of other time-saving features.

O'Reilly Media has uploaded this book to the Safari Books Online service. To have full digital access to this book and others on similar topics from O'Reilly and other publishers, sign up for free at *http://my.safaribooksonline.com*.

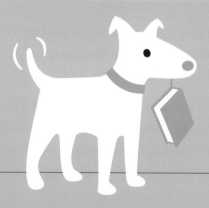

CHAPTER 1

Meet the iPod: Out of the Box and Into Your Ears in 15 Minutes

IF YOU'RE LIKE MOST PEOPLE, YOU WANT TO JUMP RIGHT IN AND GET your spiffy new iPod up and running. Apple thoughtfully includes a tiny folding pamphlet of starter info with every iPod it sells. And while it's nicely designed, you may find that it doesn't go far enough; you want more help than a few line drawings and some haiku-like instructions can give you.

This book—and especially this chapter—is designed for you.

You won't get bogged down in a bland gray ocean of print here. You'll learn how to get your iPod whistling sweet tunes in your ear in no time, and find out how to control your particular iPod model. If you want more information on in-depth 'Podding or getting the most out of iTunes, you can find that in chapters farther down the road.

But for now, let's get rolling with your new iPod. Ready?

Meet the iPod Touch

SINCE ITS ARRIVAL IN 2007, the iPod Touch has become the most popular member of the iPod family. It's also the most versatile; it runs thousands of mini-programs called apps, makes and takes FaceTime video calls, keeps you on schedule, surfs the Web, handles your email, takes text and audio notes, and serves up plenty of fun as a handheld game console. Oh, it also plays music, videos, slideshows, and podcasts, and it displays eBooks on a gorgeous screen whenever you feel like reading. Yes, the Touch is the Swiss Army knife of iPods.

The Touch gets its moniker from its responsive *touchscreen*, the smooth glass surface that lets you navigate through your music, videos, and photos with nothing more than a tap or drag of your finger.

While the Touch may have inherited its sensitive screen from the iPhone, it gets its playback stability from the flash memory that holds all your media files. No matter how hard you run or rock out, you'll probably never hear your music skip a beat. Nor is it likely you'll run out of juice: the Touch gives you about 40 hours of audio playback or 7 hours of video viewing on a single battery charge.

Speaking of video, the Touch sports the same eye-catching 3.5-inch Retina Display as the iPhone does, giving it an impressive 960 x 640 pixel resolution. To see the display in its finest form, flip the Touch sideways when you view photos, movies, and TV shows. You don't have to be content just *watching* videos, either—the Touch lets you shoot and edit high-definition movies as well, and you can upload them directly to YouTube. Need a still camera? The Touch has one of those, too.

You can buy the Touch in three memory configurations: an 8-gigabyte model that stores 1,750 songs or 10 hours of iPod-friendly video, a 32-gigabyte version that holds 7,000 songs or 40 hours of video, and a 64-gig model that stores a relatively whopping 14,000 songs and 80 hours of video. It also comes in two colors: black or white (and yes, it's no Nano in the exterior-color department).

As an entertainment device, the Touch is tops, but its ability to reach out and touch the Internet is what makes it an iPod you can do business with (if you can tear yourself away from all the fun stuff, that is). Thanks to its built-in WiFi chip and a mobile version of Apple's Safari browser, you can surf the Web whenever you're in range of a wireless network. And where there's Internet, there's email, stock-market updates, weather forecasts, YouTube videos, and online maps. You use your fingertips to point your way around the Web—or to fire up the Touch's onscreen keyboard for a little good, old-fashioned text entry.

With iOS 5, the latest version of Apple's system software for the Touch, you also get Reminders (a to-do list app), iMessages (so you can send text messages and photos to other iOS 5 users), and Newsstand (a place to park your eMagazines). Chapter 3 has more on all these new, built-in apps. And if that's not enough, you can customize your Touch with purchases from the iTunes App Store, where more than 500,000 additional mini-programs await you.

One more thing: if you've ever been out and about with your iPod and wished you could buy music or video on the fly, you can. With the Touch and a wireless network connection, this little Internet iPod can step right up to the iTunes Store and shop away.

NOTE The Touch and the iPhone may look like kissing cousins, but they have some distinct differences. For one thing, the Touch isn't a mobile phone, like the iPhone is. While this means that Touch owners get to skip The Wireless Carrier Experience, it also means there's no ubiquitous cellphone network to tap into when you run out of WiFi hotspots. (The good news: no phone bill, either.) In addition, the Touch's built-in camera—with less than a full megapixel of photo resolution—isn't as good as the iPhone 4S's 8-megapixel gem. On the plus side, without the extra hardware inside, the Touch is much more svelte.

Meet the iPod Nano

IF THERE'S ANY IPOD that's undergone a radical transformation since its introduction, it's the humble Nano. From the time it hit the scene in 2005, this sporty little player has changed its size and shape nearly every year, and the 2011 Nano is no exception: It's even smaller—and sportier—than its ancestors.

How small? A mere 1.48 inches wide by 1.61 inches high, and it weighs less than an ounce; you can clip it to your shirt and barely feel it. Unlike the models before 2010, this Nano comes with a touchscreen for tapping, flicking, and swiping your way to music, podcasts, audiobooks, and photos. Its bright color screen shows them all off in 240 x 240 pixel resolution on a 1.54-inch display.

Designed with runners and other fitness enthusiasts in mind, the Nano has a built-in pedometer that tracks your steps and helps you chart your workouts. As of 2011, you don't even need special gym shoes and an electronic sensor to have this iPod compile your workout data—it does all that on its own now.

This Nano also includes Apple's VoiceOver feature, which recites menus and song titles into your headphones when you're too busy running to look at the screen. And since it stores all your music on a nice, stable flash-memory chip, you don't have to worry about your music skipping, even if you are.

When you get tired of recorded music, switch to the Nano's integrated FM radio. Unlike standard receivers, the Nano can pause live shows for a few minutes should someone start talking at you in the middle of a song.

The Nano comes in 8- and 16-gigabyte models, and you can choose from seven anodized aluminum colors (pink, red, blue, green, yellow, silver, and a graphite gray). With a full battery charge, you'll get up to 24 hours of audio playback. That should get you through even the most intense cardio routine.

NOTE Stripped down and buffed up with a touchscreen, the current Nano offers far fewer features than pre-2010 models. It has no video camera or video playback capability; no Contacts, Calendars, or Notes features; and no built-in microphone or games. If you long for the more full-featured Nanos of the past, remember that there's always eBay or inventory-clearance sales.

Meet the iPod Shuffle

THE SMALLEST MEMBER OF Team iPod doesn't have a screen—but it doesn't need one, because it's designed for fuss-free music on the go. You don't have to worry about losing your Shuffle because, like the new Nano, it clips right onto your lapel or pocket—it's like jewelry you can rock out with.

TAKE YOUR PICK OF five standard Shuffle colors: blue, orange, green, pink, and silver. It comes with a 2-gigabyte memory chip that holds hundreds of songs, audio podcasts, and audiobooks. And even though it's called the Shuffle, you don't *have* to shuffle your music; you can play your tracks in order with the nudge of a button (see below).

The Shuffle may not have a screen, but it does include VoiceOver technology. Just press the VoiceOver button to make your Shuffle announce the name and artist of the song currently playing. Speaking of playing, you get about 15 hours of music between battery charges.

This iPod is so petite that you can't charge it with the same USB cable the other iPods use—it comes with its own little dual-function USB adapter that connects to your computer to both charge the player and load music from iTunes. In addition to the adapter, here's what you'll find in the Shuffle box:

❶ Those trademark white Apple headphones that plug into a jack on top of the Shuffle.

❷ The Shuffle itself, complete with a handy control ring that lets you adjust the volume and jump back and forth between songs.

❸ The Shuffle's VoiceOver button. Push it to hear the Shuffle announce the name of the current song or playlist.

❹ The Shuffle's On/Off switch. Slide it one notch to the left to play tunes in order (⟳) or slide it over all the way over to shuffle them (⤬).

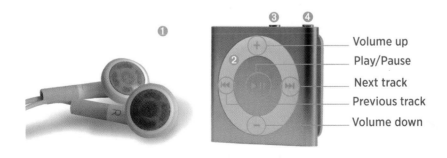

Volume up
Play/Pause
Next track
Previous track
Volume down

Meet the iPod Classic

WITH ITS SOLID, RECTANGULAR shape and horizontal screen, the faithful iPod Classic still retains the look of the original, boxy white-and-chrome iPod that started it all back in 2001.

A decade later, Apple has transformed that humble little 5-gigabyte music player with its black-and-white screen into a gorgeous full-color portable media system that can play movies, TV shows, and video games—and it still fits comfortably in the palm of your hand. Although Apple hasn't added any new features to the Classic in the past few years, it's still a beloved model, especially for media lovers who want to carry around all (or most) of their music collections with them.

That's because the Classic has more than double the storage of even the highest-capacity new-gen iPods—and quite an improvement over its original 5 gigabytes. You can stuff 160 gigabytes of music, photos, videos, and more onto the Classic. That's 40,000 songs or 200 hours of video. And you don't have to stock up on the Duracells, either, because the Classic has a rechargeable battery that can play audio for 36 hours or video for 6 hours.

The Classic comes in either silver or black. Unlike earlier iPods that sported hard glossy plastic on the front, Apple's latest version comes outfitted in a full metal jacket—anodized aluminum on the front and shiny stainless steel on the back.

Along with the click wheel—think of it as the Classic's mouse—the 2.5-inch color screen is the player's other main component. Capable of displaying more than 65,000 colors at a resolution of 320 x 240 pixels (translation: high-quality), the Classic is a great place to store and show off your latest vacation photos. In fact, you can keep up to 25,000 pictures on your 'Pod. The screen also makes it a delight to catch up on that episode of *The Daily Show* you missed, or play a few rounds of solitaire while you listen to your favorite music.

The Classic comes with a USB cable to connect with your Windows PC or Macintosh, along with those iconic see-what-I've-got white earphones. Want more stuff for your Classic? Check out the accessories mentioned in Chapter 12.

Install iTunes

BEFORE YOU CAN HAVE hours of iPod fun, you need to install iTunes, Apple's multimedia, multifunction jukebox program, on your computer. Apple's QuickTime program, a video helper for iTunes, comes along with the download. (With the modern iPod Touch, you technically don't need iTunes, but it *is* a great place to store your big video files.) To get iTunes:

➊ **Fire up your computer's web browser and point it to** *www.itunes.com/downloads*.

➋ **Click the Download Now button**. (Turn off the "Email me..." and "Keep me up to date..." checkboxes to spare yourself future marketing missives.) Wait for the file to download to your computer.

➌ **When the file lands on your hard drive, double-click the** *iTunesSetup.exe* **file**. If you use a Mac, double-click the *iTunes.dmg* file and then open the *iTunes.mpkg* file to start the installation. If your Mac is younger than 7 years old, you probably already have iTunes installed. Go to →Software Update and tell your Mac to see if there's a newer version of the program, just in case.

➍ **Follow the screens until the software installer says it's done**.

You may need to restart your computer after you install iTunes. Once you do, you're ready to connect your new iPod to your computer.

NOTE The hardware and operating-system requirements needed to run iTunes are listed below the Download Now button. If you have an older computer, it's worth a glance just to make sure your rig can handle the program. For the record, iTunes 10.5 requires Windows XP, Windows Vista, or Windows 7; or Mac OS X 10.5 and later.

Get Music into iTunes (and Later, Onto Your iPod)

ONCE YOU HAVE ITUNES running on your computer, you can start filling it up with music (and then loading your songs onto your iPod). Chapters 4 and 5 have info on song formats and technical settings, but if you've got a brand-new iPod, odds are you don't care about *that* right now. You just want to load up some music. Here are three simple ways to do that:

Import Existing Songs into iTunes

When iTunes first opens and displays your sad, empty music library, it suggests a couple of ways to get yourself some tunes—namely by buying them from the iTunes Store or converting songs from your CD collection into iPod-ready files. Those methods are described on the opposite page.

But there's another way, and it doesn't involve money or a lot of extra effort.

If you've had a computer for longer than a few years, odds are you already have some songs on your hard drive in the popular MP3 format. Since they're already on your computer, why not add them to your iPod through iTunes? They're probably sitting in a folder, waiting for you to play them.

To grab that music and add it to iTunes, choose File→Add Folder to Library (Windows PCs) or File→Add to Library (Macs). In the box that appears, navigate across your hard drive to your folder of music, select it, and click the Choose button to pull your songs into iTunes.

Boom! There you have it—your old music in your brand-new iTunes library.

> **NOTE** Now, many Windows fans may have music in the Windows Media Audio (WMA) format. The bad news here is that iTunes can't play WMA files. The good news is that when iTunes finds WMA files, it can automatically convert them to an iPod-friendly format. You can always add WMA tracks by choosing File→Add to Library and selecting the songs you want; iTunes then converts them. One last thing to remember: The program can't convert copy-protected tracks you may have downloaded from other online music stores.

Import a CD

You can also use iTunes to convert tracks from your audio CDs into iPod-ready music files. Just start up iTunes and stick a CD in your computer's disc drive. The program asks if you want to import the CD into iTunes. (If it doesn't ask, click the Import CD button at the bottom-right of the iTunes window.) If you're connected to the Internet, iTunes automatically downloads song titles and artist information for the CD (yes, strange as it may seem, music managers like iTunes don't get information about an album from the album itself; they search for it in a huge database on the Web).

Once you tell iTunes to import music, it begins adding the songs to your library. You can import all the tracks from a CD or, if you don't want every song, turn off the checkboxes next to titles you want to skip. Chapter 4 has more on using iTunes to convert CDs.

Buy Music in the iTunes Store

Another way to get music for your iTunes library and iPod is to buy it from the iTunes Store. Click the iTunes Store icon in the list on the left side of iTunes (that's called the Source list, since it identifies the source of your media, like "Library" or "Store").

Once you land on the Store's main page and set up your iTunes account (see page 160), you can buy and download songs, audiobooks, and videos. The content goes straight into your iTunes library and then onto your iPod. Chapter 7 is all about the iTunes Store.

If you buy music, apps, or books from the Store on one of your iOS devices, like your iPod Touch or iPhone, you can have iTunes automatically download copies to your computer. Page 112 tells you how.

Meet the iPod Accessories

AS YOU MAY HAVE noticed before you got preoccupied with iTunes, your new iPod came with a few other things inside its smooth plastic box. What you find inside varies by iPod model, but all of them come with three things:

❶ Apple's classic white headphones.

❷ A USB cable to connect your iPod to your computer. The iPod Touch, Nano, and Classic come with a white USB cable with a flat dock-connector port, while the Shuffle has its own USB adapter (see page 5).

❸ A little pamphlet of quick-start information that's not nearly as fun or as colorful as this book.

What you want right now is the USB cable. Connect the small, narrow end to your computer's USB port and the wide, flat end (or the adapter, if you have a Shuffle) to the iPod. The first time you connect your iPod to a computer, iTunes' Setup Assistant walks you through a few steps to get your iPod ready to go (see page 16 for a description). In addition, the iPod begins to charge, as described on page 12.

Connect or Disconnect Your iPod from Your Computer

Connecting and disconnecting your iPod from the computer to load new songs, videos, and other content is a basic fact of life for the Nano, Shuffle, and Classic. With its wireless powers, the iPod Touch doesn't need to rely on the white cord as much (except for charging), but it, too, can make occasional visits to the computer to, say, sync over huge files or get a full-system software restore (page 278).

No matter how often you need to make the iPod-computer link, you should do it properly to keep both you and your iPod happy. As the previous page explained, to make the connection, plug the smaller end of the USB cable into your computer's USB port and the wider, flatter end into the bottom of your iPod. (Shuffle owners, insert the 3.5 mm plug into your headphone jack, and the other end into your computer's USB port.)

When it comes to portable devices, what gets connected usually needs to get disconnected. Resist the impulse to yank the USB cable out of your iPod without checking it first. If you see menus or the battery icon on your 'Pod, you can safely unplug it. (Shuffle owners, see the steps below.)

But if you see the icon circled at right in iTunes, you need to *manually* eject the iPod from your computer. iTunes gives you two easy ways to do that:

❶ Click the Eject icon next to the name of your iPod in the iTunes Source list.

❷ If your iPod is already selected in the Source list, choose Controls→Eject iPod or press Ctrl+E (⌘-E).

With either method, the iPod announces onscreen that it's disengaging, displaying an "OK to Disconnect" progress bar as it breaks its connection with the computer. Once all the gray screens go away and you see the regular menus again, you can safely liberate your iPod.

Charge Your iPod for the First Time

RIGHT OUT OF THE box, your iPod probably has enough juice to run for a while without having to charge it up. Eventually, though, you'll need to go in for an electric fill-up. All you need to do is plug the iPod into your computer using the USB cable (the iPod charges itself by drawing power from the USB connector). Just make sure you have your computer turned on and that it isn't asleep.

It takes only a few hours to fully charge your iPod battery, and even less time to do what Apple calls a *fast charge*, which quickly powers up the battery to 80 percent of its capacity. That should be plenty of gas in your iPod's tank for a quick spin.

Here's how much time each iPod needs for both a fast and a full charge:

	FAST CHARGE	FULL CHARGE
iPod Touch	2 hours	4 hours
iPod Nano	1.5 hours	3 hours
iPod Shuffle	2 hours	3 hours
iPod Classic	2 hours	4 hours

If you're traveling and don't want to drag your laptop with you just to charge your iPod, you can buy an AC adapter for the USB cable. Chapter 2 has more on that.

iPod Touch Ports and Switches

THE IPOD TOUCH KEEPS most of its controls behind its sensitive screen, but it does have a few physical buttons and jacks on the outside. Here's a tour of the Touch from top to bottom:

❶ **Sleep/Wake**. Press the thin black button on top of the Touch to put it to sleep and save some battery power. If you've got a song playing, no problem: A sleeping Touch still plays—it's just the display that goes dark.

❷ **Volume**. These two buttons reside on the left side of the Touch. Press the top one to increase the sound on either the tiny external speaker or an attached pair of headphones; the bottom button lowers the volume.

❸ **Home**. Forget clicking your heels together three times to get home—just push the indented button below the Touch's screen and you'll always return home. The iPod's Home screen is where your tappable icons for music, photos, Safari web browsing, and more hang out. If you ever wander deep into the iPod and don't know how to get out, push the Home button to escape. You can also push it to wake the Touch from sleep.

❹ **Headphones**. Plug the included headphones into the small, round jack on the bottom edge of the Touch. You can also use non-Apple headphones, so long as the new gear uses the standard 3.5 mm stereo plug (most do).

❺ **Dock connector**. This thin jack is the port you use to plug in the iPod's USB cable for charging and media transfers from iTunes. Most iPod accessories (Chapter 12), such as audio docks, connect through this port as well. You may also see it referred to as the "30-pin dock connector." The Touch's own tiny external speaker sits to its right.

Set Up and Activate the iPod Touch

THANKS TO ITS IOS 5 software and WiFi chip, the Touch can jump onto the Internet over the airwaves, making it the easiest iPod to set up. Touch owners no longer have to get to a computer and unwind the USB cable to get their iPods ready for action—all that can be done wirelessly now. This, of course, means you need a WiFi network nearby. (If you don't have one, flip ahead to page 16 to learn how to set up the Touch via good old-fashioned USB cable.)

Here's how you set up your player as a brand-new iPod Touch right out of the box—providing, of course, that the tablet retained its charge on the trip from China; if power is running low, see page 12 for charge-up instructions.

❶ Press the Touch's Home button. You see a gray screen with the word "iPod" in the middle of it and a right-pointing arrow underneath it. Put your finger on the arrow and slide it to the right.

❷ Tap your preferred language for iPad screens and menus. As you can see in the image below, English is the default option for U.S. users, but tap the arrow for more choices.

❸ Pick your country or region. The United States is the default choice, but if you're not there, tap Show More.

❹ Decide whether you want to turn on Location Services. Location Services pinpoints the position of your Touch on a map, using a database of WiFi hotspots to guide it. It's great for finding restaurants close to you, but not so much for your privacy. If you leave Location Services off, you can always turn it on later by tapping Home→Settings→Location Services→On.

❺ Choose your WiFi network. If you're at home, find your personal network on the list and tap it to select it. Type in your network's password. If you're in range of a public network, you can connect to it, but be leery of typing in any personal information, like a credit-card number to set up an Apple ID. Once the iPod connects to the Internet, it takes a few minutes to activate itself with Apple's servers.

❻ Sign in with or create an Apple ID. Your Apple ID (page 160) is the online user name and password you use to buy and download apps, music, books, videos, podcasts, and more from the iTunes and App Stores. If you already have an Apple ID, sign in with it here. If not, tap "Create a new Apple ID" to go to the next screen, where you can base your new ID on an existing email address or set up a spiffy new—and free—iCloud account (see below). If you don't want to deal with this Apple ID stuff now, tap the Skip This Step link at the bottom of the screen.

❼ Set up iCloud. On this screen, you can turn on Apple's free iCloud service, where you can back up all your apps, contacts, calendars, and more to Apple's online servers. You can also restore the Touch from an iCloud backup. (Chapter 11 has more on iCloud.)

❽ Set up your email account. You can compose, send, and receive email right on your iPod, but first you have to introduce it to your mail account(s). You can use an existing account or your free iCloud mail account from Apple. Or, you can set up your mail accounts later by going to Home→Settings→Mail, Contacts, Calendars→Add Account. The iPod automatically sets up the accounts from most major services, like Gmail and Yahoo when you type in your account name and

password. You may need to drag out the account info from your Internet service provider to add an ISP-based account, like those from Comcast and Verizon.

Now, start using your Touch! You don't see these setup screens again, unless you need to replace the software on an ailing iPod (page 278). You get the option during the setup steps to restore a backup of the iPod's settings and account data from an iCloud or iTunes backup file, so you're not totally parked back on Square One. The iPod setup process has come a long way, baby.

Set Up and Sync Your Touch With iTunes

IF YOU SKIPPED THE PC-free iPod Touch setup because you didn't have a WiFi network around (or because all your stuff is on your computer), you can set up the player using iTunes instead. Just connect your iPod to the computer with the USB cable. When you do, iTunes pops up and walks you through the setup, which includes naming your gadget and choosing sync options.

If you already use iTunes to manage media on an iPhone or iPad, odds are you already have a healthy media library on your computer. And if you've had an iPod before, iTunes offers to put the content from your old player onto your new one. Depending on the size of your new iPod's drive, you may be able to fit all your stuff on it—or not, if you have more than 8, 32, or 64 GB of digital treasures on your computer. If you have less than that and want to take it all with you, just

click Done in the Setup box. iTunes loads a copy of everything in its library onto your iPod. If you have more media than your iPod has storage, iTunes loads up your 'Pod until it's full. If you want to be more selective about what you sync, see the next page.

iTunes Wi-Fi Sync

Now, just because you chose to set up your iPod with iTunes instead of doing it wirelessly doesn't mean you *always* have to dig up your USB cable when you want to put new stuff on your Touch. That's because you can now sync your 'Pod wirelessly. The iPod and the computer you're syncing with just need to be on the same WiFi network, and iTunes has to be open at the time of the sync.

To set up Wi-Fi Sync, connect your iPod to your computer. Click the Touch's icon in iTunes' Source list and click the Summary tab in the iTunes window. Scroll down to the Options area and turn on the checkbox next to "Sync this iPod over Wi-Fi." Click the Apply button and then click Sync. Remember, the computer needs to be connected to the network wirelessly, not by an Ethernet cable.

A Touch icon now stays visible in the iTunes window, where you can manually add stuff to it (as the next page explains). The Touch wirelessly syncs itself once a day when it's plugged into power. It's slower than a USB sync, but often more convenient, and you can still sync by USB when you want. In a hurry to sync over that new album? Click the Sync button in iTunes window—or, on the iPod Touch, tap Home→Settings→General→iTunes Wi-Fi Sync→Sync Now.

Manually Load the iPod Touch

IF YOU DON'T WANT to autosync your Touch, you need to load songs onto it manually. Until you do, the Touch just sits there, empty and forlorn in your iTunes window, waiting for you to give it something to play with. Here are your options:

Manual Method #1

❶ Click the Touch icon on the left side of the iTunes window (the Source list). This opens up a world of syncing preferences for your 'Pod.

❷ Click the Music tab, and then turn on the Sync Music checkbox.

❸ Click the button next to "Selected playlists, artists, and genres," and check off the items you want to copy to your iPod. (No playlists yet? See Chapter 6.)

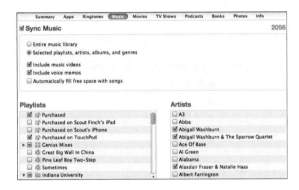

❹ Click the Apply button at the bottom of the iTunes window.

Manual Method #2

❶ This one's for those into detailed picking and choosing: Click the Summary tab and turn on "Manually manage music and videos." Now you can click the songs, albums, or playlists you want on your iPod and drag them to the Touch icon in the Source list.

Manual Method #3

❶ Every item in your iTunes library has a checkmark next to its name when you first import it. Clear the checkmark next to whatever you *don't* want on your Touch. (If you have a big library, hold down the Ctrl [⌘] key while clicking any title; that performs the nifty trick of removing *all* the checkmarks. Then go back and check only the stuff you *do* want.)

❷ Click the Touch icon under Devices in the Source list, and then click the Summary tab.

❸ At the bottom of the Summary screen, turn on the checkbox next to "Sync only checked songs and videos," and then click the Sync button.

Finger Moves for the iPod Touch

UNTIL THE TOUCH ARRIVED on the scene, iPods were controlled by a click wheel or control ring on the front of the player. The Nano has a limited version of the touch-sensitive screen, and the Shuffle and the Classic still use the circular dashboard. But with an iPod Touch, you don't need a steering wheel to get around the iPod—you just tap the onscreen icons and menus to navigate.

You'll use some moves more often than others as you navigate the Touch:

- **Tap**. Lightly touch a song title, app icon, or picture thumbnail on the screen with your fingertip. The Touch isn't a crusty old calculator, so you don't have to push down hard; a gentle tap on the glass starts a song, launches an app, or pops a picture into view.

- **Drag**. This time, keep your fingertip pressed down on the screen. As you slide it around the Touch glass, you scroll to different parts of a web page, photo, or other item that goes beyond the screen's boundaries. You also use the drag move to nudge onscreen volume sliders up and down. It's really the same concept as holding down the button on a computer mouse and dragging. A *two-finger drag* scrolls a web window within a web window (which is, fortunately, not too common on mobile sites).

- **Slide**. A slide is like a drag, but you need it on only a couple of Touch times. The first is on the "slide to unlock" screen you see when you wake the iPod from a nap (see below). The second is when you want to power down the Touch completely; press the Sleep/Wake button until the "slide to power off" slider appears.

NOTE The iPod Touch relies on the human touch—skin-on-glass contact—to work. If you have really long fingernails, a Band-Aid on the tip of your finger, or happen to be wearing gloves at the time, you're going to have problems working the Touch. You can't use a pencil eraser or pen tip, either. You can, however, find special styluses that work with the Touch screen; for example, Pogo (*http://tenonedesign.com*) makes one for $15.

- **Flick**. This move lets you speed-scroll up and down through long lists of songs, or side to side through overstuffed photo albums. To flick properly, quickly whip your finger along the length or width of the screen. (Make it a light movement—this isn't a slide or a drag here.) The faster you flick that finger, the faster the screens fly by. For example, use the flick when you're in Cover Flow mode—tap the Home screen's Music icon and hold the Touch horizontally. All your album covers appear onscreen, and you can flick through them until you find the one you want to hear.

- **Finger spread and pinch**. Can't see what you want because it's too small on the screen? To make it bigger, put your thumb and index finger together, place them on that area of the screen, and then spread your fingers apart. To go the opposite way and zoom out so things shrink back down, put those same fingers on the screen, separated this time, and then pinch them together.

- **Double-tap**. This two-steppin' tap comes into play in a couple of situations. First, it serves as a shortcut to automatically zoom in on a photo or a section of a web page. You can also double-tap to zoom in on a section of a Google map (Chapter 3).

Second, if you're watching a movie or TV show, tap the screen twice to toggle back and forth between screen aspect ratios—the full-screen view (top right), where the edges of the frame get cropped off, or the widescreen, letter-boxed view (bottom right), which movie lovers favor because it's what the film's director intended a scene to look like.

- **Two-finger tap**. Two fingers, one tap. That's what you do to zoom *out* of a Google map view (remember, you use *one* finger and *two* taps to zoom in—Google just wants to keep you on your toes).

Nano and Classic Ports and Switches

ALTHOUGH THEY STARTED OUT looking and acting similarly despite their different sizes, the iPod Nano and Classic don't have that much in common anymore. The Nano has fled the click-wheel world for a glossy touch screen, and the Classic hasn't changed much at all over the past few years.

Here's where the Nano and Classic differ:

① **Volume**. The Nano has + and − buttons on its top-left edge to control the sound output through the headphones. The Classic still clings to its click wheel for menu navigation and volume control.

② **Sleep/Wake**. The Tic Tac–shaped button on the Nano's top-right edge turns its touchscreen on or off. Press it gently.

③ **Hold**. The Classic is the only iPod left with a physical Hold switch. Slide it to the On position (with the orange spot visible) to lock down the Classic's controls so your iPod doesn't accidentally get bumped on or off when it rattles around in your pocket or bag.

Despite their design differences, the Nano and the Classic still have two things in common:

④ **Headphones**. The small, round jack on the bottom of the Nano (below) or the top of the Classic (above) is where you plug in your white earbuds.

⑤ **Dock connector**. This flat, thin jack is where you plug in the iPod's USB cable so you can connect it to your computer to sync up your iTunes library, or charge up your Nano or Classic battery.

Control the iPod Nano or Classic

THE NANO AND THE Classic let you control media in different ways. Here's how to work either 'Pod.

iPod Nano

Here are the finger moves that get your Nano singing:

- **Tap**. Gently press your finger on an icon to open its menus, or on a song title to play it.

- **Double-tap**. Tap two times to zoom in on a photo—do the same to zoom back out.

- **Swipe**. Lightly whip your finger side to side on the glass to move through the parade of icons on the Home screen.

- **Flick**. Whip your finger up and down to scroll through long playlists.

- **Drag**. Hold down a volume control and slide your finger to adjust it.

- **Rotate**. Home screen upside-down? Place two fingers on the glass and twist them in the direction you want the screen to be.

- **Press**. Hold your finger on the screen while a song plays or you look at a photo to return to the Home screen.

iPod Classic

Push any button to turn the Classic on. Then control it like so:

- ❶ **Menu**. Tap this button to return to any screen you just viewed. For example, if you visited Music→Playlists→My Top Rated, you'd press Menu twice to return to the Music menu.

- ❷ **Next/Fast-Forward**. Press here to jump to the next song in a playlist (Chapter 6), or hold it down to zip through a song.

- ❸ **Play/Pause**. This button starts a song; push it again to pause the music.

- ❹ **Previous/Rewind**. Press and release this button to play the song before the current track, or hold it down to "rewind" within a song.

- ❺ **Select**. Press here to choose a highlighted menu item. When you have a song title highlighted, the Select button begins playback.

Get Stuff onto the iPod Nano or Classic: The Quick Way

YOU DON'T HAVE TO do much to keep your iPod's music and video collection up to date with what's on your computer. That's because iTunes has a nifty *autosync* feature that automatically makes sure that whatever is in your iTunes library also appears on your iPod once you connect 'Pod to desktop PC.

The first time you plug in your new iPod (after you install iTunes, of course), the iPod Setup Assistant leaps into action, asking you to name your iPod, and if you'd like to "Automatically sync songs to my iPod." If your answer is yes, then just click the Done button. iTunes loads a copy of everything in its library that fits onto your iPod (see the note below if you have more music than the iPod has storage). That's it. Your iPod is ready to go.

You can copy photos from a specific folder on your computer and choose the language you'd like the iPod menus to appear in here as well. But if you just want to stick with the music for now, Chapter 9 can fill you in on the photo business. If you generally like the autosync feature but want more control over what goes onto your iPod, read on to find out how to make that happen.

> **NOTE** If you have a small-capacity iPod, you may already have more music than can fit on your player. If that's the case, *your* automatic option is the Autofill button at the bottom of the iTunes window. Skip ahead to page 24 to learn more about Autofill, which lets iTunes decide what to put on your 'Pod. And if you want to selectively sync certain playlists or artists, check out page 23 for the details.

Manually Load the iPod Nano or Classic

IF YOU DON'T HAVE enough room on your Nano or Classic for your whole iTunes library, or if you plan to load music onto your iPod from more than one computer (say your work PC and home PC), you'll want to *manually* manage your songs and other media. To put your iPod on manual right from the get-go, turn off the check-box on the iPod Setup Assistant screen next to "Automatically sync songs...." (If you've already done the setup thing, see page 128 to learn how to get back to Manual Land.) iTunes now refrains from automatically dumping everything onto your iPod. "But," you ask, "*how* do I get the music on there by myself?" Easy—you just drag it:

❶ **In iTunes' Source list, click the Music icon under Library**. Click the button circled below to see a list of all the songs in your music library. You can also click Ctrl+B (⌘-B) to go into Column Browser view (see page 101), where iTunes lists your music by genre, artist, and album.

❷ **Click the songs or albums you want to copy to your iPod**. Grab multiple songs or albums by holding down the Ctrl (⌘) key while clicking.

❸ **Drag your selections onto the iPod icon**. The number of songs you're dragging appears inside a red circle.

You can manually load any items in your iTunes library—audiobooks, movies, whatever—onto your iPod this way.

Fill Up Any iPod with Autofill

MOST PEOPLE'S ENTIRE MUSIC library is too big to stuff onto the wee 2-gigabyte Shuffle, or even the 8-gigabyte Touch or Nano. (Classic owners can chuckle here.) If you love all your music and don't want to spend time cherry-picking tracks to load up your iPod, Autofill it to the brim with a full serving of tunes.

If you're a Shuffle owner connecting your iPod to your PC for the first time, the iPod Setup Assistant appears. Leave the "Automatically choose songs..." checkbox turned on, click Done, and presto: iTunes grabs a random collection of songs from your library and copies them onto your tiny 'Pod. After that, each time you connect your Shuffle, a small panel appears at the bottom of iTunes, inviting you to fill up your player with a click of the Autofill button.

Although Autofill used to be a Shuffle-only feature, other iPods can use it as well, as long as you set them to manually manage music. To use Autofill with a Touch, Nano, or Classic, connect the iPod and click the flippy triangle next to its icon in the iTunes Source list. The Autofill bar appears at the bottom of the screen. Click the Autofill button to load up.

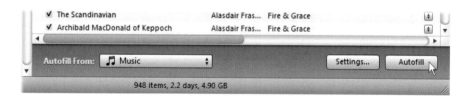

In the "Autofill From" pop-up menu, tell iTunes to snag songs from your entire library or just a particular playlist (see Chapter 6). Click the Settings button to have iTunes pick random tracks or to select highly rated songs more often. ("Ratings?" you say? Check out Chapter 5 for the details.)

After you Autofill for the first time, when you return for another batch of songs, you can turn on the checkbox next to "Replace all items when Autofilling" to have iTunes wipe the first batch of songs off your iPod and substitute new tracks.

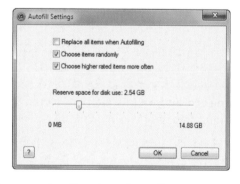

Once iTunes fills up your 'Pod, you see an "iPod sync is complete" message at the top of the screen. Click the Eject button next to your iPod's icon, unplug the player from the computer, clip it onto your shirt, and head out with your little metal square full of music.

Manually Load Your iPod Shuffle

IF *YOU* WANT TO decide what goes onto your Shuffle, opt for manual updates instead of letting iTunes choose. As with any other iPod on manual control, you drag songs and playlists you want from your iTunes library and drop them onto the Shuffle's icon in the Source list.

When you click the Shuffle icon and it displays your song list, feel free to re-arrange individual songs in the order you want to hear them—just drag them up or down. The info at the bottom of the iTunes window tells you how much space you have left on your Shuffle if you're looking to fill it to the brim.

To delete songs from the Shuffle, select one or more tracks and then press the Delete key on your keyboard. This action deletes the song from your Shuffle only, not your iTunes library; see page 138.

You can also mix and match your song-loading methods. Start by dragging a few favorite playlists over to the Shuffle, and then click Autofill to finish the job. Just make sure you turn the "Replace all items when Autofilling" checkbox off, or iTunes will wipe out the tracks you already added.

Early versions of the iPod Shuffle used to be monogamous—that is, they wanted to work with only one iTunes library at a time and would threaten to erase and replace the Shuffle's contents if you added music from a different computer. As you can imagine, this was quite a drag if you bought music on both a work and a home computer and wanted to load it up wherever you happened to be.

Thankfully, the free-spirited iPod Shuffles of today let you manually add music from multiple computers, just as you can with any other ol' iPod.

Find the Music on Your iPod—and Play It

NOW THAT YOU'VE GOT some songs on your iPod, you're ready to listen to them. Plug your headphones into the headphone jack and press the Sleep/Wake button on your Touch or Nano—or any button on the front of the Classic—to turn it on.

Find Music on Your iPod Touch

The Touch's screen is full of icons, but when it comes time to crank up the tunes, here's what you do:

❶ Tap the Music icon in the bottom-left corner of the Home screen.

❷ You see five tappable buttons at the bottom of the screen. These let you see your music sorted by playlist, artist, song, or album. The More button at the end lets you sort by composer, genre, and other categories.

❸ Tap the Songs button and then scroll (by flicking your finger) down to the song you want to play. You can also hold down the alphabet bar on the right and then drag your finger slowly to better target the scroll. Tap a song's title to hear it play. (Apple, never missing an opportunity to nibble on your credit card, has pinned a Store button in the upper-right corner in case you can't find any songs you want to hear at the moment.)

Find Music on Your Nano

Your music is just a finger-length away on the iPod Nano:

❶ **On the Home screen, tap the Music icon**. That brings up a list of categories labelled Songs, Artists, and Albums. If you're in the Songs menu, tap a title to hear it play. If you tapped Artists or Albums, tap a name or title to see the available tracks, and then tap one to listen.

❷ **Tap the screen to get playback controls**. The usual suspects like Pause, Fast-Forward, and Rewind await your gentle touch.

❸ **Tap the screen again and flick your finger right to left to get a volume control slider**. You can raise or lower the volume onscreen if you don't feel like pressing the Nano's physical volume buttons.

Find Music on Your Classic

After you pick a language, the first menu you see says "iPod" at the top of the screen. Here's how to start playing your tunes:

❶ **On the iPod menu, highlight the Music menu**. Run your thumb over the scroll wheel to move the blue highlight bar up and down.

❷ **Press the round center button to select Music**.

❸ **On the Music menu, scroll to a category so you can find your song**. You can select music by artist, album, song, genre, and so on. Scroll to the one you want, and then press the center button.

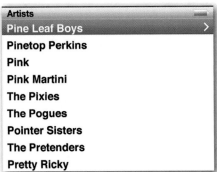

❹ **Scroll through the list on the iPod's screen**. Say you decided to look for music by artist. You now see a list of all the singers and bands whose songs sit on your iPod. Scroll down to the one you want, and press the center button. You'll see a list of the albums you have from that artist.

❺ **Scroll to the album you want to hear**. Press the Select or ▶❙❙ button to start playing the album. Press ▶❙❙ again to stop the song, or press the Menu button to retrace your steps back to the Classic's main screen.

CHAPTER 2

Bopping Around the iPod Nano, Shuffle, and Classic

THE ORIGINAL IPOD, STILL WITH US IN THE FORM OF THE IPOD CLASSIC, was simple to operate, and it still is—five buttons and a click wheel take you to all your songs, movies, games, audio books, and everything else parked on your 'Pod. Even though the player doesn't have a mouse, its controls work just like those on a desktop computer: You highlight an item onscreen and click the Classic's center button to select it. Performing this action either takes you to another menu of options or triggers an action—like playing a song, calling up a calendar, or displaying the time in Paris.

Although older iPod Nanos operate in a similar manner, today's square Nano (introduced in 2010 and updated in 2011) changes all this. This little iPod is so small that it has no room for a click wheel. Heck, it's barely bigger than the iPod Shuffle, but uses some of the same touchscreen technology that its big brother, the iPod Touch, does. You navigate the Nano not with a wheel, but with your finger—and it's a lot of fun.

No matter how you control your iPod, though, it's all about getting to your songs, photos, and other media. This chapter shows you what lies within all the menus on your Nano and Classic—and what each item does. Not to be forgotten, Shuffle owners will find special coverage of their screenless wonders sprinkled throughout.

Navigate the iPod Nano's Menus

ON THE MODERN NANO, you get to your songs, photos, FM radio, pedometer, and other fun stuff by tapping your fingers—or sliding, dragging, and flicking them as described in the previous chapter.

The Nano keeps all its menus hidden under colorful icons on its Home screen. To see all the podcasts on your Nano, for example, you just tap the Podcasts icon, and there are all your shows, in a big, flickable list.

But as you may have noticed, the Nano has a very small screen. By default, it shows you one big icon (Music, Radio, Fitness, and so on) at a time. Just flick your finger from right to left on the screen to watch the horizontal icon parade. Here's what you'll find under the icons:

- **Now Playing**. Can't name that tune? Tap this gray icon to pop up the current track's name, complete with its album artwork (if it has any) and playback controls. Tap ➊ to see a list of all the tracks on the album.

- **Music.** Tap here to see a list of icons for all the ways you can sort your song lists. You see tappable categories for Genius mixes (page 145), playlists (Chapter 6), artists, albums, songs, genres, composers, and compilations. You can also see a list of your audiobooks, podcasts, and educational iTunes U content. Tap a category to see its related tracks. For example, tap Artists to see all the songs and albums you have by that singer or band.

- **Radio**. Tap here to fire up the Nano's built-in FM radio. Page 48 has more on using the radio and its features.

- **Fitness.** The 2011 iPod Nano isn't just an audio player. It's a pedometer and a clip-on workout coach as well. Page 223 has more on those features.

- **Clock**. Tap the clock face icon to see an even bigger clock onscreen—and one with the correct time. Flick the screen left to get to the Nano's stopwatch, and flick left again to see its timer (Chapter 10).

- **Photos**. If you synced digital photos from your computer, you can view them by tapping the Photos icon and then tapping a photo album or image thumbnail. Chapter 9 has more on photo-viewing.

- **Podcasts**. If you subscribe to *podcasts*, those free audio and video shows from the iTunes Store, you'll find them under this icon.

- **Settings**. Tap here to adjust the way your Nano works. See the next section for details.

- **Voice Memos**. If you plugged in a headset and mic and recorded some audio notes (page 227), you'll see a blue Voice Memos icon as well.

The Nano Settings Menu

The Settings icon on the Nano's Home screen has submenus so you can tweak your iPod experience. Here's what you'll find under the icon and what you can do in each submenu:

- **About**. Find out how many songs and photos your Nano holds, the player's format (Windows or Mac), the amount of space left, and its serial number.

- **Music**. Turn on Shake to shuffle songs kinetically (you get a new song each time you shake your Nano-clenched fist), even out song volumes with Sound Check (or lock them in with Volume Limit), improve tracks with equalizer presets, or turn on crossfades.

Music is the only icon with submenu icons that sort your tunes by artist, album, and so on. To surface the sub-icons so you don't have to drill down through the Music menu, you can redecorate your Home screen with smaller icons that take you right where you want to go. Tap Settings→General→Home Screen. Next to Small Icons, tap On. Below the Small Icons setting, tap Music, and then tap the On buttons next to the icons you want on your Home screen. You can display four mini-icons per screen and flick between batches; the white dots at the bottom of the screen show you where you're at in the icon pages.

- **General**. The controls that set the Nano's screen brightness, wallpaper, date, time, local radio region, live-radio pause, accessibility functions, and native language all live here. Tap Settings→General→Home Screen. Next to Small Icons, tap the On button. Right below that, tap the On button next to the icons you want to see. You can turn on or off any icon, big or small, on the Nano's Home screen here, too.

- **Radio**. Pick your geographic area and turn on Live Pause (page 48) here.

- **Photos**. Configure slideshow timing and transitions here.

- **Fitness**. Set a goal for the number of steps you want to take per day or adjust your recorded height and weight for the calorie math here. Designate an inspirational "PowerSong" and pick a voice for the spoken feedback as you work out. You can also select units of measure here.

- **Reset Settings**. Choose this option to blow away all those custom settings you've been fiddling with and start fresh with the factory defaults.

Navigate the iPod Classic's Menus

LIKE ANY MODERN GADGET, the iPod uses a series of menus and submenus to control it. You can recognize the Classic's top-level, or main, menu because it says "iPod" at the top of the screen. No matter how deeply you burrow into the player's submenus, you can always get back to the main menu by repeatedly pressing the Menu button on the click wheel.

In fact, think of Classic navigation like this: Press the round center button to go deeper into menus and press the Menu button to back out, retracing your steps along the way.

The contents of your iPod menu vary a bit depending what you're doing at the time and if you've changed any of the default settings; page 41 shows how to mix and match menu items to your liking. Here's the basic lineup (you only see the Now Playing item if you have a song currently playing):

- **Music**
- **Videos**
- **Photos**
- **Podcasts**
- **Extras**
- **Settings**
- **Shuffle Songs**
- **Now Playing**

The Classic may be the oldest iPod in the family, but after the iPod Touch, it's the most versatile. The next few pages tell you a little more about each menu you see on this old-school iPod. And just as any iPod gives you choices about which song you want to play, it also lets you decide what you want displayed on your main menu. If you like the sound of that, check out page 41 later in this chapter.

What's in the Classic's Music Menu

THE CLASSIC'S MUSIC MENU gives you one-stop shopping for your iPod's audio-related options, including tunes, audio books, and podcasts.

- **Cover Flow**. Cover Flow is a visual treat, displaying gorgeous album covers that whiz by, right before your eyes. There's more on this cool feature on page 40.

- **Genius Mixes**. Your iPod includes its very own music mix-master. Chapter 6 explains the genius of Genius in greater detail.

- **Playlists**. A *playlist* is a customized list of songs that you create. Chapter 6 has loads more on creating playlists.

- **Artists**. This option groups every tune by performer.

- **Albums**. Your music, grouped by album.

- **Songs**. All the songs on your iPod, listed alphabetically.

- **Genres**. Your music, sorted by type: rock, rap, country, and so on.

- **Composers**. Your music, grouped by songwriter.

- **Audiobooks**. Your iPod's spoken-word content.

- **Search**. When you have a ton of tunes and don't feel like scrolling through your collection, use the Search function to click out the first few letters of a tune using the Classic's tiny onscreen keyboard. Songs that match your entries pop up in their own list.

What's in the Classic's Videos Menu

YOUR CLASSIC CAN WORK as a personal movie player. Before you grab the popcorn, here's what you'll find on its menu of video options:

- **Movies**. Go here to find full-length feature films you bought (and synced) from the iTunes Store, as well as your own home movies (Chapter 8).

- **Rentals**. If you opted to rent a movie instead of buying it, you'll find it waiting for you here.

- **TV Shows**. This menu holds iTunes Store–purchased TV episodes and personally recorded shows.

- **Music Videos**. A list of your collected music-video clips.

- **Video Playlists**. Just as you can create playlists of music in iTunes, you can also create playlists of videos. They live here.

- **Settings**. Click here to configure your TV playback options. For example, you can set your iPod to play video in widescreen format or adjust it for full-screen viewing. An option to turn on closed captioning is here, too.

Playing a video works just like playing a song: browse, scroll, and select. Chapters 7 and 8 tell you how to buy, sort, and organize your iPod's video collection using iTunes.

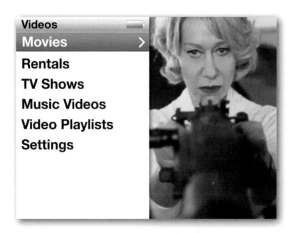

What's in the Classic's Photos Menu

READY TO TURN YOUR iPod into a pocket photo-viewer? Once you stock your Classic with images (Chapter 9 shows you how), the Photos menu lets you adjust picture-viewing preferences—including slideshow settings for picture collections—and call up your actual pics.

All Photos

Click here to view your iPod's entire photo library; individual albums are listed by name below the Settings menu. Chapter 9 shows you how to summon your pictures onscreen.

Slideshow Settings

- **Time Per Slide**. Linger up to 20 seconds on each photo, or manually click through them.

- **Music**. Select a playlist as your soundtrack, or not (for silent shows).

- **Repeat**. As with playlists, slideshows can repeat—if you want 'em to.

- **Shuffle Photos**. Toggle this setting on to display each photo in a slideshow in random order.

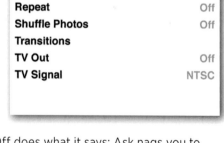

- **Transitions**. Options here include a classic Hollywood fade, a dissolve, and many more scene-changers.

- **TV Out**. To display your slideshow on a TV, select On or Ask. For slideshows you want to show on your iPod, choose Off or Ask. (Off does what it says; Ask nags you to choose between a TV and your iPod as the display for your slideshow.) Nano and Classic owners won't see the Off setting until they actually plug video-ready cables into their iPods.

- **TV Signal**. If you use a TV in North or South America or in East Asia, select NTSC; most other places use the PAL standard.

What's in the Classic's Podcasts Menu

WHEN PODCASTS FIRST APPEARED several years ago, they were almost all audio files—radio-like shows you could download and play on your 'Pod. But podcasts aren't just about audio these days—you can find plenty of video podcasts out there, too. If you want to dive in and get some shows right now, Chapter 7 explains how to download and subscribe to podcasts from the iTunes Store.

There are a couple of really great things about podcasts. For one, pretty much all of them are still free, so you have a wealth of fresh content available to put on your iPod every day.

For another, you can find plenty of nightly and weekly news programs from the major TV networks here—*Face the Nation*, *Meet the Press*, *This Week*, *Washington Week*, and so on—all blissfully commercial-free and ready to get you up to date with what's happening in the world.

Go to iPod→Podcasts to see shows you downloaded and synced up through iTunes. The iPod's menu sorts the podcasts by show name, like *BBC Digital Planet* or *Chad Vader*, with the total number of episodes listed under the title. If you haven't yet listened to an episode, a blue dot appears next to its name—which makes it easy to find your new stuff.

> **TIP** Want more free video for your iPod? Although the Classic can't stream video off the Web like the Touch can, you have other options. Rev up your favorite search engine and find upcoming movie releases. The official websites of many major motion pictures offer iPod-sized versions of the film's trailer that you can snag off the Web, pull into iTunes, and copy to your Classic. Some trailers give so much away, you may feel like you've already seen the movie (and boy, was it bad), saving yourself the price of an $8 to $13 movie ticket.

What's in the Classic's Extras Menu

HERE LIE ALL THE goodies that make the iPod more than just a music player:

- **Alarms**. Have the iPod wake you with a beep—or put you to sleep with a song (a timer setting lets you drift off to Dreamland with music).

- **Calendars**. This menu holds a copy of your personal daily schedule, synced from Microsoft Outlook or iCal.

- **Clocks**. With its built-in clock and ability to display multiple time zones, the iPod is probably the most stylish pocket watch you'll ever see.

- **Contacts**. Any phone numbers and addresses you port over from your computer reside here.

- **Games**. Kill time with a round of Klondike solitaire, test your brainpower with iQuiz, or shoot things in the Vortex.

- **Notes**. The iPod has a built-in text reader (see page 231) you can use to read brief documents and notes.

- **Screen Lock**. For stuff that's nobody's business—your address book, schedule, photos, and so on—you may want to protect your 'Pod with a four-digit passcode. To set it up, choose iPod→Extras→Screen Lock. On the Lock screen, use the click wheel to dial up four digits between 0 and 9. Press the center button to set the number and move to the next of the four boxes. Confirm your digits on the next screen. To turn on the lock, choose iPod→Extras→Screen Lock→Lock. To unlock the screen, dial in your passcode number. (If you forget the code, connect your iPod to the computer it normally syncs with to bypass the lock.)

- **Stopwatch**. Your iPod can serve as a timer so you can keep track of your overall workouts or time each lap around a track.

- **Voice Memos**. Classic owners with an optional microphone attachment (see page 227) can find their recordings at iPod→Voice Memos.

Chapter 10 has more details on many of these features.

What's in the Classic's Settings Menu

THE SETTINGS MENU HAS more than a dozen options for tailoring your iPod's look and sound.

- **About**. Look here for your iPod's serial number; the number of songs, videos, and photos on it; your model's hard drive size; and how much disk space you have left. Click the center button to go through all three screens of info.

- **Shuffle**. Turn this feature On to shuffle songs or albums.

- **Repeat**. Repeat One plays the current song over and over; Repeat All repeats the current album, playlist, or song library.

- **Main Menu**. Customize which items appear in the Classic's main menu here.

- **Music Menu**. Customize which items appear in your Music menu here, like Radio— for when you have Apple's optional FM Radio Remote.

- **Volume Limit**. Keep your (or your child's) eardrums from melting down by setting a volume limit—and locking it. Hearing loss from loud music players is a serious problem. So serious, in fact, that this setting gets its own page later in the chapter.

- **Backlight**. Specify how long your screen's backlight stays on each time you press a button or turn a dial—from 2 seconds to Always On.

- **Brightness**. If your iPod movies seem a bit dim (and not just because of Hollywood's standards), use this setting to brighten the screen.

- **Audiobooks**. If you're having trouble catching all the words as you listen to an audiobook, visit this setting. You can speed up or slow down the narration.

- **EQ**. Choose from more than 20 equalizer presets for acoustic, classical, hip-hop, and other types of music. Chapter 5 has more on equalization.

- **Sound Check**. Turn on Sound Check to level out the volume of your songs. Chapter 5 has more info.

- **Clicker**. Some people think the clicker noise the Classic makes during a long scroll sounds like ants tap-dancing. Others like the audio cue. Decide for yourself and turn the sound off or on here.

- **Date & Time**. Adjust your iPod's date, time, and time zone here.

- **Sort By**. This setting lets you change the sort order of the contacts in your iPod's address book (first name first or last name first).

- **Language**. The iPod can display its menus in most major European and Asian languages. Pick the one you want here. If your Classic gets set to a language you can't read (accidentally or by the hand of a prank-minded associate), you can restore your native tongue to the menus in a couple of ways.

For one, you can scroll all the way down to the end of the menu to the Reset All Settings option and select it. Although this pops you back to the iPod's original pick-a-language screen, it also wipes out any other settings you custom-configured.

The second method saves your settings but requires some careful counting: Start by clicking the Menu button until you get back to the main iPod menu.

Next, scroll down to the sixth line on the main screen and select it. This calls up the Settings menu, even if you can't read it. On the Settings menu, scroll all the way down, select the third line from the bottom (as shown above) and press the center button. That takes you to the big list of languages, with English right there on top. Select your language of choice, press the center button to set it, and return to business as usual.

- **Legal**. The Legal screen contains a long scroll of copyright notices for Apple and its software partners. It's not very interesting reading unless you're studying intellectual-property law.

- **Reset All Settings**. This command returns all your iPod's customized sound and display settings to their factory defaults.

Other Nano and Classic Menus: Shuffle Songs, Now Playing, and Cover Flow

BOTH THE IPOD NANO and Classic have a few other screens or controls that pop up from time to time. Here's what to expect:

Shuffle Songs

The mystical, magical qualities of the iPod's Shuffle Songs setting (*"How does my little PeaPod always know when to play my Weird Al Yankovic and Monty Python songs to cheer me up?"*) make it one of the player's most popular features. On the latest Nano, tap Music→Songs, and then tap Shuffle (✗) to start mixing up your songs. (All the way down at the bottom of the Songs list? Tap the Nano's status bar [the band up top, with the clock and battery icon in it] to jump back to the beginning of the Songs list.) On the iPod Classic, the Shuffle option appears on the main menu. Just scroll and select it to shuffle your songs.

Now Playing

As described earlier, when you tap the Now Playing icon on the Nano's screen, you see the song title, album cover art, and playback controls. But flick that first Now Playing screen to the left, and you get a virtual slider for the volume level, plus Repeat (↻), Genius (❋), and Shuffle (✗) buttons.

On the Classic, if you have a song playing but have scrolled back to the main menu to do something else, the Now Playing command appears at the very bottom of the screen. Highlight it and press Select to call up the song's Now Playing screen and get back to the music at hand. When you're on the Now Playing screen, press the iPod's center button in quick succession to get a new mini-menu with each hit, like the scrubber bar (page 45) or the chance to rate the song (Chapter 5).

Cover Flow

Although the iPod Classic doesn't have the fancy-schmancy touch-screen that the Touch and Nano do, it does have one thing in common with the Touch: Cover Flow. To see your album covers flip by as you spin the Classic's scroll wheel, choose iPod→ Music→Cover Flow.

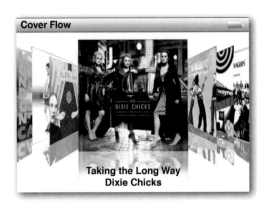

Cover Flow

Taking the Long Way
Dixie Chicks

Customize Your iPod's Menus

NANO OR CLASSIC, YOU'RE not stuck with the iPod's stock icon positions or menu items. On the Nano, you can rearrange icons across the Home screen. So if, for example, you want the Radio and Podcasts icons to appear first, you can make it so.

To redecorate your Nano's Home screen, press and hold your finger down on any one icon until they all start wiggling—they're shown at a jaunty angle in mid-wiggle here. While they're wiggling, drag the icons into your preferred order. When you're happy, press the Sleep/Wake button to stop the shaking and lock in the new arrangement. This wiggle-and-drag trick also works if you opt to display a quartet of small Home screen icons on your Nano's screen instead of having the default string of large icons. (Want the smaller icons? Tap Settings→General→Home Screen→Small Icons→On.)

Not one to be left out of the customization fun, the iPod Classic lets you arrange both your main menu and music menu screens so that only the items you like appear. For example, you could add "Calendar" as a menu item on the Classic's main screen so you don't have to dig through the Extras menu to get at it.

To do that, on the Classic, choose iPod→Settings→Main Menu. As you scroll down the list of menu items, press the center button to add (or delete) each one from the main menu. You might, for example, consider adding these commands:

- **Clock**, for quick checks of the time.

- **Games**, for quick killing of time.

- **Contacts**, to look up phone numbers and call people to pass the time.

To see the fruits of your labor, press Menu twice to return to the main screen. Sure enough, in addition to the usual commands described on page 32, you see the formerly buried menus right out front, ready to go.

Now that you've got your Classic's Main Menu screen squared away, you can do the same type of customization on your iPod's Music screen by choosing Settings→Music Menu.

Set the iPod's Clock

WHEN THE TOUCHSCREEN NANO made its debut, people joked that all you needed was a strap and the small square iPod could double as a wristwatch. (See page 226 on how to make *that* happen.) While it does display the time in digital form in its status bar on most screens, you can also check the time on an old-fashioned analog clock face by tapping the Clock icon on the Home screen.

- To get to the clock on the Nano, tap Settings→ General→Date & Time. On this screen, tap Date, Time, or Time Zone (useful when traveling) to make adjustments. You can also opt for a military-style 24-hour clock, have the clock appear when you wake up the Nano (flick to the right to dismiss it), or switch the clock face between 16 different designs.

- To make adjustments to your current clock for things like daylight saving time, the current date, the time zone—or to opt for the military-style 24-hour clock display—choose iPod→Settings→Date & Time.

  The iPod Classic lets you have multiple clocks for your world travels (see Chapter 10). To create a new clock, choose Clocks and press the Classic's center button. A box appears with a choice of Add or Edit. Scroll to Add, and then click the center button to select it.

- To change the city a clock represents on the Classic, click it with the iPod's center button and then select Edit. Pick the geographic area you want from the Region menu, and then choose a city on the next screen.

- To delete a Classic clock, select it, press the center button, and choose Delete.

TIP You can ask your Classic to display the current time in its title bar whenever music is playing. Just choose iPod→Settings→Date & Time→Time in Title. Press the center button to toggle the title-bar clock on or off.

Use the iPod Classic as an Alarm Clock

THE IPOD CLASSIC'S ALARM clock can give you a gentle nudge when you need it. To set your alarm:

❶ **Choose Extras→Alarms→Create Alarm**. Press the center button. The alarm gets set to On, and you land on a screen full of choices, described below.

❷ **Choose Date**. As you turn the click wheel, you change the date for your wake-up call. Press the center button as you pick the month, day, minutes, and so on.

❸ **Choose Time**. Repeat the wheel-turning and clicking to choose the hour, minute, and AM/PM setting for the alarm. When you get back to the Create Alarm menu, click Repeat if this is a standing alert, and then choose the alarm's frequency: daily, weekly, and so on.

❹ **Choose Alert Sound**. It's time to decide whether you want "Beep" (a warbling R2-D2–like tone that comes out of the iPod's built-in speaker) or music from a selected playlist. If you choose music, it plays through your headphones (assuming they haven't fallen out) or to an external set of speakers if you have some (see page 265).

❺ **Choose Label**. What's alarming you—a class, a meeting, time to take a pill? Pick a name for your alarm here.

If you wake up early and want to turn off the alarm, go to Extras→Alarms→[Name of Alarm]→Alarm and press the center button to toggle it off. You can also delete an alarm with the Delete option at the bottom of the menu.

Search for Songs on the iPod Classic

AS YOUR MUSIC COLLECTION grows, scrolling to find a song or album can leave you thumb-weary. Sometimes, you may not even remember if you *have* a certain song on the Classic, given its 160 gigabytes of song space. The Classic's Search feature lets you drill down through your massive library to locate specific songs, albums, and so on with a few spins of the click wheel. It works like this:

❶ Choose iPod→Music→Search.

❷ On the screen that appears, use the click wheel to highlight a letter from the alphabet. Press the center button to select the letter.

❸ The iPod immediately presents a list of matching titles, winnowing it further as you select more letters. Use the iPod's Rewind/Previous key as a backspace button to wipe out letters you don't want.

❹ Once the title you want appears onscreen, click the Menu button (to jump up to the results list), and then scroll down to select your song.

TIP iPod Shuffle owners, you can have the iPod *recite* your playlist titles so you can pick the one you want. If you haven't already done so, turn on the Shuffle's VoiceOver feature—connect the Shuffle to your computer, click its icon in the iTunes Source list, and click the Summary tab. Turn on the checkbox for Enable VoiceOver, and then click Apply. After you download and install the VoiceOver software, it syncs up audio menus for your Shuffle's content, and you can hear more than just the music.

To hear the name of the current track, press the VoiceOver button (the silver nub between the headphone jack and the On/Off/Shuffle button). To hear an audio menu of your playlists, hold down the VoiceOver button until it beeps. The Shuffle recites the playlist names, and you can click the Next or Previous buttons to move through them. Press the Play/Pause button or the VoiceOver button again to hear the playlist. To leave the Playlists menu, press and hold the VoiceOver button for a second.

VoiceOver on the iPod Nano works differently because it also describes what's *on* the screen. To turn it on, choose Settings→General→Accessibility→VoiceOver→On. VoiceOver changes how you control the Nano, with some gestures requiring *two* fingers. Apple has more info at *http://support.apple.com/kb/HT4046*.

Jump Around Within Songs and Videos

SOMETIMES, YOU JUST HAVE to hear the good part of a song again or watch that scene in a movie once more because it was so cool the first time. If that's the case, the iPod gives you the controls to make it happen.

This jump-to-the-best-part technique is called *scrubbing*, so if a fellow iPodder tells you to scrub over to 2:05 in a song to hear a great guitar solo, he's not talking about cleaning the bathtub.

On the iPod Nano, tap the Now Playing icon. When the cover of the current selection appears, tap the screen to summon the playback controls. Flick once to the left to pull the second page of controls into view and drag the time bar's round, white handle either forward or backward to get to the part of the song you want to hear.

On the iPod Classic, hold down the Rewind/Previous and the Fast Forward/Next buttons on either side of the click wheel to zip back and forth through a song or video clip.

If you want to get to a specific time in a song or video, press the Classic's center button and then use the click wheel to scroll over to the exact spot in the track's onscreen timeline. For an audio file, a small diamond appears in the timeline when you press the center button so you can see where you are in a song.

TIP   Need some soothing sounds at the end of a long day—but don't want the iPod Classic on all night if you drift off? Have it sing you to sleep with the Sleep Timer feature. Choose Extras→Alarms→Sleep Timer and then pick the amount of time you want the Classic to play: 15, 30, 60, 90, or 120 minutes. (You can choose to turn the timer *off* here as well.) Once you pick a time, press Play and relax. The Sleep Timer item in the Alarms menu displays a countdown of the time left, but hopefully you'll be too sleepy to notice.

Adjust the iPod's Volume

The iPod Nano has a set of plus (+) and minus (–) buttons on its top edge, and the Shuffle's control ring has its pluses and minuses (literally) as well, all so you can pump up (or down) your music's volume. On the Classic, the volume knob is virtual. Run your thumb over the click wheel to see the timeline bar at the bottom of the screen switch to a volume-level indicator.

If you want to protect your hearing, use the Volume Limit setting. Parents who worry that their kids are blasting music too loudly can set a volume limit and lock it in with a numeric password:

❶ On the Nano, tap Settings→Music→Volume Limit; on the Classic, choose iPod→Settings→Volume Limit.

❷ On the next screen, drag your finger on the volume slider (Nano) or use the click wheel and the volume bar (Classic) to select a maximum level.

❸ The Nano automatically remembers the maximum volume level; you can return to the Home screen by pressing and holding your finger anywhere on the screen. If you want to lock in that level, tap the Lock Volume Limit button on the Volume Limit screen. On the next screen, tap in a four-digit code to prevent anyone without the code from going in and changing the level.

On the Classic, once you dial in the max volume level, press the center button to set it. You can press the Menu button to leave the Volume Limit screen or press Play/Pause and use the click wheel to dial up a four-digit passcode.

On the iPod Shuffle, you set a volume limit on the *iTunes* side. Connect the Shuffle to your computer, click its icon in the Source list, and click the Summary tab. Scroll down to the Options area and turn on the checkbox for "Limit maximum volume." Use the onscreen slider to increase or decrease the Shuffle's loudness potential; you can also click the lock icon here to prevent little hands from making big changes to the setting. When you're done, click the Apply button.

Charge Your iPod Without Your Computer

The USB 2.0 cable (or USB adapter, if you have a Shuffle) that comes with your iPod has two jobs:

- To connect your iPod to iTunes.

- To draw power from your computer to charge up your iPod's battery.

There may be times, however, when your battery is in the red and you're nowhere near your computer. You may be on the road, nowhere near an electrical outlet. Then it's time to turn to other options, including these:

- **Get a car charger that connects to the standard 12-volt power outlet in most cars**. Several companies make auto chargers for the iPod for around $20, and you can find them at Apple Stores (including *www.apple.com/ ipodstore*); retail stores that sell iPod gear, like Best Buy; and specialty iPod-accessory web shops like Griffin Technology (*www.griffintechnology. com*).

- **Use a USB power adapter**. Many iPod accessory shops sell wall chargers as well as car chargers, and some give you one of each in a set. Apple also makes its own matching white cube to go with your USB cable. These power blocks typically have a jack on one side that accepts your iPod's USB cable (and connected iPod), and a set of silver prongs on the other side that plugs into a regular electrical outlet. Chapter 12 has more on finding power for your 'Pod, and you can get Apple's AC adapter for around $29 in iPod-friendly stores or online at *www.apple.com/ipodstore*.

Griffin Technology's $40 PowerDuo charger set for iPod

> **TIP** If you find the iPod Classic's backlight doesn't stay on nearly as long as you'd like, you can change the amount of time it shines by going to iPod→Settings→Backlight. Once you're there, scroll to the amount of time you'd like to see the light, in increments of between 2 and 30 seconds or Always On. That last one's a real battery killer, though, as all that illumination needs power.

Play FM Radio on the iPod Nano

FORGET ABOUT THOSE BOXY transistor radios of yore—your sleek new iPod Nano can pull down an FM signal from the airwaves and bring live broadcasts right to your ears. For stations transmitting RDS (Radio Data System) information, the Nano even displays the name of the song, the artist, and the station's call letters onscreen. One thing: You need to listen to the radio through headphones or a set of connected external speakers, because the cord doubles as the radio antenna. Here's how it all works:

- **Play and tune the radio**. Tap the Radio icon on the Home screen, and then tap the ❶ icon in the bottom-right corner of the screen. On the Radio menu, tap Local Stations and then hit the Refresh button to have the Nano round up a list of all the stations in your area. Tap a station to listen to it. If you want to flip through stations until you find something that sounds good, tap the Now Playing icon to call up a screen with the tuning controls. Tap ◄◄ or ►►I to sample stations up and down the dial; press and hold the arrows to scan FM stations. Press ► to listen or ■ to turn off the radio. You can also flick the tuner bar on the screen. On stations that support it, you can tap ❶ in the lower-right corner of the screen and then tap Recent Songs to see a list of the tunes you've just been listening to.

- **Add favorite stations**. When you land on a station you really like, tap the star icon down on the bottom-left corner of the tuner screen. To see your list of favorite stations, tap ❶, tap Favorites, and then tap the station in the list to hear it. To edit the list, swipe the Favorites screen from left to right, tap the Edit button that appears, tap ⊖ next to the station you want to ditch, and then tap the Delete button to confirm your decision.

- **Pause live radio**. To pause a broadcast, tap the Now Playing or Radio icon. Swipe to the left to get to the second screen, where the Live Pause controls live. Tap II to pause playback and ► to resume playing. A progress bar at the bottom shows you how long you've been in Pause mode. Like TiVo, you can fast-forward or rewind through the audio stored in the progress bar—just tap ↺ or ►► to jump in 30-second blocks or press and hold down the ►► icon to skip ahead in 10-second hops.

- **Tag songs**. If you see a little tag icon (circled here), the station supports iTunes tagging. When you hear a song you *have* to have, tap the tag icon. When you sync your Nano to your computer, the songs appear in a Tagged playlist in the Store area of the Source list. You can listen to previews there—and *buy* the songs, naturally.

Play Games on an iPod Classic

THE IPOD CLASSIC IS a personal entertainment machine on many levels and comes with three games: Klondike, iQuiz, and Vortex. To find any of your games on the Classic, go to iPod→Extras→Games.

Klondike

The iPod has a Vegas-style Klondike solitaire game. To play, you get a row of seven card piles, on which you alternate black and red cards in descending numerical order. Use the click wheel to pass a virtual hand over each stack. Click the center button when you get to the card you want to move to the bottom of the screen. Then scroll the hand to the pile where you want to place the card and click the center button again to make the play. Click the facedown card (upper left) for three new cards to play.

iQuiz

Complete with colorful flashing graphics and a cheesy, '70's-style game show soundtrack, iQuiz picks your brain with contemporary multiple-choice questions in several trivia categories like music, movies, and TV. The game brings its own questions to the screen, but it also taps into your iPod to find out how much you know about your own library.

Vortex

Most computers and handheld devices wouldn't be complete without some brick-bashing version of the old Pong-against-the-wall game. Vortex scales up the basic concept to 360 degrees of brick-smashing 3-D fun. Use the scroll wheel to move the bat around the edges of the circular Vortex and audibly smash through the rotating bricks.

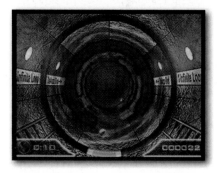

NOTE Even the very first iPod in 2001 came with a game but it was an *Easter egg*, or hidden feature. To find it, you had to select About on the iPod's menu and hold down the center button until the classic Brick game (also known as Breakout) appeared. The original 1970s Breakout arcade game, incidentally, was engineered by Steve Wozniak with help from Steve Jobs—who both went on to found Apple.

CHAPTER 3

Touring the Touch

TRADITIONAL IPODS MAY HAVE THEIR CLICK WHEELS AND BUTTONS, but the iPod Touch brings a whole new level of control to your fingertips. In fact, your fingertips *do* control the way you use this very special 'Pod. Instead of scrolling and clicking through menu after menu, this touchscreen-outfitted iPod gives you a set of icons on its Home screen. Tap one and you instantly go wherever you want to—whether that's onto the Web, amongst your favorite tunes, or into your photo collection. And the Touch not only shows off pictures, it *shoots* them, too—along with videos.

The Touch comes preloaded with colorful little programs that let you send and receive email from all your accounts, keep tabs on the weather, track the stock market, and record your to-do lists. But you're not limited to standard-issue software—thanks to the iTunes App Store, you can turn your Touch into a personalized pocket computer with its own games, productivity programs, eBooks, and more.

This chapter gives you a close-up look at where to find everything on your Touch and how to customize it to your preferences.

Turn the Touch On and Off

WHILE ITS NICE, BRIGHT interactive touchscreen gets most of the attention, the Touch does have a few physical controls—a quartet of buttons along its edges and front. Two of these buttons let you turn the Touch on. One is the narrow little Sleep/Wake button on the Touch's top-right edge. The other is the Home button on the front of the Touch (described in detail on the next page).

The Sleep/Wake button serves a second purpose, too—it puts the Touch in Sleep mode. Give it a gentle press to put the Touch down for a nap in power-saving standby mode.

To wake up a sleeping Touch, press the Sleep/Wake button once more or press the Home button.

If you want to turn your Touch off completely, the Sleep/Wake button acts as an On/Off button, too—just press and hold it down for a few seconds. The screen fades to black, and the no-nonsense "slide to power off" red arrow appears. Drag the arrow to the right to power down your 'Pod.

When it's time to play again, press the Sleep/Wake button to turn the Touch back on.

The Home Button and Home Screen

EVEN WITH ITS SIMPLE design, the Touch has one very promi-nent physical button, smack-dab on the player's glass front: the Home button. You'll press this one a lot, because it's the portal to all the stuff stored on your Touch.

Most people associate the word *Home* with peace and stability, and this button lives up to that notion. No matter where you are in the Touch—16 levels up in a game, deep into the new U2 album, or out on the Internet, pressing the Home button always brings you back to the main Touch screen. You don't even have to click your heels three times.

When you turn on your brand-new Touch, the Home screen will probably look some-thing like this, with its included apps in their standard order. The Touch divides the icons into two groups: One is the four-by-four grid in the main part of the screen, and the other is the single row of four icons along the bottom. You can have up to 11 flickable pages of icons on the Touch's Home "screen," but no matter which page you flick to, the four icons anchored to the bottom row always stay onscreen.

Want to rearrange the icons—including that bottom row of four—so you can put your most-used apps up front? Press down on an icon until it wiggles, and then drag it to a new location. When you're done rear-ranging, press the Home button to make the icons sit still again. Once you fill up the first Home screen with icons, swipe your finger to the left to go to the next screen of icons. Swipe your finger the other way to go back to that first screen. (If you find all this finger dragging, well, a drag, you can rearrange your icons more easily in iTunes; see page 77 to learn how.)

The Home button can do other tricks, too, like letting you switch quickly from one app to another (page 91) and forcing misbehaving apps to quit. If an app is stuck onscreen, hold down the Sleep/Wake button until the red "power off" slider appears (opposite page). Let go of Sleep/Wake and hold down the Home button until the app closes—and you're back Home. And you can summon the Touch's camera from the Lock Screen by pressing the Home button twice quickly to get a ◘ icon that takes you right into the Camera app.

What's in the Music Menu

SINCE YOU HAVE AN iPod, you probably want to play some music, right? To do that, tap the Music icon; you'll see your audio collection sorted into all kinds of helpful categories, like songs, artists, and albums. Click a category to reveal its list of songs, musicians, or albums. Flick your finger up and down the screen to scroll through a list. In any category that goes right to a song list, tap a song's title to hear the tune. For other categories, like Artists or Albums, click a name or title in the list to see all the songs in that category, and then tap a song title to play it.

Icons on the bottom row of the Touch's Music screen take you to the first four categories, which vary depending on whether you synced up Genius Mixes (Chapter 6) from iTunes. Here's what the categories look like:

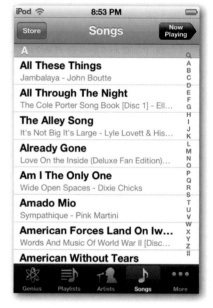

- **Genius**. If you *did* sync Genius Mixes, tap this button to play them.

- **Playlists**. If you didn't go for a Genius Mix sync session (or haven't gotten to it yet), Playlists shows up as the first icon. In case you haven't heard of a *playlist*, it's a collection of songs that you think sound good together A playlist for a gym routine could contain high-energy dance tracks, for example. (Chapter 6 shows you how to create a playlist.).

- **Artists**. To sort your music by band or performer, tap Artists. Even if your collection has just one measly track from an obscure bar band, the band's name will show up proudly next to Elvis Presley and The Beatles. Tap the band's or artist's name to see the available tracks, and tap a song to start playing it.

- **Songs**. Tap here to see a complete list of the songs on your iPod, nicely arranged in alphabetical order. If you don't feel like flicking forever to get down to "Zing! Went the Strings of My Heart," tap the vertical index bar to jump to a specific letter—and all the songs that start with it.

> **NOTE** If you didn't sync Genius Mixes to your iPod, the fourth category before the More button is Albums. There's more on More—and Albums—on the next page.

The last icon in the row is aptly named More. Tap it to see *more* ways to sort your audio collection, including these categories:

- **Albums**. Far from its roots on discs of black vinyl, the notion of "album" still thrives on music players everywhere, whether you have the complete set of tracks or not. Tap here to see all your music grouped according to the name of the album it appears on.

- **Audiobooks**. Tap here to see the narrated books you bought and downloaded from the iTunes Store or Audible.com (Chapter 7). Tracks you ripped from audiobook CDs don't show up here automatically; you have to edit the file type first (to do that, see page 120).

- **Compilations**. Soundtracks, tribute records, and any other album with tracks from multiple artists is usually considered a *compilation*. If iTunes doesn't automatically tag these albums as compilations, you can do it yourself by heading to page 120.

- **Composers**. All your music, listed by songwriter, resides here.

- **Genres**. If you're in a jazz, country, pop, or other music-specific mood, tap Genres to see all the music in a particular category.

- **iTunes U**. College lectures, educational videos, and other academic pursuits from the iTunes U campus in the iTunes Store live here.

- **Podcasts**. All those radio-like shows you can download free from the Web huddle together under this menu. Tap a show title to see a list of individual episodes. A blue dot means it's a new, unheard episode, while a half-blue dot means you started listening and stopped somewhere along the way.

As you tap around your collection, your Touch is ready if you want to add to it right there: A Store button in the top-left corner of most screens awaits your impulses.

TIP Don't like Apple's order of things and want to put your lists where *you* want them? Tap the More button and, on the next screen, tap the Edit button in the top-left corner. On the black Configure screen, drag the ghostly white list icons down into the bottom row in the order you prefer them. Once you get your favorite icons within easy reach, tap Done.

What's in the Videos Menu

VIDEO COMES IN MANY forms these days: movies, TV shows, podcasts, and more. If you have moving images on your Touch, they're in one of these categories:

- **Movies**. Hollywood blockbusters from the iTunes Store, movies you made yourself, and trailers you snagged off the Web all live happily here.

- **TV Shows**. Don't have time for TV the traditional way (on the couch and with a beverage)? When you grab TV shows from the iTunes Store, you see them in this part of the Videos menu.

- **Music Videos**. You find music videos you bought from the iTunes Store (or those that come with some albums) here.

- **Video Podcasts**. Podcasts aren't just audio-only these days; look here for full-blown video productions. (You see only one listing for each podcaster, along with the number of episodes you've got.)

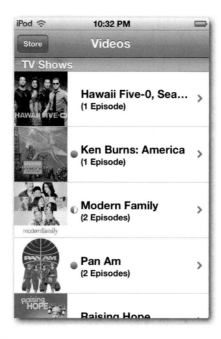

A thumbnail photo next to each video gives you a hint as to its content, and information like running time or number of episodes appears here as well.

Tap a title to play a video. If you have multiple episodes of a TV show or podcast, tap the show title and then tap the name of the episode you want to watch. Rotate the Touch to landscape view and enjoy the show. (Flip ahead to Chapter 8 if you want to know more about video *right now*.)

What's in the Photos Menu

WHO NEEDS TO DRAG around a photo album or a laptop full of slideshows when you've got a Touch? And with the current Touch, you not only have a picture viewer, you get a whole digital camera and camcorder in the mix, too.

Odds are, though, you probably took most of your photos with a standard digital camera. As Chapter 9 explains, you can transfer copies of your favorite pictures and photo albums onto the Touch through iTunes. And when you do, they land here in the Photos app.

Give the Photos icon (the happy sunflower) a tap on the Home screen, and all those pictures await you in the iPod's Photo library. Many photo-organizer programs, like Adobe Photoshop Elements and Apple's iPhoto, let you sort pictures into albums, and you can see those same albums in the Photos app, if you opted to sync them over. The number in parentheses next to the album name reveals how many photos live there.

The Camera Roll album at the top of the screen collects all the photos you take and the videos you shoot with the Touch itself; you can import them back into your computer using your photo-organizer app. Other images that come right to the Touch—like screenshots you snap or photos you save from email messages—land here, too. Chapter 9 has all the photographic details.

What's in the Settings Menu

THE TOUCH IS A powerful little media machine, and you fine-tune the way it works in the Settings menu. Here's what you find by tapping the Settings icon on the Home screen:

- **Airplane Mode**. When the flight attendant tells you to turn off all Internet devices, tap Airplane Mode to On—that turns *off* your WiFi, the airborne data streams the pilot is worried about.

- **WiFi**. Turn the iPod's WiFi antenna on or off here—or see what wireless network you're currently connected to.

- **Notifications**. Many apps can alert you to news and updates (like football scores) with "push" notifications that automatically pop up onscreen. Turn the alerts on or off here.

- **Sounds**. The Touch can make all sorts of external noises, from ringtones for FaceTime calls to keyboard clicks. Set your sounds (and volumes) here.

- **Brightness**. If you don't like the Touch's Auto-Brightness sensor adjusting your screen, override it and make your own adjustments here.

- **Wallpaper**. Tap here to change the background image for your Touch's Lock (at left in photo) and Home (right) screens. You can use Apple's stock snaps or your own pictures.

- **General**. Here you'll find the Touch's About menu (listing the iPod's serial number, software version, and number of songs, videos, apps, and more), plus network info, Bluetooth settings, and the On/Off switch for the GPS-like Location Services feature. You control wireless settings, like those for iTunes Wi-Fi Sync and over-the-air software updates, from here as well. You can also restrict Spotlight searches to certain file types, set up a passcode for your Touch, and adjust the date and time. The Keyboard settings let you turn off (or on) the iPod's spell-check and auto-correction features. In the International area, you can choose the iPod's display language or switch to a foreign-language keyboard. The Accessibility options include VoiceOver settings, spoken-word alerts, and high-contrast screen text. You can also reset all the settings you've fiddled with—and even erase all the iPod's content.

- **iCloud**. Tap here to set preferences for syncing your personal data—contacts, calendars, mail, notes, reminders, bookmarks—as well as your Photo Stream (page 212) and data backup to Apple's free online storage locker.

- **Mail, Contacts, Calendars**. Tap here to set up an email account right on the Touch. You can adjust all other mail-related preferences here, too (like how often the Touch looks for new messages), and delete unwanted accounts. Scroll farther down for the Contacts settings, where you can change the way the Touch sorts your contacts—first name first or last name first. In the Calendars area, you get time zone controls to make sure your events are set for your own location, and a toggle to turn event invitation alerts on or off. Chapter 10 has more on syncing contacts and calendars.

- **Twitter**. If you use the popular microblogging service, log into your account here to tweet photos, links, and more right from the Touch.

- **FaceTime**. Turn the FaceTime feature on here, and set up the email account you want to use with it so FaceTime callers can find you.

- **Safari**. Specify the Safari web browser's default search engine (Google, Yahoo, or Bing), and whether you want the Autofill feature to fill in website user names and passwords on your behalf. The security settings are here, too: Turn on warnings for potentially fraudulent websites, block annoying pop-up ads and cookies, or clear your browser cache—which erases all the accumulated page parts left behind from your web surfing. Chapter 11 has more on this fun stuff.

- **Messages**. Set up your iMessage account to use Apple's free text-messaging service for iOS 5 devices here. Page 66 has more on iMessage.

- **Music**. You can set the iPod to shuffle with a shake (or not), turn the Equalizer and Sound Check features off or on (Chapter 5), set limits for maximum volume, and choose to display lyrics and podcast titles here.

- **Video**. Instruct the Touch to pick up playing a video where you left off, and turn closed captioning on or off. If you're connecting your iPod to a television, the TV Out settings for pumping video to the big screen also reside here.

- **Photos**. The settings for your Touch slideshows are here, including the time each slide stays onscreen, the animated transition between shots, and whether the Touch repeats the show or shuffles the slides.

- **Notes**. Tap here to pick one of three fonts for your little yellow iPod notes.

- **Store**. The name of the iTunes account you use to buy apps and music gets displayed here. Tap Sign Out to log out.

- **Individual application settings**. Certain apps, like Facebook and iBooks, have their own settings screen. Tap the app name to see and adjust the settings. Facebook, for example, lets you reload screens with a shake of the Touch and set up push alerts.

Other Icons on the Touch Home Screen

THE MUSIC, VIDEOS, AND Photos icons on the Touch Home screen definitely get a workout, but several other icons await your gentle tap as well:

- **FaceTime**. Tap here to start the cameras rolling with Apple's mondo-cool video-chat program. New Touch owners can yap up a storm with other Touch-carrying folks, and with iPhone 4 peeps as well. Page 65 has more.

- **Calendar**. You can sync a copy of your schedule from your computer's copy of Outlook, iCal, or Entourage. Chapter 10 tells you how.

- **Camera**. Tap this icon to turn on the Touch's built-in camera. With a few screen taps, you can snap digital pictures of something in front of you or use the Touch's front-facing camera to capture a self-portrait. A little onscreen slider lets you switch from shooting still photos to capturing video. Flip ahead in this chapter for more on using the Touch's camera.

- **YouTube**. Wirelessly watch video from one of the world's most popular (and time-consuming) websites. Chapter 8 has more on YouTube and other iPod video.

- **Maps**. Get directions or even *find yourself*. You'll read more on Maps later in this chapter.

- **Weather**. Temperatures and forecasts for your favorite cities live here. Tap ❶ to flip the screen to add towns, and swipe a finger across the screen to whip through them. Tap ❷! to get Yahoo's event info for that locale.

- **Notes**. When you need to jot down information in a hurry—like a grocery list or an idea for the Great American Novel—tap here. The Touch keyboard slides up, ready for action. Tap **✚** to add a new note, and tap 🗑 to delete an existing one. To call up a previously typed note, tap its name in the main Notes list. To email or print a note, tap ↗.

You can sync notes between your Touch and Microsoft Outlook 2003 and later or Mac OS X Mail 10.5 and later. Just connect the Touch to your computer, click its icon in the Source list, and click the Info tab in the main part of the iTunes window. Scroll down, turn on the checkbox next to the option for syncing notes, and then click Apply or Sync. If you have MobileMe, Google, Yahoo, or AOL mail accounts set to sync wirelessly, you can sync their Notes as well. Tap Settings→Mail,

Contacts, Calendars; tap the name of your account; and then tap the Notes button to On. You can also sync notes through iCloud (page 254).

- **Reminders**. A to-do list to keep you organized; see page 67 for more..

- **Clock**. You can have one clock in your pocket—or keep time in several cities around the world at once. Chapter 10 has the details.

- **Game Center**. Want to play a game? Turn to page 64.

- **Newsstand**. This app keeps all your eMagazines in one place (page 70).

- **iTunes**. This happy purple icon leads to shopping fun in the iTunes Store—without wires. Chapter 7 tells you what to expect once you get there.

- **App Store**. Tap here for games, eBooks, and more to tickle your Touch.

- **Stocks**. Check your portfolio to see how the market is doing. To add your stocks to your palm-sized Big Board, tap the tiny ➊ in the bottom-right corner. The screen spins around, giving you a place to type in ticker symbols. Flick the bottom panel to browse through three screens of information about a selected stock, including a quick-look chart of its 52-week performance, sales graphs, and recent headlines about the company. Turn the Touch sideways and tap to see the stock's trading price rise and fall over a day, a week, a month, 3 months, 6 months, 1 year, or 2 years. Tap ➍! to get company info from Yahoo Finance.

- **Mail**. Tap here to check your email—or send messages. There's more on the Mail app and setting up your accounts later in this chapter.

- **Safari**. Take a web journey. Tap the Safari icon to fire up the browser; check out Chapter 11 for details on how to use it.

- **Contacts**. Keep in touch on your Touch with the iPod's address book. See Chapter 10 for instructions on syncing old contacts or making new ones.

- **Calculator**. Tap the Calculator icon to get a big, bright math machine, ready to divide and conquer. Hold the Touch in landscape mode to get a scientific calculator for trigonometry and other math functions.

- **Voice Memos**. Turn your Touch into an audio recorder. Chapter 10 explains how.

Map Your Way with WiFi

THE TOUCH'S RELIANCE ON a WiFi signal doesn't make it a very good navigational device when you're away from your home network or a coffee shop (unless you have a personal portable hot spot, like the Verizon MiFi). There are plenty of times, however, when getting directions and finding places on a map from the comfort of a WiFi connection comes in handy.

To plot your course, tap the Maps icon on the Home screen. Here are some of the things you can do with Maps and a network connection:

- **Find yourself**. Tap the compass icon in the bottom-left corner (circled) to have the Touch pinpoint your current location within a few hundred yards. (While the Touch doesn't have a GPS chip inside it, it does have software that calculates your position based on a big database of WiFi hot spots.) To find yourself, you need to make sure you have Location Services turned on. To do that, tap Settings→General→Location Services→On.

- **Find an address**. In the Address box at the top of the screen, type in an address—or tap the icon to call up your Contacts list, where you can select the friend or business you want to map. Then tap the Search button to see a red pushpin drop onto that location.

If your location has an orange icon next to it (), you can see what that address looks like in real life with Google Street View. Tap , and when the

photo of the location appears, drag your finger around the screen to see the image from all directions and angles. When you're done, tap the mini map (the circle in the bottom-right corner, shown right) to go back to the regular map.

- **Options for map addresses**. Tap the Directions button at the bottom of the screen. When you see your address marked on the map next to the push-pin, tap the 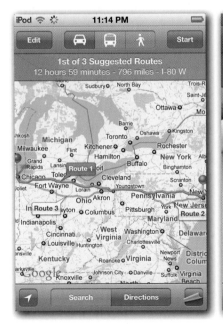 icon to advance to a screen where you can get directions to or from that address. Your other options include adding the address to a contact file (great for filing away restaurants you want to visit again), or sharing it by email (the Touch's Mail program pops up). You can also book-mark it for future reference. (Tap the ⊞ button to call up a screen with tabs for Bookmarks, Recents [for recent locations], and Contacts.)

- **Find your way**. Tap the Directions button at the bottom of the screen. A two-field box appears. If you don't want to use your current location as the starting point, tap ⊗ in the Start box, and then type in a point of origin. In the End box, type in your destination. Press the Route button. The Maps app returns turn-by-turn directions for travel by car, mass transit (if applicable), or on foot. It also shows available alternate routes. Tap the icon for your means of the transportation, and then tap the Start button to get going. Tap ← or → to move through the directions. If you want to see a text list of the directions, tap the ⊿ icon in the bottom-right corner (the map appears to curl up in cool iPod 3-D), and then tap the List button.

  While on this screen, you can also choose the look of your map: a regular cartographic version, a satellite image, or a hybrid of both. Tap Show Traffic if you want to see current road congestion and maybe take that antacid *before* you leave the house. If you have an AirPrint-compatible printer, tap the Print button to take a copy of the map with you.

Play Around in Game Center

UNLESS YOU'RE PLAYING SOLITAIRE, games are usually more fun when you play with someone. Once you sign up for the Touch's new Game Center, you can compete against thousands of other Game Center players around the world. You can add pals to a Friends list for quick competitions, do battle with strangers in multiplayer games, and join the race to the top of each game's leaderboard.

Here's how to get started with Game Center:

❶ Tap the Game Center icon on the Touch's Home screen and sign up for an account or type in your Apple ID (page 160); games you buy and download get billed to this account. Pick an online nickname—it may take a few tries to find an available one. You can also add a photo to your profile.

❷ Configure your settings so you get invitations to games, and so Game Center members can find you based on your email address.

❸ If you didn't turn them on before, you can get push notifications from the Game Center for game invitations and updates.

❹ Add some friends by tapping the **+** icon. Here, you can send a message to an email address or a Game Center nickname. After your buds accept your friend requests, you can send game challenges by tapping the Friends button and then tapping a name. (Tap the Requests button to see pending friend requests from other players.) And after you sign up a few friends, Game Center reccomends new ones for you.

❺ Once you have your account set up, it's time to get a game. Tap the Games icon and then tap Find Game Center Games. Not every App Store game is hooked into Game Center, so it's best to pick them from within the app. At the top of the Games screen. tap Game Recommendations to see suggestions from Game Center itself.

❻ Play. Tap the Friends button to pick a buddy, tap the name of a game, and then tap Play. Your pal gets a game invite, and once she accepts your challenge, throw down and start whooping.

If your invitation goes ignored, tap the Auto-Match button to have Game Center pair you with an available player, or send a request to another friend. Even when you play solo, you can check player standings right after you finish a game (or later by tapping Games→[Name of Game]→Leaderboards).

Make FaceTime Calls

SINCE THE EARLY DAYS of science-fiction movies and TV shows, the video-phone has been a staple of fantasy communication. Cheap webcams and tele-conferencing systems made the fantasy real, but they're *so* last year (and so stationary). For modern convenience, the Touch makes and takes video calls thanks to FaceTime, its built-in mobile video-chat app.

To use FaceTime, you need an Apple ID (Chapter 7) and a WiFi connection. You also need folks to talk to, namely other new Touch owners and people running around with iPad 2s and iPhone 4/4S models who have time to chat.

Once you have all that, getting started with FaceTime is easy:

❶ Tap the FaceTime icon on the Home screen and sign in with your Apple ID. Fill in your vitals, like your geographic region and email address, so other FaceTimers can find and call you.

❷ Once you have your account set up, tap the Contacts icon on the Home screen, tap the name of the person you want to call, and then tap the FaceTime button at the bottom of the Contacts screen. Since iPhone 4/4S owners can use their phone numbers for FaceTime calls, a screen pops up asking what connection (phone digits or email address) you want to use for the call. Tap your choice. If you don't have anybody in your Contacts file, visit Chapter 10, which explains how to import your computer's address book or add entries on the Touch itself.

❸ When your buddy picks up the call, hold your Touch up so they can see you and start chatting. You see them, too. If the little picture-in-picture window of your face is in the way, use your finger to drag it to a new part of the screen.

❹ After you wave goodbye, tap the End button to hang up.

If you need to temporarily turn off the sound during a call (like when the baby starts screaming), tap the Mute icon (🎤).

Want to show your friend what you're seeing without physically flipping the Touch around? Tap the 📷 icon in the bottom-right corner to switch to the Touch's rear camera. Tap the icon again to return the view to you.

Use iMessage

THANKS TO THE IMESSAGE app in iOS 5, iPod Touch owners now have a way to send free, unlimited text messages, photos, and videos to people who are also running iMessage on their iPads, iPhones, and Touches. It works over a WiFi connection on the iPod Touch. Setting up iMessage takes just a few steps:

❶ On the Home screen, tap open the iMessage app. The first time you start it up, it asks you to enter your Apple ID. (If you've blown off Apple's previous 18 attempts to get you to sign up for an account, tap Create New Account and follow along onscreen.) The email address you use with your Apple ID is the one people need in order to send you iMessages.

❷ To add more email addresses to your iMessage account, tap open the Settings icon on the iPod Touch's Home screen and in the left column of icons, tap Messages. Tap the "Receive At" line and then type in the addresses. (The Settings screen also has a button to turn off iMessage if you don't want to be pestered.)

❸ Once you sign up, you can send messages to others who have registered with Apple. Tap open iMessage on the Home screen, tap the ☑ icon, and then enter the address of your recipient. Type your message in the text field at the bottom of the screen and then tap the Send button.

Tap ◉ if you also want to send a picture or video from your Camera Roll—or shoot a new pic for the occasion.

To see your previous iMessage conversations, tap the Messages button in the upper-left corner of the screen. A list of earlier chats appear onscreen. From here, you can tap open a conversation to review or restart it. To whack old chatter, tap the Edit button, select the conversations, tap the ⊖ icon next to each one, and then tap the Delete button.

Unlike a cellphone text plan, which ties your message Inbox to your mobile number, iMessage works by email address. This means you can get your messages on several iOS 5 devices to keep your conversations going. And, unlike a cellphone text plan, iMessage is *free*—making it an affordable way to keep up with your pals, as long as they're all using iOS 5 gadgets, too.

Use Reminders

FOR LONG-TIME USERS OF iOS, one vital app has been missing for years: a to-do list. Apple has finally checked this task off its own to-do list and introduced the new Reminders app. Reminders is wonderfully easy to use, and you can jot down your chores in a straightforward list or assign them to a future date. Here's how add a task either way:

- **By List.** Tap open the Reminders icon on the iPod's home screen. Tap the List button, tap the **+** button in the upper-right corner, and then type in what you need to accomplish, like "Buy Pampers."

- **By Date.** Tap the Date button at the top of the screen. If the task needs to be completed in the next few days, find the day in the date bar along the bottom of the screen and then tap the **+** button to enter your item. For a date far in the future, tap the calendar icon in the upper-left corner to reveal the next three months, as shown here, and then tap the day you need a reminder.

As you complete your chores in either List or Date view, tap the empty square next to the task to check it off. Here are a couple of other things you can do with the Reminders app:

- In List view, swipe left to right to see a list of completed tasks and get that proud feeling of accomplishment.

- Tap an entry to add to it or see more information about the task. On the Details screen, you can tap to add a reminder for your reminder (in the form of an onscreen notification; see page 69), repeat the alert, add a note about the task, or even delete the whole thing.

Can't remember exactly when you did something? Search your reminders by tapping the Search icon in the top-left corner on either the List or Date screens. In the search box, type in keywords to bring up results that may jog your memory.

User Twitter

TWITTER, FOR THOSE WHO haven't been paying attention the past few years, is a microblogging service; it lets you update friends about your activities or musings. Millions of people use it to report what they see or feel, check for public announcements, and share links to photos and web pages. You have 140 characters per message to express your thoughts. And it's free.

If you already have a Twitter account—and use it—get ready to let out a joyous holler, because iOS 5 lets you tweet (post updates) directly from many iPod Touch apps, including Safari, Maps, YouTube, Camera, and Photos. Just tap the ☛ icon in those apps to see the Tweet menu option.

Technically, Twitter's not a built-in app, but so many iPod programs offer a tweet option that it's best covered in this part of the book. To get full use of the Twitter experience with your iPod apps and see reactions to the things you share, you can install the Twitter app right from the Settings screen:

❶ Tap Home→Settings→Twitter.

❷ Tap the Install button to snag the program from the App Store. (You need to have an App Store account and password to get the app, so check out page 160 if you don't.)

❸ If you already have a Twitter account, you don't need to install the app if you just want to tweet out links and photos from your Touch. Type in your Twitter user name and password on the settings screen and tap Sign In.

❹ If you're new to this Twitter thing but want to take the plunge right on your iPod, tap the Create New Account button and follow along.

So now that you have Twitter installed and your personal Twitter account set up, what do you do with it on your Touch? If you're an experienced Twitter user, you've probably already put this book down and gone off to post a few tweets to your pals.

If you're brand-new to Twitter, you should take a spin over to the Support area of Twitter's site. The company has set up its own online guide for using the service, as well as using the search feature to find out what everyone else is tweeting about. The guide is at *http://support.twitter.com/groups/31-twitter-basics*.

Use Notifications

THE IPOD'S NATIVE APPS can keep track of your life, from bugging you about meetings to reminding you to buy milk on the way home. Once you visit Settings→Notifications and turn on alerts for the apps you want to hear from, you'll get little onscreen notifications no matter what you're doing on the iPod.

But with all the various apps on board, wouldn't it be great to have *one* place where you can review pressing matters, like calendar appointments, email messages, or pending to-do list items?

Thankfully, there is such a Dashboard of Your Life. It's called the Notifications screen. To see it from anywhere or any app on your Touch, just place your finger at the very top edge of the screen and drag it downward, like you're pulling down a miniature window shade. The Notifications screen appears.

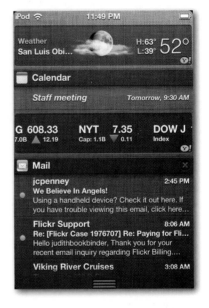

You can get a quick hit of data and jump to any listed app or message by tapping it. Notifications also appear on the iPod's Lock Screen so you don't miss anything when you're not using your Touch. To go right to a notice, put your finger on the app's icon or message and slide it to the right. This both unlocks the Touch and opens the app that's badgering you for attention.

By default, the Notifications screen shows you basic info-nuggets, like pending reminders, calendar appointments, stock prices, or any new email messages that have arrived. But like most things on the Touch, you can customize your Notifications screen by adding apps it, removing them, or resorting them.

To do all this, tap Settings→Notifications. You can sort the displayed apps manually or by time (meaning the newest updates appear highest up). To manually sort the apps, tap the Edit button in the top-right corner and use the grip strip (≡) to drag them into a new order. Tap an app's name to turn its notifications on or off—or to further customize its display with one of two different onscreen styles (a small, top-of-the-screen "banner" or a larger, middle-of-the-screen "alert").

No matter when a notification popped onto your screen, you can always get a recap by dragging down the Notifications screen. To dismiss it, put your finger at the bottom of the iPod screen and flick upwards. Consider yourself notified.

Use Newsstand and iBooks

Even though you may not use it—or haven't had reason to yet—the Touch's new built-in Newsstand app organizes all the digital newspapers and magazines you buy through the App Store. And Apple's iBooks app, while not built-in, is easy to snag from the App Store so you can buy and download electronic books to read as well.

Yes, even though the Touch's screen *is* much smaller than the iPad's, the Touch is still a handy way to haul around dozens of magazines and hefty books in convenient electronic form—it's like a bookstore that fits in your pocket, and the Touch is easier to hold and read on crowded trains, planes, and other tight spots.

First up, Newsstand. This app sits quietly on the iPod's Home screen, waiting for you to download an electronic magazine or newspaper so it can display the material proudly on its virtual shelves.

"Hey," you say, "That all sounds great, but how do I find and subscribe to digital magazines and newspapers in the first place?" Apple, in its quest to sell you more content, has made it extremely easy: Just launch the Newsstand app and tap the Store button in the top-right corner, as shown at the right.

The Newsstand whisks you to a special part of the App Store, one with electronic periodicals you can buy, subscribe to, and download to your Touch. The Store displays each ePublication as though it were an app, offering price, ratings, and other information. Tap a title to learn more, buy a single issue, or sign up for a subscription. The bill for your purchase goes to the credit card linked to your Apple ID (page 160).

If you need to cancel, renew, or adjust a subscription, log into your Store account with your Apple ID. You can do that right from the Touch by opening the iTunes Store app, flicking to the bottom of the screen, and tapping either your account name (if you're signed in already) or Sign In. Tap View Apple ID, log in, and flick down to Subscriptions. Tap Manage and then tap the name of the ePublication you want to change.

If you sign up for a subscription, the Newsstand app automatically grabs each new issue and sends you a notification (if you have your settings configured to do so). The app also lists the number of new e-rags in a red circle on the Newsstand icon. Tap it open to see what awaits you on the faux-IKEA shelves.

On to iBooks. The first time you visit the App Store (page 166), you'll likely get a note from Apple asking if you'd like to download a free copy of its iBooks app so you can read eBooks. If this appeals to you, tap the Get iBooks button (you can always go back and download it later from the Apple Store).

Once you install iBooks, you see it also has a Store button that beckons you to tap it. When you do, you're swept right into the section of the App Store that sells electronic books. After you find something to read, tap the price to buy it—and to have it billed to your iTunes account. If you're not sold yet, tap the Get Sample button to download a portion of it to evaluate. Tap the Library button to leave the Store and return to your personal book collection.

The books you download appear in the iBooks app. Tap a book cover to open the title and start reading. You can read your book in either portrait (vertical) or landscape (horizontal) mode.

By tapping the electronic page onscreen, you can summon the controls for navigating and customizing your reading experience. For instance:

- Tap ≔ to go to the book's table of contents or list of pages you've bookmarked.

- Tap ☀ to adjust the screen brightness.

- Tap ₐA to make the type larger or smaller, pick a different typeface, or add a light-brown sepia tone to the page to make it easier to read.

- Tap Q to search for text within the book—or on Google and Wikipedia.

- Tap 🔖 to bookmark your place. If you're reading the book on different iOS devices, iBooks offers to sync your bookmarks between them.

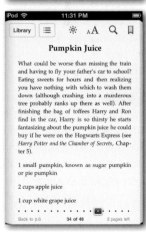

With your fingertip, use the brown slider at the bottom of the page to skip around in the book. When you're done reading, tap the Library button in the top-left corner of a book's page to close it and return to your Library. You can also open, read, and store PDF files in the iBooks app. Page 230 shows you how.

Use the Touch Keyboard

THE TOUCH HAS FOUR buttons but no keys—and no physical keyboard. All your text input for web addresses, email messages, Game Center sign-ups, and more come from the Touch's virtual keyboard. This keyboard magically appears onscreen whenever you tap an area that requires typed text.

Trained typists (or those with large fingers) may find the keyboard annoying at first, but most people feel it gets easier the more they use it. To enter a letter, tap the key you want. As your finger hits the screen, a bigger version of the letter balloons briefly into view so you can visually confirm your keystroke.

The keyboard works in portrait (vertical) mode, but it's wider and easier to use in landscape (horizontal) view. It's a regular old QWERTY keyboard, with a few special keys.

❶ **Shift (⇧)**. Need a capital letter? Tap this key first (it takes on an eerie white glow to show you it's in action) and then type your letter, which should appear in uppercase. After all that excitement, the ⇧ key returns to normal and your letters go back to lowercase.

❷ **Backspace/Delete (⌫)**. One of the most popular keys ever. Press this one to back up and erase previously typed letters. Tap once quickly to erase the first letter to the left. Hold it down to have it gobble letters a bit faster, like a reverse Pac-Man. Hold it down even longer, and it whacks entire words at a time for a speedier deletion experience.

❸ **?123**. The Touch keyboard has a finite amount of space, and not enough room for *all* the keys the average person needs. Tap this button when you need to type in numbers or punctuation, and the keyboard switches to a whole new set of keys. Tap the same key—which is now an **ABC** key—to return to the letters keyboard. (Want to get to a special character more quickly? Press and hold the **?123** key until the keyboard changes, and then drag your finger over to the punctuation or number you need.)

Need even more characters? The Touch has a third keyboard tucked away. When you're on the **?123** keyboard, a **#+=** key appears. Tap it to get more obscure characters, like math symbols, brackets, and currency signs.

When you type letters into a note, an email message, a web form, or anyplace that's not a URL, the Touch adds a return key to the keyboard so you can jump down from one line to the next. This key transforms itself to say "Join" when you type in a WiFi password, "Go" when you enter a web address, and "Search" when you enter keywords into the Safari search box.

To make up for its limited real estate, the Touch keyboard includes shortcuts that help you work faster:

- **Web addresses**. When you type in Safari's web address box, the keyboard adds a few characters to aid your URL entry, including an underscore, a slash, and a hyphen key. It also provides a *.com* button so you can finish off that address. For URLs that end with other suffixes, like *.edu, .org, .us,* or *.net,* press and hold the *.com* button to see them all, and then slide your finger over to the one you need. Tap the Go button to take off.

- **Accented or special characters**. Need an accented letter, say an *á* instead of a regular *a*? Press and hold the *a* character to reveal a whole bunch of accented choices, and slide your finger onto the one you need. This trick works on most letters that take accent marks. You can also use it to get international currency symbols by holding down the *$* key, or to get a *§* when you hold down *&*.

- **Keyboard settings shortcuts**. Tap Settings→General→Keyboard to turn on (or off) all the iPod's keyboard helper settings, like auto-capitalization (the next letter after a period gets capped), auto-correction (for catching typos), and the spell-checker that underlines suspect words in red. There's also the Enable Caps Lock setting that kicks you into all-caps mode with a double-tap of the Shift (⇧) key and the "." shortcut that inserts a period and a space when you double-tap the space bar.

If you want to type in another language altogether, tap International Keyboards and select the language you want—the Touch offers around 50 keyboards, including those for Arabic, Cherokee, and Korean. Tap a language in the list to add its keyboard. When you're ready to type with international flair, tap ⊕ on the keyboard (it's to the left of the space bar, as shown on the opposite page) and you can switch between languages and keyboard layouts.

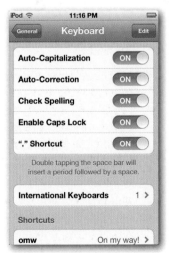

You can also add text shortcuts for commonly used phrases. Just flick down to Shortcuts and tap Add New Shortcut.

Cut, Copy, Paste, and Replace by Touch

THE TOUCH HAS COME a long way as a device that can handle the conventions of modern word-processing. There's no Ctrl or ⌘ key on its keyboard, though, so Apple incorporated tap-friendly commands for those convenient cut-copy-paste functions right into the Touch.

❶ To cut or copy from text you can edit (like an outgoing email message or a note you created), double-tap a word to highlight it. A **Cut | Copy | Paste** box pops up. To select more words, drag the blue dots on either end of the selected word. Then tap Cut or Copy.

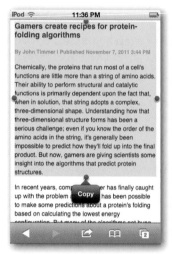

❷ For pages you *can't* edit (like incoming emails), hold your finger down until a magnifying glass and an insertion-point cursor appear. Drag it to the text you want to copy. When you lift your finger, a Select or Select All box appears. Select gives you the blue dots you can drag to highlight more text. Select All highlights all the text. Lift your finger, and you get a Copy button. A web page works differently: When you lift your finger, you get only a Copy button.

❸ Tap the place where you want to paste the text—or jump to a different program and tap within it to get the Paste button.

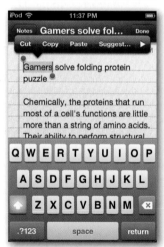

❹ Tap the Paste button to add the text to the new location.

Make a mistake and wish you could undo what you just did? Give the Touch a shake and then tap the Undo Edit button that appears onscreen.

TIP If all this tiny typing is denting your productivity when you have to do some serious text input, consider getting a wireless Bluetooth keyboard for your Touch. True, you have to haul around a big chunk of gear—unless you're at home in front of the TV. To use an external keyboard, turn on the iPod's Bluetooth chip by choosing Settings→General→Bluetooth→On and then follow the instructions that came with the wireless keyboard for connecting it to the Touch.

In addition to the Cut, Copy, and Paste options in apps where you can edit text (like Notes or Mail), you can replace a misspelled word with one that's spelled correctly—or look up its definition in the onboard dictionary by selecting it and tapping Define. If you have the Touch's spell-check function turned on (flip back two pages), the Touch highlights typos (and unknown words) with a red underscore so they stand out as you proofread. (You *do* proof important messages, right?) These are the words you want to replace.

You can also replace one word with a closely related one (for those times when you typed close to, but not quite, the right word).

To get the Suggest option, double-tap (or Select) a word onscreen. When the **Cut | Copy | Paste | Suggest...** box appears (top right), tap Suggest. The Touch offers up a few alternate words. If you see the one you *meant* to type, tap it to replace the text. If it can't find a similar word, you see a "No Replacements" message.

But enough about text—want to copy a photo or video into a message-in-progress or some other program? Hold your finger down on the screen until the Copy button pops up, as shown in the bottom-right photo. Tap the Copy button and then tap within the message body to get a Paste button. Tap it to insert your image or video.

If you want to copy *multiple* items, like pictures out of a photo album, tap the 🖪 icon in the top-right corner. Next, tap the photos you want to copy; blue checkmarks appear in the corners to confirm your selection. Tap the Copy button on the top-left of the toolbar, switch to the program where you want to deposit your pics (like a mail message under construction), and then press the glass until the Paste button appears.

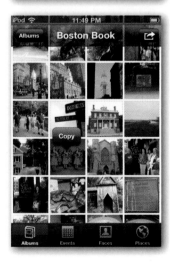

TIP Hate the Touch correcting your typing as you go? Choose Settings→General→Keyboard→Auto-Correction→Off.

Install (and Uninstall) New Apps

PROGRAMS FROM THE APP Store give your Touch all sorts of new powers. If you're eager to try some out, here are two ways to trick out your Touch:

- **Buy apps in the iTunes Store**. In iTunes' Source list, click iTunes Store and then click the App Store link on the main Store page. After you shop, connect the Touch to your computer and sync 'em up. Chapter 5 explains the fine art of syncing.

- **Buy apps on the Touch**. When you've got a WiFi connection, tap the blue App Store icon on the Home screen and browse away. At the top of the Featured screen, you can see what's new and hot—or what the iTunes Genius (page 143) thinks you might like. At the bottom of the screen, you find apps grouped by category and by the "Top 25 Apps." A Search icon (Q) awaits if you're looking for something specific. When you find an app you want, tap the price icon; it turns into a Buy button. Hit that, type in your iTunes Store name and password (even if you're downloading a free application), and the download begins. After the program finishes loading and installing, tap its icon to launch it.

It's a fact of life: Sometimes apps don't work out. They're not what you thought they'd be, they're buggy (it happens), or they take up too much precious Touch space. Here are two ways to uninstall an app:

- **Remove apps in iTunes**. Connect the Touch to your computer, click its icon in iTunes, and then click the Applications tab. In the list, deselect the apps you want to remove and then click Sync to uninstall them.

- **Remove apps on the Touch**. On the Home screen, press and hold the unwanted application's icon until an ⊗ appears in the wiggling icon's corner. Tap the ⊗, confirm your intention to delete, and wave goodbye to that app. Press the Home button to return to business as usual.

NOTE See a red, circled number on the App Store icon? You've got updates waiting for that number of apps; tap the icon to go into the App Store and see what they are. Tap the name of one of the programs, or tap the Price button (don't worry, updates are free), and then tap Install. The App Store updates the program after you type in your password. For multiple-app updates, tap Update All in the top-right corner.

Manage Apps in iTunes

EARLIER IN THIS CHAPTER, you learned how to rearrange the icons on your Touch's Home screen. And after reading the previous page, you may now have a *ton* of groovy new app icons all over your Touch—but not in the order you want them. Sure, you can drag wiggling icons all over the 11 pages of your Home screen, but that can get a little confusing and frustrating if you accidentally drop an icon on the wrong page.

Fortunately, iTunes lets you arrange all your Touch icons from the comfort of your big-screen computer:

❶ **Connect the iPod to your computer**. Click its icon in the Source list.

❷ **Click the Apps tab**. You now see all your applications—plus giant versions of each page of your Touch Home screen, all lined up vertically on the right side.

❸ **Select the icons you want to move**. Once you click an icon on the large screen, drag it to the desired page thumbnail displayed along the right side of the screen to move it there. It's much easier to group similar apps on a page this way—you can have, say, a page of games or a page of online newspapers. You can even change the four permanent icons in the gray bar at the bottom of the Touch screen.

❹ **Click Apply or Sync**. Wait just a moment as iTunes rearranges the icons on your Touch, so they mirror how you have them in iTunes.

Snap and Edit Photos with the Camera

FOR YEARS, MANY TOUCH owners have pined for a hardware feature that iPhone owners could take for granted: a camera. In 2010, Apple granted that wish and then some—the Touch now has *two* cameras, one on the front and one on the back. Together, they provide the hardware you need for FaceTime video calls, shooting quick video clips, and snapping off still photos.

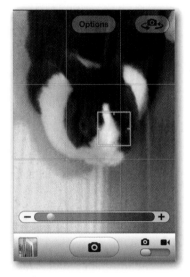

This section deals with the Touch as a still camera; flip ahead two pages to shoot and edit video. As digital cameras go, the Touch's camera isn't exactly a multi-megapixel powerhouse—it's relatively low-quality compared to your regular camera or even the iPhone 4S. (But at least the Touch now *has* a camera.)

To start using it, tap the Camera icon on the Touch's Home screen. Make sure the little slider in the bottom-right corner is set to 📷 (still camera) and not 🎥◀ (video camera). Then line up your shot and press the shutter button (📷) in the middle of the bottom toolbar. The Touch makes a little shutter-click noise, just like an old-fashioned film camera.

The Touch saves your newly snapped picture in Photos→Camera Roll. A thumbnail of the last shot you snapped also appears in the bottom-left corner of the screen; tap it to jump right to the photo in the Camera Roll album.

The Touch camera, while not exactly overloaded with the features of a standalone point-and-shoot camera, does offer a few controls for better photos:

- **Exposure adjustment**. Lighting is an important part of photography, and while the Touch doesn't have a flash, it does let you adjust the *exposure* (the overall lightness or darkness) of an image. If you have a shot lined up, but one part of the frame is cast in shadows, tap a lighter area of the image. A blue-white square appears briefly onscreen and the Touch readjusts its overall exposure settings based on that area. Now snap the picture.

- **Zoom**. Pinching the screen with your fingers to readjust the photo's exposure brings up the zoom slider (shown above). If you want to narrow in on your subject and lose distracting background elements, drag the slider to the right until you have the framing you want. Drag the slider the other way to zoom back out.

- **Grid**. Tap the Options button to overlay the screen with a nine-square grid to help you align and compose your shots.

In iOS 5, you can do basic image-editing on your iPod. Just tap open a photo that needs fixing and tap the Edit button at the top of the screen. You can tap:

- ❶ **Rotate.** Tap the Rotate button to spin a vertical shot into a horizontal one or flip it upside down.

- ❷ **Enhance.** Tap here to have the iPod analyze the picture and improve its contrast, exposure, and saturation.

- ❸ **Red Eye.** If your subject has glowing red demon eyes from your camera flash, tap the Red Eye button to give those devil peepers a neutral color.

- ❹ **Crop.** Tap here to chop out the boring, distracting, or ex-boyfriend parts of a picture. In Crop mode, tap the Constrain button to conform to standard photo sizes, like 4 x 6, and then tap the yellow Crop button.

Hate that change you made to a pic? Tap the Cancel button to reverse it. Once you like an edited photo, tap the Save button to put a copy in your Camera Roll.

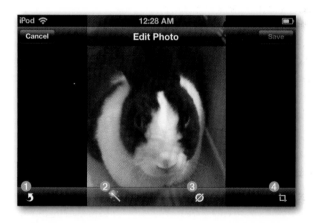

To change cameras and take a self-portrait with the front camera (circled below left), tap the Switch Cameras icon in the upper-right corner of the photo screen. As shown on these pages, you can take photos in either portrait (vertical) or landscape (horizontal) mode. The Touch's rear camera (circled below right) sits in the corner on the back, so be careful when you shoot with it or you may get a stunning portrait of your own finger.

Shoot and Edit Videos on the Touch

CELLPHONES AND POCKET CAMCORDERS that can shoot video clips have boomed in popularity over the years—which could explain the noticeable increase in YouTube videos of cats riding Roomba vacuum cleaners. Thanks to its back camera that shoots high-definition video (at a resolution of 720p and at 30 frames per second), the Touch now joins the video party. Warn your pets.

Shooting a video on the Touch works a lot like shooting a still photo. And even though you can tap an area of the screen to adjust the exposure, there's no zoom feature for video as there is for still photos.

Tap the Camera icon on the Touch's Home screen to get started. When you want to shoot videos, make sure the slider on the gray toolbar is set to record video (■◀) and not to snap still photos (▢).

The tiny microphone next to the camera lens on the back of the Touch records audio to go along with your video.

You can hold the Touch vertically or horizontally to shoot video, but portrait-shot clips may get shrunk or letterboxed if you upload them to a video-sharing site that's geared to display video in the more cinematic horizontal orientation. When you're ready to start filming, tap the ● button. It flashes red to indicate that you're recording.

The time stamp in the upper-right corner of the screen shows the current length of your video-in-progress. When you're ready to virtually yell "Cut!", tap the ● button again to stop recording.

Once you do, the Touch stores your clip in Photos→Camera Roll. To see what you shot without leaving the Camera app, tap the thumbnail preview at the end of the gray toolbar to call up the clip. Tap ▶ to play it back.

Editing Video on the Touch

Do you have a video where all the good action is in the middle? You know, the one where the first 5 minutes capture your voice trying to wheedle your toddler into dancing for Grandma—while the last 2 minutes show the inside of your shirt pocket because you forgot to turn off the camera? That stuff is easy to fix on the Touch.

Here's how to trim off the unnecessary parts on either end of a clip (you can't edit *within* a clip):

❶ Open the video you want to edit.

❷ Tap the screen to call up the editing controls. The frame-viewer bar at the top of the screen displays scenes from the clip.

❸ Press the outer edge of the frame-viewer so it turns yellow, and then drag either end of the yellow bar to isolate just the frames you want to keep. Tap the Trim button to cut away the detritus.

After you press the Trim button, the Touch offers you a choice of cutting the original clip (which makes this edit permanent) or saving the edited video as a whole *new* clip—while leaving the original version intact.

TIP   The Touch offers rudimentary tools for quickly chopping video. If you want a more complete pocket movie studio that lets you add titles, transitions, theme music, and more, hit the App Store and check out programs like ReelDirector ($4) or Apple's own iMovie for iPhone/Touch ($5).

Share and Upload Photos and Videos

NOW THAT YOU'VE TAKEN all these great photos and videos on your Touch, don't you want to share them with the world—or at least your friends and relatives? You can do that several ways:

- **Email**. It's easy to share selected photos and short videos directly with friends. Just tap Photos→Camera Roll to see your photos and videos (if you have the Camera app open onscreen, tap the thumbnail preview in the toolbar to jump to your collection). No matter how you get there, hit the ☞ button, tap the thumbnails of the photos and videos you want to send, and then tap Share. A mail message appears with your files attached, ready for you to address and send. (You can also use the ☞ button to select files for deletion out of the Camera Roll.)

- **Message**. Tap the ☞ icon on a selected photo or video to send it as an iMessage (page 66) to friends with iOS 5 devices.

- **Print**. If you have an AirPrint printer (page 258), tap ☞ for the Print option.

- **Tweet**. Got Twitter? Select a photo and tap ☞ to see the Tweet command.

- **Upload to YouTube**. With a video clip open onscreen, tap the ☞ button and select Send to YouTube. There's an option to email it from here, too.

- **Transfer to the computer**. Connect your Touch to your Windows PC or Mac and use the Import command in your photo-organizer program (like Adobe Photoshop Elements, iPhoto, or Image Capture) to copy over photos and videos. Once you have the files on your computer, you can post them to your blog or a photo-sharing site.

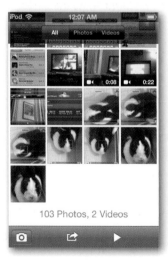 

Cover Flow in Motion

THE TOUCH CAMERA IS great, but if you like moving pictures—or pictures that *really* move—check out Cover Flow. Designed to show off your music collection to maximum effect, Cover Flow is basically a parade of album artwork that also lets you start playing music right away.

To use Cover Flow, tap the Music icon on the Home screen to get into your audio library. Instead of tapping through lists with the Touch in portrait mode, rotate it to landscape (horizontal) view. The text-based lists go away, replaced by full-color album covers. Flick your finger across the screen to see them whiz by.

An album cover doesn't tell you what songs are on it, so stop flicking covers and tap one to see its track listing. You can also tap the ❸ button in the lower-right corner to spin the cover around and see the song list. To hear a song play, tap its title in the list. To pause the song, tap ‖ in the lower-left corner; press ▶ to start it up again.

To flip back to the album art, tap the track listing (▤) or the ❸ button again. When you've exhausted the sheer visual excitement of Cover Flow (or you have to do something else for a while), turn the iPod back to portrait mode (upright) to return to your lists and screen icons. Cover Flow may not do much for some people, but it sure is pretty to watch.

TIP With all the audio and video files—not to mention email messages, contacts, calendar appointments, and other stuff—on your Touch, you may wish for a quick way to find a specific item. Wish no more. On the first Home screen, swipe your finger to the right to get a handy search box. Type in the name of the app or title you seek and tap the Search button to retrieve it.

Explore the Now Playing Screen

THE TOUCH SHOWS OFF photos and videos quite nicely, and it even makes your music look good. Cover Flow (see the previous page) is one example, but even if you're just listening to an album, you get a big visual reminder of what you're listening to. This is called the Now Playing screen.

In addition to lovely giant cover art, the Now Playing screen displays icons and information along its top edge to control your music. Here's what everything means, starting from left to right:

- **Back arrow (←)**. Just like the Back button on a web browser, tap here to go back to the screen you were on before you landed here.

- **Song information**. The top-center of the Now Playing screen displays the name of the current song, the artist performing it, and the album it's on.

- **Track listing (▤)**. The information in the middle of the screen tells you the current song's name. Tap this icon to see all the tracks you have from this album. (You can also double-tap the album cover, which spins around to reveal the list of tracks on the album.)

TIP   Have you ever wanted a computer like the ones on *Star Trek*, where you could just speak a music playback command out loud and have the machine respond and obey? You can do that easily on the latest Touch models (or even on a slightly older model with Apple's headset/microphone combo) thanks to the Voice Control feature. To use it, hold down the Home button until the blue Voice Control screen appears and beeps. Then speak your commands clearly into the Touch.

Sample commands include "Play artist Beyoncé" or "Play album 'Let It Be'." Say "Shuffle" to shuffle or "Genius" to hear similar tracks. "Play" and "Pause" work as commands, and you can even ask, "What's playing?" To turn off Voice Control, say "Stop" or "Cancel." If English isn't your native tongue, you can change the language that Voice Control responds to by choosing Settings→General→International→ Voice Control→[Language].

Sure, it's not quite the Siri personal assistant that rides along with the iPhone 4S, but it can be fun to boss the Touch around when you want to listen to music.

When you tap the ▤ button on the Now Playing screen to see an album's song list in high-contrast white type on a black background, a blue triangle identifies the track currently playing. If you're tired of that tune, tap a different song title to hear that one instead.

Looking at your song titles on this screen gives you the opportunity to add your own personal star ratings. As the song plays, swipe the row of dots along the top part of the screen to convert them into stars. You can rate songs from 1 to 5 stars, and the ratings you add to your songs here get synced back to iTunes when you connect Touch to computer. Chapter 5 has more on star ratings.

When you tire of looking at track names and rating songs, you can return to the full-screen album art view by tapping the tiny album cover in the top-right corner.

Like Cover Flow, the Now Playing screen looks the coolest when you have big, bright, colorful album covers for your song files. If you purchased your music from the iTunes Store or another online music emporium, the album art came with it. If you ripped the tracks yourself and didn't add any album artwork, you probably see a boring old gray music note. If you find this aesthetically unappealing, flip to page 122 for art lessons.

Control Music on the Now Playing Screen

THE NOW PLAYING SCREEN is more than just a pretty face for your music. You can also manage current-song playback from this screen. Here's what the various icons mean, starting with that strip along the bottom of the screen:

- **Play/Pause (▶/II) button**. The Now Playing screen usually means something is playing; you pause the song by tapping **II**, and restart it by tapping ▶.

- **Previous, Next (I◀◀, ▶▶I)**. To hear a currently playing song from the beginning again, tap **I◀◀**. If you're already at the beginning of a song, tap **I◀◀** to go to the previous track. Conversely, if you want to skip a long fade-out and blow on through to the end of a song, tap the **▶▶I** key. Tapping the same key at the end of a song takes you to the next track.

Miss the days of fast-forwarding or rewinding cassette tapes to hear the quality parts of a song? Press and hold **I◀◀** or **▶▶I** to simulate the process on the Touch. The longer you keep the button pressed, the faster the song leaps by.

- **Volume**. Sure, your Touch has physical volume buttons on its outer edge, but sometimes you don't feel like readjusting your grip on the player to scootch the volume up a notch for that cool saxophone solo in the middle of a song. With the volume slider at the bottom of the screen, you can boost or reduce the sound by dragging the big white dot with the tip of your finger. (If you do use the physical volume buttons while looking at the Now Playing screen, you see the onscreen slider move magically by itself.)

If you have an Apple TV or an AirPort Express that you've connected to your TV, home-entertainment sound system, stereo, or set of powered speakers (page 266), you also see the AirPlay icon (◪) on the playback control bar. Tap it and choose an output source from the list on the screen.

But wait, there's more to the Now Playing screen! It's just not real obvious until you tap the screen again to call up another layer of playback controls—the ones that like to stay out of the way unless you really want them. (Tap the screen again to hide them when you're done.) Here they are:

- **Loop**. Certain songs are so good that you want to play them over and over and over again. To make that happen, tap the Loop button (🔁) button twice until it looks like 🔂. If you want to put the album itself on repeat, tap the Loop button only once, so that it turns a nice shade of blue (🔁).

- **Like**. If you're logged into Ping (page 170), tap the 👍 icon to tell your pals you like the song.

- **Scrubber bar**. This slider at the top of the screen shows you the total length of the song, how much time has elapsed, and how much is left to go. Drag the white dot (formally known as the "playhead") to a different time to skip to that part of the song. The "2 of 19" (or whatever) number above the scrubber bar tells you where this track falls in the album or playlist.

- **Genius playlist**. Tap the ⚛ icon to make a Genius playlist based on this song. Chapter 6 has the details.

- **Ping post**. Tap the ● icon to share your thoughts about the track on Ping.

- **Shuffle**. If you like to mix things up, the Touch can shuffle the tracks in the current album or playlist for you. Just tap the 🔀 button. When it turns blue, the Touch plays the songs in random order. Tap 🔀 again to turn off Shuffle and return to the standard playback order.

If you're listening to an audio podcast, you might see three other icons:

- **Email podcast**. Tap ✉ to email a link to the podcast.

- **30-second playback**. Tap the ⏪ icon to replay the last half-minute of audio in case you missed something.

- **Playback speed**. Tap 2X to hear the audio in double time, tap ½X to hear it slowed to half-speed, and tap 1X to hear it at its normal speed.

Set Up Mail Accounts

WHEN YOU'RE NEAR A WiFi hot spot, the Touch is a traveling email machine that lets you read, write, and send messages. And just as there are two ways to get apps on the Touch, there are two ways to set up your email accounts.

- **Sync mail settings with iTunes**. You get email on your computer, right? If you're using a dedicated program, like Microsoft Outlook or Apple Mail, you can copy those account settings over to the Touch. Connect the Touch to your computer, click its icon in iTunes, and then click the Info tab. Scroll down to Sync Mail Accounts and turn on the checkbox next to it. All the email accounts you have configured on your computer are listed underneath, so turn on the checkboxes next to the ones you want to tote around on the Touch. Click Sync or Apply to copy the settings—but not your computer-based messages—over to the Touch.

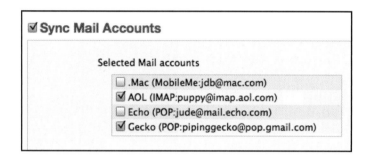

- **Set up mail accounts on the Touch**. Tap the Mail icon. You can set up a free iCloud account (page 254) or, if you use Exchange, Gmail, Yahoo, or AOL, tap the appropriate icon. If you don't use any of those, tap Other. On the next screen, type in your name, email address, password, and a brief description ("Gmail," say). If you tapped Other, type in the account settings you got from your Internet provider when you signed up. Click Save, and the program fetches your mail. Need help sorting through email geekery, like the difference between IMAP and POP? Check out this book's Missing CD page at *http:// missingmanuals.com/cds/ipodtmm10/*.

Use Email on the Touch

MAIL ON THE TOUCH looks and works pretty much like any other email program. You can:

- **Check mail**. Tap the Mail icon on the Home screen. If you have just a single account on your Touch, you see just one Inbox. If you're juggling multiple mail accounts, the Inboxes area of the Mailboxes screen displays the name of each account, the number of new messages in each, and the overall number of new messages. You can get to the individual mailbox folders for each account (like Sent and Saved) by tapping their names in the Accounts list. Tap the ↻ button in the bottom-left corner to check for new messages.

- **Read mail**. When you have an Inbox open on the screen, tap a message preview (pictured in the bottom screen at right) to open it. A blue dot means you haven't read that message yet. If you open the message and want to remember to read it again later, tap Details on the From line and then tap the blue Mark Unread link that appears.

- **Write mail**. To compose a new message, tap the ✐ icon in the bottom-left corner of the mailbox screen or in an open message. An empty message form and the Touch's keyboard appear, ready for you to write and send mail. To format text, select it, tap the ► icon on the menu, tap **B**/<u>U</u>, and then pick a style.

- **Delete mail**. Tap the 🗑 icon at the bottom of the screen to trash an open message. Delete a message without opening it by swiping your finger across its Inbox preview and tapping the red Delete button that appears. To trash bulk mail in bulk, tap the Edit button in the upper-right corner of the Inbox screen. Tap the preview of each message so a red checkmark appears, and then tap Delete to whack them all at once.

On the Edit screen, you can also move messages to another mail folder, tap the Mark button to flag messages (🚩) for later, or mark them as unread.

Organize Apps in Folders

AS MENTIONED EARLIER IN this chapter, you can have up to 11 Home-screen pages on your Touch and flick across them to find the apps you want. But some app-loving folk can quickly fill up all 11 screens with icons. Also, some people would prefer a tidier way to group their apps than dragging them around to different pages.

This is where Home screen *folders* can make everything better. You can have up to 12 apps in a single folder—which looks like an icon with little icons nestled inside it (right). Putting apps in folders saves screen space and keeps them corralled. By default, most new Touches come with one folder from the start: the Utilities folder, which contains the Contacts, Calculator, and Voice Memos apps.

To create a folder, press and hold an icon until it wiggles, and then drag that icon on top of one you want to put in the same folder. When you do, you automatically create a folder and see a bar with a generic name for it, like "Games." You can keep this name or replace it with one of your own. Once you set up a folder, you can drag up to 10 more apps in to fill it up. Tap the screen to close the folder.

To launch an app inside a folder, tap the folder to open it, and then tap the app you want to use.

If you change your mind and want to pull an app out of a folder, open the folder and press and hold the app's icon to start the Wiggle Dance. Now you can drag it out of the folder and back to its place on the Home screen proper.

To get rid of a folder altogether, press an icon to get them all wiggling. Drag *all* the apps out of the folder and back to the Home screen. When the last app is out, the folder disappears.

TIP Can't remember what folder you stuck an app in? Flick to the left from the first Home screen, type the app's name into the Spotlight search bar, and tap it open when it appears in the results list.

Multitask on Your Touch

PUTTING APPS IN FOLDERS helps you organize your Touch screen more precisely, but it doesn't save you a lot of time when you're in the middle of one thing and want to switch over to use another app real quickly—like if you're reading email and want to nip out and turn on your Pandora radio app to hear some tunes as you shovel out your Inbox. Who wants to go all the way out to the Home screen for that?

Fortunately, the Touch has a shortcut. When you're in an app, click the Home button twice. A row of four icons sprouts from the bottom of the screen, shoving the app you're currently using up to the top of the screen (top-right).

These four icons represent the apps you've recently used. Tap one to quickly switch to it. Turn on Pandora, check your sports scores, do whatever it is you wanted to do. When you finish, double-click the Home button again. When the row of icons appears, tap the icon of the app you were previously using to return to it.

If the app you want isn't in this initial row of four, flick the icons from right to left until you find the one you want.

To kill apps in the hidden row that you haven't used in forever (because they may be hogging memory), press down on an icon until the ⊝ symbol appears. Tap it to remove the app from the recently used list—but not from the Touch itself. Press the Home button when you're done.

In addition to your most recent apps list, the Home button double-click offers another time-saver. Instead of flicking right to left to see the recent apps, flick left to right to see the Music playback controls (bottom right). These can save you the trouble of going all the way back to the Now Playing screen to skip a playlist track. And if

you get agitated when the Touch reorients itself into landscape view when you try to read an eBook or write a message in bed, tap the first icon, the circular arrow in the left corner. This locks the Touch into portrait mode no matter which way you hold it—until you tap this icon again to unlock the screen.

iTunes Basics

IF YOU READ CHAPTER 1 TO FIND A SPEEDY WAY TO GET YOUR IPOD set up and ready to play, you've already dipped a toe into the iTunes waters. But as you may have guessed, beneath its pretty surface, iTunes is a deep well of media-management wonders.

Even if you haven't bought any music from the iTunes Store yet, you can use the program to import music from your CD collection. Once you check everything into your iTunes library, the program makes it easy to browse and search through all your treasures—and automatically mix your music. You can add song ratings, lyrics, and artwork to your music files, too.

Yes, iTunes is a powerful media organizer. So powerful, in fact, that this chapter focuses on its most basic and useful functions—like what its controls do and how to import music from CDs. Chapter 5 focuses on advanced iTunes features, and Chapter 6 tells you how to create customized song playlists. Chapter 7 is all about blowing your bucks at the iTunes Store, and Chapter 8 spotlights the video side of iTunes.

So turn the page to get to know iTunes better.

The iTunes Window: An Introduction

ITUNES IS YOUR IPOD'S best friend. You can do just about everything with your digital files here—convert songs on a CD into iPod-ready tunes, buy music, listen to Internet radio stations, watch videos, and more. Here's a quick tour of the main iTunes window and what all the buttons and sliders do.

The gray-tinted Source panel on the left side of iTunes displays all your media libraries and connected devices. Click an item in the panel to display its contents in the main window (number 6 above), like so:

❶ Click any icon in the Library group to see what's in your various media libraries. As you add music, movies, and other stuff to iTunes, click the appropriate icon to find what you're looking for—a song, a TV show, and so on. Programs you buy for the iPod Touch land here under Apps. Want to change what iTunes lists? Press Ctrl+comma (⌘-comma) to call up iTunes' Preferences menu, and then click the General tab. In the "Sources" area, turn on (or off) the checkboxes for, say, Ringtones or iTunes U.

❷ In the Store area, click the shopping-bag icon to buy new stuff from the Store, or click the Purchased icon to see what you've already bought. The Ping icon takes you to iTunes' music social network (page 170). The Downloads icon shows items downloading from the Store, or files ready for you to snag, like the latest episode of a podcast. The icon for Apple's iTunes Match service (page 113) lives here as well.

③ If you have a music CD in your computer's drive, it shows up in the Devices area, as will a connected iPod. Click the gray Eject icon next to the device name to safely pop out a disc or disconnect an iPod.

④ In the Shared area, you can browse the media libraries of other iTunes fans and stream their music if you have iTunes' Home Sharing feature turned on (page 110). The stacked music-note icon also lets you know that you can copy music and videos between machines.

⑤ iTunes keeps all your custom song lists—whether the iTunes Genius automatically created them or you lovingly handcrafted them—in the Genius and Playlists sections. The iTunes DJ feature, which quickly whips up party mixes, lives here, too.

⑥ When you click a name in the Source list—Music, in this case—iTunes' main window displays all the items in that category. The three columns that appear above the main song list let you browse your collection by genre, artist, and album. Naturally, this part of the window is called the Column Browser. It's shown here in the top position, but you can display it on the left by choosing View→Column Browser→On Left.

The outer edges of the iTunes window are full of buttons and controls. Here's what they do:

⑦ Play and pause a song or video—or jump to the next or previous track. The volume slider adjusts the sound level.

⑧ The center of the upper pane shows you the song currently playing. To the right of that, you have handy buttons to change views within the main window and a search box so you can find songs fast.

⑨ The bottom-left corner includes shortcut buttons for (from left to right) making a new playlist, shuffling or repeating your playlists, and displaying album artwork or video stills.

⑩ The lower-right corner of iTunes is where the Genius controls hang out. When you have a song selected, click the whizzy electron–shaped icon to create a Genius playlist (Chapter 6) based on that tune. The boxed-arrow icon toggles the iTunes sidebar panel on (great if you love Ping) and off (if Ping isn't for you). If you're the proud owner of an Apple TV or AirPlay-compatible speakers (page 266), the AirPlay icon sits in this row too, waiting for you to click it and select an output source for the song or video currently playing in iTunes.

Change the Look of the iTunes Window

DON'T BE MISLED BY the brushed-aluminum look of iTunes: You can push and pull various window parts like saltwater taffy.

- To toggle iTunes' three-pane Column Browser (previous page) open or closed, press Ctrl+B (⌘-B). You can adjust how much of the browser you see by dragging the tiny dot (circled) at the top of the song-list window up or down. If you prefer to see the browser as rows of vertical columns anchored along the left side of the iTunes window, click View→Column Browser→On Left.

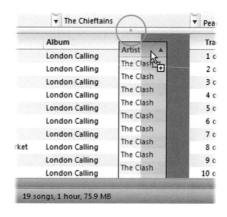

- iTunes divides the main song list into columns you can sort or rearrange. Click a column title (like Name or Album) to sort the list alphabetically. Click the title again to reverse the sort order. Change the order of the columns themselves by dragging them, as shown above.

- To adjust a column's width, drag its right-hand vertical divider line (it's easiest to grab it in the column title bar).

- To resize all the columns so they expand to precisely fit their contents, right-click (Control-click) any column title and choose Auto Size All Columns. This option appeals to those who like things organized in regimental formation.

- To add (or delete) columns, right-click (Control-click) any column title. From the pop-up list of column categories (Bit Rate, Date Added, and so on), choose the column you want to add or remove. Checkmarks indicate currently visible columns. Once you add a column, you can click its title to sort your songs by that characteristic.

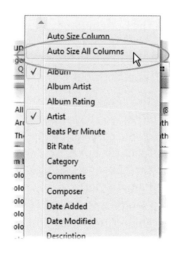

Change the Size of the iTunes Window

LOVELY AS ITUNES IS, it takes up a heck of a lot of screen real estate. When you're working on other things, you can shrink it down. In fact, iTunes can run in three sizes: small, medium, and large.

❶ *Large.* This is what you get the first time you open iTunes. Hate the social networking nags from Ping, or the hard-sell "suggestions" for purchases from the iTunes Store in the sidebar on the right? Close it by clicking the square button in the lower-right corner.

❷ *Medium.* Need something smaller in a flash? Switch back and forth between large and medium by pressing Ctrl+M (Shift-⌘-M) or by choosing View→Switch to Mini Player.

❸ *Small.* To really scrunch things down, start with the medium-size window, then drag the resize handle (the diagonal lines in the lower-right corner) leftward. To expand the panel, reverse the process.

Tired of losing your iTunes mini-player among an array of windows on your screen? You can make it *always* visible, so that it sits on top of other open windows, documents, and assorted screen detritus. Open iTunes Preferences (Ctrl+comma [⌘-comma]), click the Advanced tab, and turn on the checkbox next to "Keep Mini Player on top of all other windows." Now you won't have to click frantically around the screen trying to find iTunes if you get caught listening to your bubblegum-pop playlist at work.

Import Selected Songs from Your CDs

IN CHAPTER 1, YOU learned how iTunes simplifies converting (also called *rip-ping*) songs from your compact discs into small, iPod-ready digital files: Pop a CD into your computer's disc drive and iTunes walks you through the process. If you're connected to the Internet, iTunes downloads song titles and other album info. A few minutes later, you've got copies of those songs in iTunes.

If you need time to think about *which* songs you want from each CD, no problem. Summon the Preferences box (Ctrl+comma [⌘-comma]), click the General tab, and then change the menu next to "When you insert a CD" to "Show CD."

So now, if you don't want to rip an entire album—you may not want anything from Don McLean's *American Pie* besides the title track, for example—you can exclude songs you *don't* want by removing the checkmarks next to their names. Once you pick your songs, click the Import CD button in the bottom-right corner of the screen.

TIP If you know you want all the songs on that stack of CDs next to your computer, just change the iTunes CD import preferences to "Import CD and Eject" to save yourself some clicking.

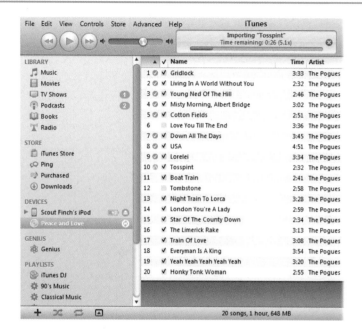

	✓	Name	Time	Artist
1 ◎	✓	Gridlock	3:33	The Pogues
2 ◎	✓	Living In A World Without You	2:32	The Pogues
3 ◎	✓	Young Ned Of The Hill	2:46	The Pogues
4 ◎	✓	Misty Morning, Albert Bridge	3:02	The Pogues
5 ◎	✓	Cotton Fields	2:51	The Pogues
6		Love You Till The End	3:36	The Pogues
7 ◎	✓	Down All The Days	3:45	The Pogues
8 ◎	✓	USA	4:51	The Pogues
9 ◎	✓	Lorelei	3:34	The Pogues
10 ◎	✓	Tosspint	2:32	The Pogues
11	✓	Boat Train	2:41	The Pogues
12		Tombstone	2:58	The Pogues
13	✓	Night Train To Lorca	3:28	The Pogues
14	✓	London You're A Lady	2:59	The Pogues
15	✓	Star Of The County Down	2:34	The Pogues
16	✓	The Limerick Rake	3:13	The Pogues
17	✓	Train Of Love	3:08	The Pogues
18	✓	Everyman Is A King	3:54	The Pogues
19	✓	Yeah Yeah Yeah Yeah Yeah	3:20	The Pogues
20	✓	Honky Tonk Woman	2:55	The Pogues

20 songs, 1 hour, 648 MB

You can Ctrl+click (⌘-click) any box to deselect all the checkboxes at once. To turn them all on again, Ctrl+click (⌘-click) a box next to an unchecked song. This is a great technique when you want only one or two songs from a CD; turn off *all* the checkboxes, and then turn on only the tracks you want.

As the import process starts, iTunes moves down the list of checked songs, converting each one to a file and, in Windows 7, dropping it in your Music→iTunes→iTunes Media→Music folder; on Mac OS X systems, songs go in the Home→Music→iTunes→iTunes Media→Music folder. (If you've had iTunes for years, your iTunes Media folder is probably still called iTunes Music, and there's a separate Music folder inside it.) An orange squiggle next to a song name means that iTunes is currently converting the track. Feel free to switch to other programs, answer email, surf the Web, or do any other work as iTunes rips away.

Once iTunes finishes up, each imported song bears a green checkmark, and the program signals its success with a melodious little flourish. Now you have some brand-new songs in your iTunes music library.

TIP Don't like all those checkboxes next to song titles cluttering up your screen? Turn them off in the Preferences box shown on the opposite page. Press Ctrl+comma [⌘-comma] to get the box, and then click the General tab. Turn off the checkbox next to "Show list checkboxes" (ironic, huh?). If you wan an all-over streamlined look, turn off the little icons next to Source-list items by turning off the checkbox next to "Show source icons."

Change Import Settings for Better Audio Quality

IPODS CAN PLAY SEVERAL digital audio formats: AAC, MP3, WAV, AIFF, and one called Apple Lossless. Feel free to safely ignore that last sentence, as well as the rest of this page, if you're *happy* with the way music sounds on your iPod or through a pair of external speakers.

If you find the audio quality lacking, however, you can change the way iTunes encodes, or *converts*, songs when it imports them from a CD. You get two main options in iTunes' Import Settings box (Edit [iTunes]→Preferences→General, and then click the Import Settings button). They are:

- **Audio format (use the drop-down menu beside "Import Using")**. Some formats tightly compress audio to save space. The trade-off: lost sound quality. Highly compressed formats include AAC (iTunes' default setting) and MP3. Formats that use little or no compression include WAV and AIFF; they sound  better, but they take up more space. Apple Lossless splits the difference: better sound quality than AAC and MP3, but not as hefty as WAV or AIFF.

- **Bit rate (beside "Setting")**. The higher the number of bits listed, the greater the amount of data the file contains, and the larger the file size. The advantage? Better sound quality.

To see a song's format and other technical information, click its title in iTunes, press Ctrl+I (⌘-I), and then click the Summary tab in the Get Info box.

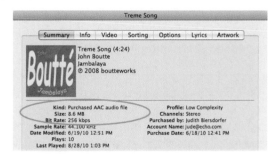

Four Ways to Browse Your Collection

INSTEAD OF JUST PRESENTING you with boring lists, iTunes gives you four ways to browse your media collection—some of them more visual than others. Click the View button at the top of iTunes to switch among them.

- **List view** is the all-text display favored by people who find comfort in the predictable layout of Excel spreadsheets (see page 94 for an example). Press Ctrl+B (⌘-B) to toggle on and off the browser that shows your music in vertical (or horizontal) panes grouped by genre, artist, and album. Press Ctrl+Alt+3 (Option-⌘-3) to jump back to List view from another view.

- **Album List view** displays an album cover in the first column if you have five or more tracks from an album. (Go to View→Always Show Artwork to override the five-track minimum.) Press Ctrl+Alt+4 (Option-⌘-4) to see Album List view.

- **Grid view** presents your collection in a nifty array of album covers and other artwork. There's a lot you can do in Grid view, so flip the page for more. Press Ctrl+Alt+5 (Option-⌘-5) to switch to the Grid.

- **Cover Flow view**. If you *really* like album art, this is the view for you. Ctrl+Alt+6 (Option-⌘-6) is the shortcut. Your collection appears as a stream of album covers. To browse them, press the left and right arrow keys on your keyboard, or drag the scroll bar under the albums. Click the little Full Screen button by the slider to turn your whole screen into Cover Flow, complete with playback controls. If you have an iPod Touch, you also get the joy of Cover Flow to Go (page 83).

Get a Bird's-Eye Look at Your Collection with Grid View

ALTHOUGH IT'S BEEN AROUND since iTunes 8, Grid view is still probably the most eye-catching way to see your media library. It's like laying out all your albums on the living room floor—great for seeing everything you've got without the hassle of having to pick it all back up. More picturesque than List view and not quite as moving as Cover Flow, Grid view is the middle road to discovering (or rediscovering) what's in your iTunes library.

Grid view can display your collection four ways: grouped by album, artist, genre, or composer. Click each named tab at the top of the screen to see your music sorted by that category. (If you don't see the tabs, choose View→Grid View→Show Header.) Here's how to work the Grid:

- Hover your mouse over any tile to get a clickable Play icon that lets you start listening to music.

- Double-click a cover in Albums view to display both the album cover and song titles in List view.

- If iTunes stacks multiple albums when you sort by artist, genre, or composer, hover your mouse over each tile to rotate through the album covers. If you want to represent the group using a particular cover or piece of art, right-click it and choose Set Default Grid Artwork. You can do the opposite for art you *don't* want to see: right-click the group and choose Clear Default Grid Artwork.

- Adjust the size of the covers by dragging the slider at the top of the window.

One thing about Grid view, though: It's pretty darn depressing unless you have artwork on just about everything in your collection. If you don't, and you see far too many generic music-note icons, Chapter 5 shows you how to art things up. And if you hate Grid view, don't use it—iTunes displays whatever view you were using the last time you quit the program.

Search for Songs in iTunes

YOU CAN CALL UP a list of all the songs with a specific word in the title, album name, or artist's name by clicking the Source pane's Music icon (under Library) and typing a few letters into the search box in iTunes' upper-right corner. With each letter you type, iTunes shortens the list it displays, showing you only tracks that match what you type.

For example, typing *train* brings up a list of everything in your music collection that has the word "train" somewhere in the song's information—maybe in the song's title ("Mystery Train"), the band name (Wire Train), or the album name (*Train A Comin'*). Click the other library icons, like Movies or Audiobooks, to comb those collections for titles that match a search term.

Another way to search for specific items is to use the Column Browser mentioned earlier in this chapter. (If you can't see it, press Ctrl+B [⌘-B].) Depending on how you configured the browser in View→Column Browser, it reveals your music collection grouped by genre, artist, or album. Hit the same keys again (Ctrl+B [⌘-B]) to close the browser.

Shuffle Your Music in Many Ways

WITH ITS ABILITY TO randomly pluck and play songs, iTunes' Shuffle feature has won over a huge number of fans, especially those who don't want to think about what to listen to as they noodle around the Internet. To start shuffling, click the twisty-arrows icon in the bottom-left corner of the iTunes window.

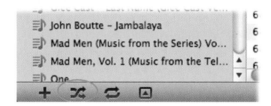

You're not stuck with a single shuffling method, either. Some days you may feel like mixing up your music song by song, and other days you may be in the mood to change things up by album.

To control just what iTunes shuffles, choose Controls→Shuffle and select Songs, Albums, or Groupings from the submenu. ("Grouping" is a way to keep certain tracks together in your iTunes library, like separate movements in a piece of classical music that are part of a larger work; page 119 has details.)

Animate Your Songs: iTunes Visualizer

VISUALIZER IS THE ITUNES term for an onscreen laser-light show that pulses, beats, and dances in perfect sync to your music. The effect is hypnotic and wild, especially when summoned midway through a sluggish day in the office.

Choose View→Visualizer to select from the iTunes Visualizer (lots of Disco in Space moments) or the iTunes Classic Visualizer (trippy psychedelic patterns-a-go-go, as shown below).

❶ To summon the scenery, choose View→Show Visualizer. The show begins immediately. To see a tiny menu of even more controls for the Visualizer or Classic Visualizer, press the / key and then the letter of the desired command listed onscreen. It's a great way to fiddle.

> **TIP** The keyboard shortcut for turning the Visualizer on and off is Ctrl+T (⌘-T).

❷ If you find the iTunes window too constraining for all this eye candy, play it full-screen by going to View→Full Screen (View→Enter Full Screen). The keyboard shortcut to this coast-to-coast visual goodness is Ctrl+F (Ctrl-⌘-F) .

True, you won't get a lot of work done, but when it comes to stress relief, visuals are a lot cheaper than a hot tub.

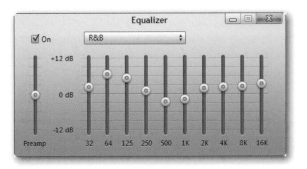

iTunes Power Moves

NOW THAT YOU'VE SEEN HOW EASY ITUNES MAKES IT TO CONVERT your favorite CD tracks into small, great-sounding files, it's time to do some serious tune-tweaking. Apple's music-management program lets you do things like rate albums and individual songs, tap into Internet radio, share music and videos with other folks on your network, and even download your past and present purchases to your iPod or other iOS devices.

You can also use iTunes as an editor: It gives you the tools you need to change song formats, edit on-stage banter from live recordings, and apply preset or customized equalizer settings to tracks. Once you get everything to your liking, you'll learn how to add, delete, and manually manage the music on your 'Pod.

Finally, you'll learn how iTunes can help with a vital—but often ignored—part of music management: backing up your catalog for safekeeping in case your hard drive croaks and takes all your songs and videos with it.

You're the Critic: Rate Your Music

ALTHOUGH THERE'S NO WAY to give a song two thumbs up in iTunes, you *can* assign an album—or each song in your collection—a rating of from one to five stars. Then you can use the ratings to produce playlists of nothing but the greatest hits on your hard drive.

First, a couple of notes: If you assign an *album* a rating, then *all* the songs on the album get the same number of stars. If you rate just a few tracks on an album, the album's rating reflects the average of the *rated* songs—so an album with two five-star songs and a bunch of unrated tracks gets five stars.

❶ To add ratings, first make sure you turn on the Album Rating and/or Rating columns in iTunes' View Options box (Ctrl+J [⌘-J]).

❷ Highlight the song you want to rate by clicking it. iTunes displays five dots in the Rating column (in the iTunes main window). When you click a dot, iTunes turns it into a star. Now either drag your mouse across the column to create one to five stars, or click one of the dots itself to apply a rating (click the third dot, for example, and iTunes gives the song three stars).

❸ Once you assign ratings, you can sort your song list by star rating (click the Album Rating or Rating column title), create a Smart Playlist of only your personal favorites (File→New Smart Playlist; choose Album Rating or Rating from the first drop-down menu), and so on.

You can even rate songs from within your iPod, and iTunes records the ratings the next time you sync up.

To rate a song on your iPod Classic, start playing it and tap the Select button a few times until you see dots onscreen. Use the scroll wheel to transform those dots into the number of stars you want to give the song. Your star ratings show up on the iPod's Now Playing screen. To rate songs on the Touch, swipe the dots on the Now Playing screen (page 85). On the Nano, tap the Now Playing art, tap ❶, and then swipe the dots to convert them to stars.

TIP If you're more menu-oriented, you can add stars from the iTunes menu. With a track selected, choose File→Rating, slide over to the submenu, and apply the rating. This is also the place to go if you change your mind: Choose None to return a song to its pristine, unrated condition.

Listen to Internet Radio

NOT SATISFIED WITH BEING a mere virtual jukebox, iTunes also serves as an international radio—without the shortwave static. You can tune in everything from mystical Celtic melodies to Zambian hip-hop. Computers with high-speed Internet connections have a smoother streaming experience, but the vast and eclectic mix of music is well worth checking out—even with a dial-up modem. Just click the Radio icon in iTunes' Source list to see a list of stations.

Stations are roughly organized by genre like Blues, Classical, and Country. Click a genre to see its list of stations. Beyond these broad groupings are specialized categories, like College/University, Sports Radio, and Golden Oldies, which includes a channel devoted to nothing but big-band music. There's even a station called Bad Song Radio that promises "nonstop bad songs all the time."

Once you listen to all the stations listed in iTunes, hit the Internet. You can find more radio stations at *www.shoutcast.com*. Windows 7 and Mac OS X users can play them through iTunes by clicking the yellow Tune In button. (If this is your first time at Shoutcast, a prompt asks how you want to hear the stream—click the button for iTunes.) XP users, save the offered *.pls* file to your desktop and then drag and drop it on Playlists. Click the resulting "tunein-station" playlist.

> **TIP** Radio stations do a great job of making song volumes consistent from song to song—and you can do the same with iTunes. Open the Preferences box (Ctrl+comma [⌘-comma]). Click the Playback icon or tab, and turn on the box for Sound Check. You also need to turn on Sound Check on your iPod. On the Classic, choose Settings→Sound Check. On the iPod Touch or Nano, choose Settings→Music and then tap Sound Check "On." The next time you connect your iPod to your computer, iTunes makes the necessary audio adjustments.

Share Your iTunes Music and Videos

NOW THAT YOU'VE BUILT a fabulous media collection, you may feel like sharing it. You can, under one condition: Your fellow sharers need to be on the same computer network. For instance, family members on your home network: kosher. Cousin Ferdinand, living in another state: not kosher.

The power to share music—that is, stream it between computers—has been with iTunes for years. But iTunes' Home Sharing feature, introduced way back in iTunes 9, lets you do more than just stream songs; you can actually *copy* music and videos from one computer to another.

Sounds great, doesn't it? Home Sharing does have its limits, though. For starters, you can share content among only five computers. Each also needs the following:

- A connection to the same (wired or wireless) network.

- A copy of iTunes 9 or later installed.

- The name and password of a single iTunes Store account or App Store account (see Chapter 7 if you need one).

Once you have all these things in hand, it's time to share:

❶ In the iTunes Source list, click the Home Sharing icon. (If you don't see the cute little house-shaped graphic, choose Advanced→Turn On Home Sharing. If you get told to authorize the computer for that iTunes account, choose Store→Authorize Computer.) On the screen that appears, type in an iTunes account name and password.

❷ Click the Create Home Share button.

❸ Repeat these steps for every computer you want to share with on your network (up to four others).

Once you set up all the computers, each of their iTunes libraries appears in everyone's Source list. Click the triangle beside the icon for the library you want to explore. After iTunes hits the network, icons for that library's contents appear in your own iTunes window. Click a shared Music icon and then double-click a song title in your iTunes window to hear it.

In addition to streaming audio files, you can stream videos, but their large size can make them skippy. This is where the power to *copy* files from one shared machine to another comes in handy.

Copy Files with Home Sharing

You can copy files between shared iTunes libraries two ways: *manually* or *automatically*. The manual method works well when you want to occasionally raid someone's media collection for random albums or videos. But if everyone listens to the same audiobook or just has to have every new album that comes into the house, the automatic method saves time and effort.

- **The manual method**. In the shared library, select the title (or Ctrl-click [⌘-click] to select multiple titles) of the audio or video files you want to copy to your Windows PC or Mac. Click the Import button in iTunes' bottom-right corner and wait as your selections pour into your own library. If, in the shared library, you want to see only the

items that you *don't* have, jump down to the Show pop-up menu at the bottom-left of the iTunes window and choose "Items not in my library."

- **The automatic method**. With the shared library onscreen, click the Settings button at the bottom-right of the iTunes window. Turn on the checkboxes next to the types of content, like music, that you want to automatically Hoover onto your own machine. Click OK.

But what if you don't want to share *everything* in your library? Or if you want to password-protect your stuff from siblings or other annoyances? That's where the Sharing preferences box comes to the rescue.

Call up the iTunes Preferences box (Ctrl+comma [⌘-comma]) and then click the Sharing tab. Turn on "Share my library on my local network." You can choose to share your entire collection or selected playlists. (You can also tell your computer to look for other people's music here.)

To secure your library, turn on the checkbox for "Require password" and give your cypher to trusted network buddies. If *they* lock up *their* media, you'll need their passwords, too. Finally, click the General tab in this same preferences box. The name you type in the Library Name box will show up in your friends' iTunes Source lists.

Use iTunes In the Cloud

IT'S EASY TO BUY digital goods from the iTunes Store, but how do you easily get the stuff you buy on one gadget onto all your computers and iOS devices if you're not home to use Home Sharing (page 110)? That's where Apple's confusingly named service iTunes In the Cloud comes in. It acts an online record-keeper for all the apps, music, and books you buy (and TV Shows, if you're downloading to a Windows PC or Mac). Once you buy something from the Store, iTunes in the Cloud *knows* it and can download copies to all the computers and devices that use the same Apple ID. As with many things in the Appleverse (as well as automobiles), you have two ways to copy files across devices: automatic and manual. Here's how to do either:

- **Automatically download purchases**. To have iTunes on your computer automatically download to your iPod Touch a copy of the music, apps, and books you buy on other devices, choose Edit [iTunes]→Preferences→Store. Under Automatic Downloads, turn on the checkboxes next to Music, Apps, and/or Books; you need to manually download TV shows, which is described next. Click OK.

  To make your iPod Touch reach out and grab stuff you bought through iTunes on your computer, go to the iPod's Home screen and tap Settings→Store. Sign into your iTunes account and tap the On button next to Music, Apps, and/or Books to snag each type of file.

- **Manually download purchases.** If you just want certain things from your Store purchases, you can download what you want when you want it. On your computer, click the Store link in the iTunes Source list and log into your account. In the Quick Links panel, click the Purchased link. On the next screen, you can see the music, TV shows, apps, and books you bought; click the All button to see everything, or the "Not in My Library" button to see items your computer lacks. Click an item's title and then click the Cloud icon to download it.

  To get selective on the Touch, tap iTunes open from the Home screen and then tap the Purchased icon at the bottom of the Store screen. Tap All to see everything you've ever bought, or "Not on this iPod" to see a list of the things missing from your player. Tap the Cloud icon and type in your iTunes Store name and password to download the stuff to your 'Pod.

Use iTunes Match

YOU MAY BE SAYING to yourself, "Well, this iTunes In the Cloud thing is great in case my hard drive dies, but I didn't buy everything in my library from the iTunes Store. What about all the tracks I ripped from my CD collection?"

You have two options here. First, you can back up your computer (and iTunes library with it) to an external drive or set of discs with free software, like Windows' Backup utility or Apple's Time Machine for Mac OS X (page 133). Second, for $25 a year, you can use Apple's iTunes Match subscription service. iTunes Match safely stores any song in your music library on Apple's iCloud servers. You can download a copy to any of your iOS devices and computers (up to 10 total, and five of them can be authorized with the same Apple ID) so your library is always with you.

For home-ripped tracks that the iTunes Store also sells (it has 20 million songs), iTunes Match adds new Store copies to your iCloud account. For more obscure tracks, ones that the Store doesn't sell, iTunes Match uploads a copy of each rare gem from your computer to iCloud (and yes, that means Apple is wading around in your personal music files).

To use iTunes Match, you need an Apple ID (page 160), an Internet connection, and an iPod Touch, iPad, or iPhone running iOS 5. Then there's the money part—you also need a credit card to pay $24.99 a year for an iTunes Match subscription, which covers up to 25,000 songs. And finally, you need some time while iTunes Match uploads your rare tracks to iCloud.

To sign up for iTunes Match, open iTunes on the computer, choose Store→Turn On iTunes Match, and then click the Subscribe button. After you sign up, your music and playlists are added to your big giant iCloud library, including any tracks that iTunes had to upload.

Now you need to get your iPod into the mix. Tap Settings→Music. Flip on iTunes Match; it nags you if you haven't signed up for a subscription yet. And while this initially removes all the songs from your Touch, you can grab them again by tap-

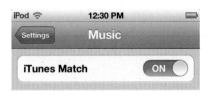

ping the Cloud icon and downloading at will. To see the tracks you've already downloaded, along with tracks you *can* download, tap Settings→Music→Show All Music→On.

The iTunes Match deal is not without its drawbacks. For one, you're on the hook for $25 a year to rent your online music locker. The service also disables the Genius Playlists and Mixes on the iPod Touch, which may bum you out. But hey, you've got all your music—right up there in the Cloud, whenever you need it.

Change a Song's File Format

SOMETIMES YOU'VE GOT A song in iTunes whose format you want to change—you might need to convert an AIFF file before loading it onto your iPod Shuffle, for example. First, head over to Edit→Preferences (iTunes→Preferences), click the General tab, and then click the Import Settings button. From the Import Using pop-up menu, pick the format you want to convert *to* and then click OK.

Now, in your iTunes library, select the song you want to convert and choose Advanced→Create MP3 Version (or AIFF, or whatever format you just picked).

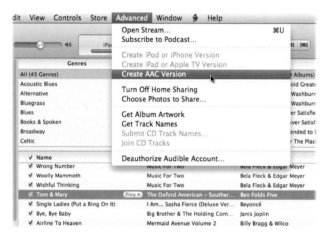

If you have a whole folder or disk full of potential converts, hold down the Shift (Option) key as you choose Advanced→Convert to AAC (or your chosen encoding format). A window pops up, which you can use to navigate to the folder or disk holding the files you want to convert. The only files that don't get converted are protected ones: Audible.com tracks and older tracks from the iTunes Store that still have copy protection built in. If you bought a song after January 2009, though, odds are you have a high-quality iTunes Plus track (see page 177) that's delightfully free of such restrictions.

The song or songs in the original format, as well as the freshly converted tracks, now reside in your library.

TIP Although you have intentionally created a duplicate of a song here, you may have other unintended dupes from home sharing, ripping the same album twice, or other accidental copying. To find these duplicates—and recover a little hard drive space—choose File→Display Duplicates. iTunes dutifully rounds up all the dupes in one window for you to inspect and possibly delete. Just make sure they are true duplicates, not, say, a studio and a live version of the same song. (To search for *exact* duplicates, hold down the Shift [Option] key and choose File→Display Exact Duplicates.) Click the Show All button to return the window to your full collection.

Set Up Multiple iTunes Libraries

THERE'S HOME SHARING AND then there's home, sharing. Many families have just one computer. If everyone uses the same copy of iTunes, you soon hear the Wiggles bumping up against the Wu-Tang Clan if you shuffle your music tracks or when you autosync multiple iPods. Wouldn't it be great if everyone had a *personal* iTunes library to have and to hold, to sync and to shuffle—separately? Absolutely.

To use multiple iTunes libraries, follow these steps:

❶ **Quit iTunes**.

❷ **Hold down the Shift (Option) key on your Windows PC or Mac keyboard and launch iTunes**. In the box that pops up, click Create Library. Give it a name, like "Tiffany's Music" or "Songs My Wife Hates."

❸ **iTunes opens up, but with an empty library**. If you have a bunch of music or videos in your main library that you want to copy over to this one, choose File→Add to Library.

❹ **Navigate to the files you want and add them**. If the songs are in your original library, they're probably in Music→iTunes→iTunes Media→Music (Home→Music→iTunes→iTunes Media→Music), in folders sorted by artist name; videos are in TV Shows or Movies. Choose the files you want to add.

To switch among libraries, hold down the Shift (Option) key when you start iTunes, and you'll get a box that lets you pick the library you want. (If you don't choose a library, iTunes opens the last one used.) Tracks you copy go into whatever library you have currently open. And now that you have those files in that library, you can switch back to the other library and get rid of them there if you want.

TIP Ever want to check the contents of your Podcasts or Movies libraries without leaving your current Music playlist? Just right-click (Control-click) on the Podcasts, Movies, or other Source-list library icons and then choose Open in New Window.

Improve Your Tunes with the Graphic Equalizer

IF YOU'D LIKE TO improve the way your songs sound, you can use iTunes' graphic equalizer (EQ) to adjust various frequencies in certain types of music. You might want to boost the bass tones in dance tracks to emphasize the booming rhythm, for example.

To get the equalizer front and center, choose View (Window)→Equalizer to unleash some of your new EQ powers.

❶ Drag the sliders (bass on the left, treble on the right) to accommodate your listening tastes (or the strengths and weaknesses of your speakers or headphones). You can drag the Preamp slider up or down to compensate for songs that sound too

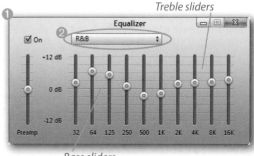

loud or too soft. To create your own presets, click the pop-up menu and select Make Preset.

❷ Use the pop-up menu to choose one of the canned presets for different types of music (Classical, Dance, Jazz, and so on).

You can apply equalizer settings to an entire album or to individual songs.

❸ To apply settings to a whole album, select the album's name (either in Grid view or in the iTunes browser pane). Then press Ctrl+I (⌘-I) and

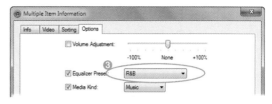

click Yes if iTunes asks whether you're sure you want to edit multiple items. In the box that pops up, click the Options tab and choose your preferred setting from the Equalizer Preset pull-down menu.

> **NOTE** *Equalization* is the art of adjusting the frequency response of an audio signal. An equalizer emphasizes, or boosts, some of the signal's frequencies while lowering others. In the range of audible sound, *bass* frequency is the low rumbly noise; *treble* is at the opposite end of the sound spectrum, with high, even shrill, notes; and *midrange* is, of course, in the middle, and it's the most audible to human ears.

④ You can apply equalizer presets to individual songs as well. Instead of selecting the album name in the iTunes window, click the song name, and then press Ctrl+I (⌘+I). Click the Options tab and choose a setting from the Equalizer Preset menu.

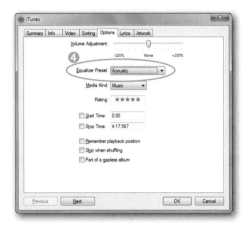

⑤ Finally, you can change the EQ settings right from your song lists by adding an Equalizer column. Choose View→View Options and turn on the Equalizer checkbox. A new column appears in your track lists, where you can select EQ settings.

TIP   The iPod itself has more than 20 equalizer presets you can use on the go. To set your iPod Touch's equalizer, choose Settings→Music→EQ. Flick down the list of presets until you find one that matches your music style, and then tap it. Your iPod now lists the preset's name next to EQ on the Settings menu. The process works pretty much the same way on the other iPods. You can tap your way into the Nano's EQ controls by going to the Home screen and choosing Settings→Music→EQ. The iPod Classic's EQ menu is at iPod→Settings→EQ.

Change a Song's Start and Stop Times

GOT A SONG WITH a bunch of onstage chit-chat before it starts, or after the music ends? Fortunately, you can change a song's start and stop times to skip the boring parts and hear only the juicy middle.

To change a track's stop time, play the song and observe the status window at the top of iTunes. Watch for the point in the timeline where you get bored. Then:

❶ Click the track you want to adjust.

❷ Choose File→Get Info (Ctrl+I [⌘-I]) to call up the song's information box.

❸ Click the Options tab and take a look at the Stop Time box, which shows the full duration of the song.

❹ Enter the new stopping point for the song, the one you noted earlier.

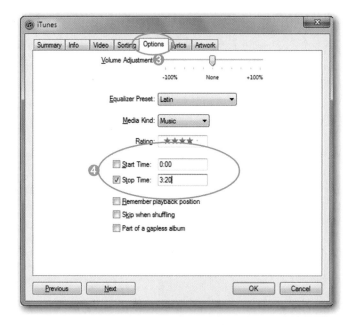

You can perform the same trick at the beginning of a song by adjusting the number in the Start Time box. The shortened version plays in iTunes and on your iPod, but the additional recorded material isn't really lost. If you ever change your mind, go back to the song's Options box and turn off the Start Time or Stop Time checkbox to return the song to its original length.

Edit Song Information

TIRED OF ITUNES NAMING so many songs "Untitled"? You can change song titles in iTunes—to enter a song's real name, for example, or to fix a typo—in a couple of ways.

In the song list, click the text you want to change, wait a moment, and then click again. The title now appears highlighted, and you can edit the text—just as you do when you change a file name on a desktop computer.

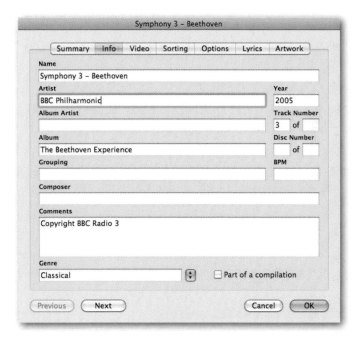

Another way to change a song's title, artist name, or other information is to click the song in the iTunes window and press Ctrl+I (⌘-I) to summon the Get Info box. (Choose File→Get Info if you forget the keyboard shortcut.) Click the Info tab and then type in the new track information.

Too much work? Try Advanced→Get CD Track Names to hunt down titles from the Internet, though if the track is something deeply obscure or homemade, the Gracenote database that iTunes uses may not know the name, either.

TIP Once you've got a song's Get Info box onscreen, use the Previous and Next buttons to navigate to other tracks grouped with it in the iTunes song list. That way, you can rapidly edit all the track information in the same playlist, on the same album, and so on, without closing and opening boxes the whole time.

Edit Album Information

YOU DON'T HAVE TO adjust your track information on a song-by-song basis. You can edit an entire album's worth of tracks simultaneously by clicking the album name in the iTunes column browser (or by clicking its cover in Grid view) and pressing Ctrl+I (⌘-I) to bring up the Get Info box.

Ever careful, iTunes flashes an alert box asking if you really want to change the info for a bunch of things at once. Click Yes.

You can make all sorts of changes to an album in the four-tabbed box that pops up. Here are a few examples:

❶ Fix a typo or mistake in the Album or Artist name boxes.

❷ Manually add an album cover or photo of your choice to the whole album by dragging it into the Artwork box.

❸ Click the Options tab and change the equalizer preset for all the songs. Right below that, use the Media Kind menu to change a mislabeled Music file to, say, Audiobook for proper sorting (see page 94).

❹ Have iTunes skip the album when you shuffle music—great for keeping winter holiday music out of your summer barbecue album rotation.

❺ Tell iTunes to play back the album without those two-second gaps between tracks by choosing "Gapless album" (perfect for opera and *Abbey Road*!).

Fetch Missing Album Covers

SONGS YOU DOWNLOAD FROM the iTunes Store often include artwork—usually a picture of the album cover. iTunes displays the picture in the lower-left corner of its main window (you may need to click the Show Artwork icon at the lower left). Covers also appear in the Album List, Grid, and Cover Flow views. But even if you rip most of your music from your own CD collection, you're not stuck with artless tracks. You can ask iTunes to head to the Internet and find as many album covers as it can.

You need a (free) iTunes Store account to make this work, so if you haven't signed up yet, flip ahead to Chapter 7 to learn how. To make iTunes go fetch, choose Advanced→Get Album Artwork. Since Apple has to root around in your library to figure out which covers you need, you get an alert box warning you that the company will be getting (and then dumping) personal information from you (but it's not laughing at your Bay City Rollers tracks).

If you have a huge library, this may take a little while, so make yourself a sandwich while iTunes gets to work. When it finishes, you should have a healthy dose of album art whizzing by in Cover Flow view or filling up the grid in the middle of the iTunes window.

If iTunes can't find certain album covers on its own, it displays a list of the missing artwork. You can use this helpful accounting to hunt for and place the art yourself, as described next.

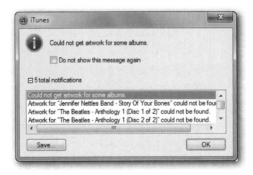

TIP Some album swag in the iTunes Store goes beyond cover artwork. Albums with the iTunes LP feature often include performance videos, animated lyrics, photos, liner notes, and more. Just look for albums with the iTunes LP badge in the store.

Replace Album Covers Manually

DESPITE ITS BEST INTENTIONS, sometimes iTunes can't find an album cover (or retrieves the wrong one). If that happens, take matters into your own hands by manually adding your own album artwork—or a photo of your choice. If Pachelbel's *Canon in D* makes you think of puppies, you can have baby dachshunds appear in iTunes every time you play that song.

❶ To add your own art to a song, pick a photo or image—JPEG files are the most common.

❷ If you found the cover on Amazon (*hint*: a great source!), save a copy of it by dragging it off the web page and onto your desktop or by right-clicking (Ctrl-clicking) it and choosing the "Save Image" option in your web browser.

❸ With your image near the iTunes window, select the song and click the Show Artwork button in the bottom-left corner of the iTunes window.

❹ Drag the image into the iTunes Artwork pane to add it to the song file.

TIP You can also add artwork by clicking a song title, typing Ctrl+I (⌘-I) to bring up the Get Info box, and then tapping the Artwork tab. Then click the Add button to call up a navigation box that lets you choose an image from your hard drive.

Find and Add Lyrics to Your Song Files

YOU CAN SAVE LYRICS with a song file just as you do album art. To add lyrics, select a song in iTunes and press Ctrl+I (⌘-I) to call up the Get Info box. Then click the Lyrics tab.

Here, you can either meticulously type in a song's verses or look them up on one of the hundreds of websites devoted to cataloging them. Once you find your words, getting them into iTunes is a mere cut 'n' paste job away. If you want to add lyrics to all the songs on an album, or to several songs on the same playlist, click the Next button (circled). That advances you to the next song, thereby saving you repeated keystrokes invoking the Get Info command.

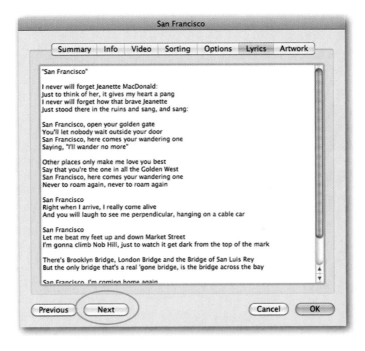

TIP Some types of iTunes files don't support the lyrics function. AAC and MP3 files are perfectly happy with lyrics, but QuickTime and WAV files can't handle them. So you need to convert that WAV of "Jumping Jack Flash" if you want to have a gas, gas, gas with lyrics.

View Lyrics on the iPod

NOW THAT YOU'VE SPENT all that time grooming your song files and adding lyrics, wouldn't it be great if you could take the fruits of your labor with you? The good news is, you can—all the info in an iTunes song file transfers over when you sync your iPod (except, of course, in the case of iPod Shuffles, which lack the whole screen thing needed to view images and text).

When you're out strolling with your iPod Classic and have a song playing, press the center button to cycle through all the information about the song. After four or five taps, the lyrics appear on the iPod's screen, making it a handheld karaoke machine you can sing along with as you go down the street. Got an iPod Touch? Just tap the album cover to see the lyrics. On the Nano, tap Now Playing on the Home screen and then tap the album art to make the song controls appear. Swipe to the left until you see your lyrics.

TIP As you click through iPod Classic screens to get to your lyrics, check out the shortcut to shuffling songs that Apple has slipped into the menus. Right before you get to the lyrics screen, you get an option to shuffle songs or albums.

What iTunes Can Tell You About Your iPod

ITUNES NOT ONLY LETS you decide which songs and videos end up on your iPod, it also helps keep your iPod's own internal software up to date, see how much space you have left on your player, and change your music, video, and podcast synchronization options.

When you connect your iPod to your computer, it shows up in the iTunes Source list (under Devices). Click the iPod icon to see all your options. Each tab at the top of the screen lets you control a different kind of content, like music or photos.

On the Summary screen (first tab), iTunes tells you:

❶ The size of your iPod, its serial number, and whether it's formatted for Windows or the Mac.

❷ Whether your iPod has the latest software (and if you're having problems, you get the chance to reinstall it).

❸ Whether iTunes automatically synchronizes your iPod or whether you need to update its contents manually. (Automatic means everything in iTunes ends up on

your iPod—space permitting, of course; manual means you get to pick and choose.) If you have a Touch, Nano, or Shuffle, you can turn on VoiceOver prompts to hear your iPod identify things like song titles, menu names, and so on. If you have an iPod Touch, a Backup section for iCloud or iTunes is displayed right above the Options area on the Summary screen.

❹ The bar at the bottom of the window uses color to identify the different media types filling up your iPod. Click the bar to see the information displayed in number of items, the amount of drive space used, or the number of days' worth of a particular type of media.

❺ Click the flippy triangle next to the iPod in the Source list to see its contents, like your music, audiobooks, and any playlists you've made.

Adjust Your iPod's Syncing Preferences with iTunes

ONCE YOUR IPOD IS connected and showing up in iTunes, you can modify all the settings that control what goes onto (and comes off of) your media player. Thanks to iTunes' long, scrollable screen full of checkboxes and lists in most categories, it's easier than ever to get precisely what you want on your 'Pod.

So where do you start? See those tabs all in a row toward the top of iTunes? Click each one to see the preferences for that type of media. (The tabs vary slightly depending on the type of iPod you have; the Touch even has a Ringtones tab for your Skype phone calls.) Here's what you'll find there:

❶ **Summary**. Key iPod hardware info here: drive capacity, serial number, and software version (and a button to update the software when Apple releases a new version). The Options area lets you choose syncing preferences and whether you want to turn your iPod into a portable data drive for carrying around big files.

❷ **Apps**. Here's where you sync all those wonderful little programs you downloaded from the App Store to your computer and then to your iPod Touch.

❸ **Music**. Click this tab to synchronize all your songs and playlists—or just the ones you like best. Keep scrolling down—you can sync by artist and genre as well.

❹ **Movies**. Full-length movies can take up to a gigabyte or more of precious 'Pod space, so iTunes gives you the option to load all, selected, or even just unwatched films.

❺ **TV Shows**. As with movies, you can selectively choose which TV shows (or episodes thereof) you bring along on your iPod.

⑥ **Podcasts**. Your pal iTunes can automatically download the podcasts you've *subscribed* to through the iTunes Store (see Chapter 7); here, you can decide which ones you want to listen to on the go.

⑦ **iTunes U**. Over the years, the iPod has found a place as a learning tool in the Groves of Academe. But you don't need to be a registered student at any of the major universities to take advantage of the free audio lectures and video presentations in the iTunes U section of the Store. You download the content here, and then sync up your 'Pod.

⑧ **Books**. This literary tab lets you selectively sync up your audiobooks and your Touch's electronic iBooks files.

⑨ **Photos**. The Touch, Nano, and Classic can all display little copies of your digital photos. Click this tab to select where you want iTunes to look for them (like in an iPhoto or Photoshop Elements folder) and which photo albums you want to bring with you.

⑩ **Info**. It's not just an all-purpose media player! The iPod Classic and Touch are happy to carry copies of all the addresses and phone numbers listed in your computer's address book (from Microsoft Outlook, the Mac OS X Address Book, and other programs). Scroll down the screen until you find an option to grab Outlook or iCal calendars. On the Touch, you can sync up web browser bookmarks and email account settings from your computer, too. If you have a free iCloud account (page 254), you can add the Touch to your collection of über-synced computers and iPhones to keep your info current across all your Internet-connected hardware.

⑪ **Nike + iPod**. If you're using the Nano's pedometer feature or the Nike + iPod app on your Nano or Touch, you can set the device to upload your workout results to the *www.nikeplus.com* website so you can track your fitness progress online.

NOTE   The iPod Touch, Nano, Shuffle, and iTunes have features for the visually impaired to navigate audio content by verbal cues instead of onscreen menus. On the Touch's Summary screen in iTunes, click the Configure Universal Access button, and then click the button to enable VoiceOver. On the Touch itself, you can turn the feature on or off at Settings→General→Accessibility. On the Nano, tap Settings→General→Accessibility, choose your speech options, and then tap VoiceOver to On. For the Shuffle, connect it to iTunes and turn on the checkbox next to Enable VoiceOver on the Summary screen. Using VoiceOver does change the way you control the iPod (especially the Touch), so be sure to read up on the feature at *www.apple.com/accessibility/*.

Load Songs onto an iPod from More Than One Computer

ITUNES' AUTOSYNC FEATURE MAKES keeping your iPod up to date a breeze, but there's a big catch: You can sync your iPod with only *one* computer. Lots of people have music scattered around multiple machines: a couple of different family Macs, an office PC and a home PC, and so on. If you want to load up your music from each of these sources, you have to change your iPod settings to *manual management*. That's easy to do. Just connect your iPod to iTunes, select it in the Source list, and then click the Summary tab in iTunes. Then:

- Scroll down to the Options area and turn on the checkbox next to "Manually manage music and videos." Click the Apply button in the bottom-right corner of iTunes to cement the change.

- Don't forget to manually eject your iPod from iTunes when you want to safely remove it from your computer. (Manual updates give you total control, but as Uncle Ben said in *Spider-Man*, "With great power comes great responsibility.") Eject the iPod by either clicking the Eject button next to the iPod's name in the iTunes Source list or by pressing Ctrl+E (⌘-E) to properly free the player from the computer.

TIP Your iPod's Summary screen (in iTunes) shows whether your iPod is formatted for Windows or a Mac. If you have a new iPod and want to use it with both a PC and a Mac, connect it to the PC first and have iTunes format it for Windows. A Mac can read the Windows format just fine, but Windows won't recognize the Mac format without special software. The iPod Touch, however, will talk to either type of computer, no matter which one you use it with first.

Manually Delete Music and Videos from Your iPod

PEOPLE WHO CHOOSE TO autosync their iPods don't have to worry about taking stuff off of their players. They can choose which playlists and media to automatically copy over to their iPods—or they can just delete unwanted items out of iTunes and resync their 'Pods to wipe the same files off the player.

But if you're a manual manager, you have to delete unwanted files yourself. (You can, however, have iTunes automatically update your podcast subscriptions; see Chapter 7 for more about podcasts.)

❶ To delete files from your iPod, connect it to your computer and click the iPod icon in iTunes' Source list.

❷ Click the flippy triangle next to the iPod icon to get to the media library you want to clean up. To delete songs, for example, click the Music icon.

❸ In the list that appears on the right side of iTunes, select the unwanted track. If you have a bunch of items you want to clear off your iPod in one fell swoop, Ctrl-click (⌘-click) to select multiple tracks. With the tracks selected, press the Delete key on the keyboard, and then confirm your choice in the iTunes alert box that appears. This removes the files from your iPod but doesn't whack them out of the iTunes library, where you can always reload them if you find you miss those songs after all.

Copy Your Music from iPod to iTunes

TO PREVENT RAMPANT PIRACY across the seven seas of Musicdom, Apple originally designed the data transfer between iTunes and the iPod as a one-way trip—you could copy music *to* a connected iPod, but not *from* an iPod to your computer. This is still pretty much Apple's way, although you can now copy iTunes Store purchases from your iPod to iTunes; Chapter 7 has the details.

But there are times when perfectly honest people need to get their songs off of their iPods—like when your computer dies and takes your iTunes library with it.

The Web is full of tips and tricks for harvesting content off of an iPod and getting it back into iTunes, often by fiddling with system settings in Windows or Mac OS X. These methods can vary based on which iPod and which version of an operating system you have. Thankfully, there's also The Shareware Option. Several helpful folks have developed free or inexpensive programs to copy content from your iPod to your computer:

- **TouchCopy**. The program costs $25, but it works with Windows PCs and Mac OS X—and on all iPod models (*www.wideanglesoftware.com/touchcopy*).

- **YamiPod**. A free program that runs off of the iPod itself and exports music back to Windows, Mac, and Linux systems (*www.yamipod.com*).

- **SharePod**. This freeware program for Windows, pictured at right, can copy music and videos back to your PC and also edit playlists, artwork, and song tags (labels) (*www.getsharepod.com*).

- **Senuti**. The name makes sense when you realize it's iTunes spelled backward. Senuti is a $19 shareware program for the Mac that lets you copy all (or just some) of the music on your iPod back to iTunes (*www. fadingred.org/senuti*).

Move Your iTunes Media Folder to an External Drive

MEDIA LIBRARIES GROW LARGE, and hard drives can seem to shrink as you add thousands of songs and hundreds of videos to iTunes. You may, in fact, think about using a big external drive for iTunes storage. That's just dandy, but you need to make sure that iTunes knows what you intend to do.

If you rudely drag your iTunes Media (or Music) folder to a different place without telling iTunes, it thinks the songs and videos in your collection are gone. The next time you start the program, you'll find a newly created, empty Media/Music folder. (While iTunes remains empty but calm, *you* may be having heart palpitations as you picture your media collection vanishing in a puff of bytes.)

To move the Media/Music folder to a new drive, give iTunes a heads-up. Before you start, make sure iTunes has been putting all your songs and videos in the iTunes Media/Music folder by opening the Preferences box (Ctrl+comma [⌘-comma]) and confirming the folder location. Then:

❶ Click the Advanced tab and turn on the checkbox next to "Keep iTunes Media folder organized."

❷ Click the Change button in the iTunes Media folder location area and navigate to the external hard drive.

❸ Click the New Folder button in the window, type in a name for the iTunes library, and then click the Create button.

❹ Back in the Change Media Folder Location box, click the Open button.

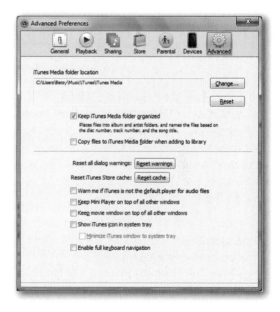

❺ Click OK to close the iTunes Preferences box.

❻ Choose File→Library→Organize Library and then check "Consolidate files."

Ignore the ominous warnings (*"This cannot be undone"*) and let iTunes heave a complete copy of your iTunes folder to the external drive. Once you confirm that everything is in the new library, trash your old iTunes Media folder and empty the Recycle Bin or Trash to get all those gigs of hard drive space back.

Where iTunes Stores Your Files

BEHIND ITS STEELY SILVER-FRAMED window, iTunes has a very precise system for storing your music, movies, and everything else you add to it. Inside its own iTunes folder on your hard drive (which, unless you moved it, is in Music→iTunes [Home→Music→iTunes]), the program keeps all your files and song information. (If you're running Windows Vista, then your iTunes folder is at User→<user name>→Music→iTunes, and Windows XP users can find it at My Documents→My Music→iTunes.)

Your iTunes Library file, *iTunes Library.itl* (*iTunes Library* on Macs with old versions of iTunes), is a record of the names of all the songs, playlists, videos, and other content you added to iTunes. It sits inside the iTunes folder. Be very careful not to move or delete this file if you happen to be poking around in the iTunes folder. If iTunes can't find it, it gives a little sigh and creates a new library—one that doesn't have a record of all your songs and other media goodies.

But even if you *do* accidentally delete the Library file, your music is still on your computer—even if iTunes doesn't know it. That's because all the song files are actually stored in the iTunes *Media* folder (or *Music* folder; see the Tip below), which is also inside the main iTunes folder. You may lose your custom playlists if your Library file goes missing, but you can always add your music files back (File→Add to Library) to recreate your library.

TIP Depending on whether you updated an older version of iTunes, your iTunes Media folder may actually be an iTunes Music folder. If you have a Media folder, iTunes neatly groups things like games, music, TV shows, movies, and other content in their own subfolders, making it much easier to find your downloaded episodes of *Mad Men* among all the song files. If you want to reorganize, media-style, choose File→Library→Organize Library and choose "Upgrade to iTunes Media organization."

Back Up Your iTunes Files

IF YOUR HARD DRIVE dies and takes your whole iTunes folder with it, you could be in for a major media migraine, depending on your backup situation. You can easily recover music, apps, TV shows, and books you purchased from the iTunes Store now, thanks to iTunes In the Cloud (page 112), but your hand-ripped tracks from your personal CD collection and music purchased from other online stores (page 183) are gone unless you're an iTunes Match subscriber (page 113). But iTunes Match doesn't upload copies of your video clips and full-length movies, so those may have just disappeared into the ether as well.

That's why it's important to back up the iTunes library—if not your whole computer—unless you're one of those types who *likes* starting over from scratch.

❶ If you just want to back up your iTunes collection to set of CDs or DVDs, fire up your disc-making program and burn a copy of your iTunes folder to the recordable platters. (The previous page explains how to find your iTunes folder and files.)

❷ Use a dedicated program to back up your computer's contents to an external hard drive or recordable discs. Plenty of third-party options are out there (many offered as part of system security suites or included with new USB external hard drives), but your computer itself may have built-in tools. For example, Mac OS X 10.5 and later includes Apple's Time Machine utility (shown here), which works with most external hard drives and makes frequent snapshots of your computer's contents throughout the day. Find it at Home→Applications→Time Machine; bring your own dedicated external hard drive.

Windows Vista and Windows 7 also include a backup program. Go to Start→Control Panel→System and Maintenance→Backup and Restore to find it and set it up. (If you use Windows XP, you may first have to install the backup program from your system discs, depending on which version of the operating system you have; Microsoft has details at *http://support. microsoft.com/kb/308422.*)

Online backup services like Mozy (*www.mozy.com*), iDrive (*www.idrive.com*), and Carbonite (*www.carbonite.com*) are alternatives to using a USB drive. You typically get 2 gigabytes of free storage and then pay as little as $5 a month.

CHAPTER 6

The Power of Playlists

A *PLAYLIST* IS A GROUP OF SONGS YOU GATHER FROM YOUR ITUNES library that you think go well together. You can include pretty much any set of tunes arranged in any order. For example, if you're having a party, you can make playlists out of the dance music in your iTunes library. If you're in a 1960s Brit-girl pop mood, you can whip together the hits of Dusty Springfield, Lulu, and Petula Clark. Some people may question your taste if you, say, mix tracks from *La Bohème* with Queen's *A Night at the Opera*, but hey—it's *your* playlist.

Creating playlists has become something of an art form since the iPod arrived in 2001. You can find books filled with sample playlists. Academics around the world write papers about group dynamics and cultural identity after studying how people create playlists—and which ones they choose to share with others. You can publish your own playlists in the iTunes Store (see page 147) so others can bear witness to your mixing prowess. Some nightclubs even invite people to hook up their iPods so they can share their playlists with the dance-floor audience.

If you don't have time to make your own playlists, Apple lends you an expert hand. Its Genius feature lets you create one-click mixes of songs that sound like they were actually meant to go together.

So get cracking and create a playlist (or 42) of your own.

Make a New Playlist in iTunes

TO CREATE A PLAYLIST, press Ctrl+N (⌘-N) in iTunes. You can also choose File→New Playlist or click the **+** button at the bottom-left corner of the iTunes window.

All freshly minted playlists start out coldly named "untitled playlist." Fortunately, iTunes highlights this generic moniker so it's ready for editing—just type in a better name: "Cardio Workout," "Hits of the Highland Lute," or whatever you want to call it. As you add playlists, iTunes alphabetizes them in the Playlists area of the Source list.

Once you create and name a spanking-new playlist, you're ready to add songs or videos. You can do so several ways, so choose the one you like best.

Playlist-Making Method #1

❶ If this is your first playlist, open the playlist in its own window so it's easy to see what's going on. To make that happen, double-click the name of the playlist in the Source panel. You end up with your full library in one window and your empty playlist in the other. (If this is your first playlist, iTunes pops up an intro screen; ignore it and go to step 2.)

❷ Go back to the main iTunes window and drag the song titles you want from your library over to the new playlist window. (Make sure you click the Music icon in the Source list to see all your songs.) Drag songs one at a time, or grab a bunch by selecting tracks one after the other; just Ctrl-click (⌘-click) each title.

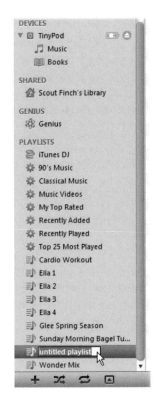

Playlist-Making Method #2

❶ Not a fan of multiple windows? No problem. You can add songs to a playlist by highlighting them in the main iTunes window (Ctrl-click [⌘-click] each one) and dragging them to the playlist.

❷ If you've created lots of playlists, you may need to scroll down iTunes' window to get to your new one.

Playlist-Making Method #3

❶ You can also pick and choose songs in your library and then create a playlist out of the highlighted songs. Select tracks by Ctrl-clicking (⌘-clicking) the titles.

❷ Choose File→New Playlist From Selection, or press Ctrl-Shift-N (⌘-Shift-N). The songs you selected appear in a brand-new playlist. If all of them came from the same album, iTunes names the playlist after the album (but it also highlights the name so you can change it).

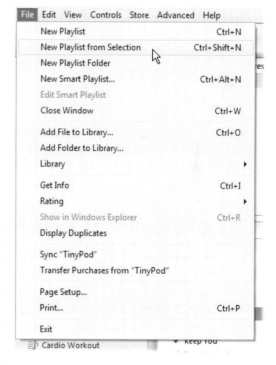

Don't worry about clogging up your hard drive. When you drag a song title onto a playlist, you don't *copy* the song, you just tell iTunes where to find the file. In essence, you're creating a shortcut to the track. That means you can have the same song on several playlists, but only one copy of it resides on your computer.

That nice iTunes even gives you some playlists of its own devising, like "Top 25 Most Played" and "Purchased" (a convenient place to find all your iTunes Store goodies listed in one place).

Change an Existing Playlist

IF YOU CHANGE YOUR mind about a playlist's tune order, drag the song titles up or down within the playlist window. Just make sure to sort the playlist by song order first (click the top of the first column, the one with the numbers listed in front of the song titles).

You can always drag more songs into a playlist, and you can delete titles if you find that your list needs pruning. Click the song in the playlist window, and then hit Backspace (Delete). When

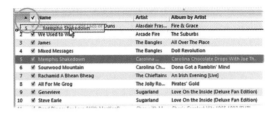

iTunes asks you to confirm your decision, click Yes. Remember, deleting a song from a playlist doesn't delete it from your music library—it just removes the title from that particular playlist. (You can get rid of a song for good only by pressing Backspace or Delete from within the iTunes library; select the Music icon under "Library" to get there.)

You can quickly add a song to an existing playlist right from the main iTunes window, no matter which view you happen to be using: Select the song, right-click (Control-click) it, and then, in the pop-up menu, choose Add to Playlist as shown below. Scroll to the playlist you want to use and then click the mouse button to add the track to that playlist.

If you want to see how many playlists contain a certain song, select the track, right-click (Control-click) it, and choose Show in Playlist in the pop-up menu.

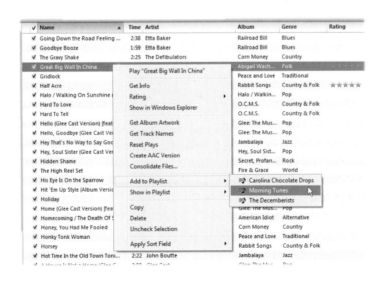

Add a Playlist to Your iPod

ADDING THAT FABULOUS NEW playlist to your iPod doesn't take any heavy lifting on your part. In fact, if you set up your iPod to autosync with iTunes, the only thing you need to do is grab your USB cable and plug in your iPod. Once iTunes recognizes the iPod, it copies any new playlists over to it.

You can also tell iTunes to sync different playlists to different iPods—helpful if you're in a multiple-iPod-owning household and you all share the same computer and iTunes library. Just plug in your iPod, select it in the Source list, and then click the Music tab. In the Sync Music area, click the button for "Selected playlists" and then turn on the checkboxes for the playlists you want.

If you manually manage the syncing process, adding new playlists is a total drag—literally, because dragging is all you have to do. With your iPod connected, select the playlist you want to transfer (Ctrl-click [⌘-click] to snag more than one), and then drag it onto the iPod's icon. That's it.

TIP If you find that your Source list is longer than the line for a Justin Bieber concert, you can save some space by putting batches of song mixes, like "Dinner Party" or "Cardio Workouts," inside *playlist folders* in the Source list. Making a folder is easy: just choose File→New Playlist Folder. Once the new folder appears in the Playlists area of the Source panel, give it a name and then drag a bunch of playlists onto the folder icon. To open the folder and crank up a playlist inside, click the flippy triangle next to the folder name to reveal the playlists. Click the triangle again to close the folder and shorten your Source list.

Delete a Playlist

ONCE THE PARTY'S OVER, you may want to get rid of that iTunes playlist. Start by clicking it in the Source list, and then press the Backspace (Delete) key. iTunes presents you with a warning box, double-checking that you really want to vaporize the list. (Again, this maneuver just zaps the playlist itself, not the songs you had in it. Those remain available in the main iTunes window.)

If you have your iPod set to autosync, then any playlist you delete from iTunes will disappear from your iPod the next time you plug in and sync your player.

If you manually manage your iPod and all its contents, connect the player and spin open the flippy triangle next to its name in the Source list. That gives you a look at all its libraries and playlists. Click the one you want to dump and then hit the Backspace (Delete) key.

Make and Edit Playlists on the iPod Touch and Nano

PLAYLIST INSPIRATION CAN STRIKE anywhere, and you may not be sitting in front of iTunes when it does. Thankfully, the Touch and Nano let you follow your whims wherever you may be. All you need are songs and a finger. Here's how:

- **Create the playlist**. On the Touch's Home screen, tap the Music icon. Tap Playlists. Near the top of the Playlists screen, tap Add Playlist and type in a name for it. A master list of all your songs appears. Each time you see one worth adding, tap its name (or the ⊕ button). You can also tap one of the icons at the bottom of the screen, like Playlists, Artists, or Albums, to find the stuff you want. At the top of every list is an "Add All Songs" option that does just that—adds all the songs listed to your playlist-in-progress. When you finish, tap Done. Your playlist is ready for its debut.

  On the Nano's Home screen, tap Music→Playlists. Tap the Playlists title bar at the top of the screen and then tap the Add button. Tap the name of the category—Songs, Albums, you know the drill—and then tap the ⊕ next to the item you want to add. Swipe left to add stuff from several categories, so you can, for example, stick in a podcast for your post-jog cooldown walk. Tap Done when you finish. Your creation is called New Playlist 1, but you can change that after you sync the Nano with iTunes.

- **Delete or edit the playlist**. To whack a whole playlist on the Touch, tap Home→Music→Playlists→[Playlist Name]→Delete. On the Nano, tap Home→Music→ Playlists. Tap the title bar on the next screen, press Edit, tap the Delete symbol (⊖), and then press the Delete button to remove the whole playlist. Tap the Clear button to keep the playlist name, but zap its songs.

  To edit an existing playlist on the Touch or Nano, tap Home→Music→Playlists→[Playlist Name]→Edit; tap the title bar on the Nano to see the Edit button. Tap the Delete symbol (⊖) and then press the Delete button to remove a song, or tap **+** (or the Add button on the Nano) to browse for and add a new song. See that "grip strip" (☰) at the right edge of the screen? Press and hold it with a finger and drag the strip up or down to rearrange the order of the songs. Tap Done when you finish.

Make a Playlist on an iPod Classic

THE IPOD CLASSIC MAY be older than the Touch and Nano, but it, too, lets you create playlists right there on the player. They sync back to iTunes the next time you connect. The iPod Classic calls its song collections "On-The-Go" playlists:

❶ Scroll through your iPod's list of songs until you get to the title of the first one you want to add to a playlist.

❷ Hold down the iPod's center button for a few seconds until a new set of menus appears. Choose "Add to On-The-Go."

❸ Scroll to the next song you want to add and repeat the process.

❹ When you're done adding songs, press the iPod's menu button until you get to the Music menu; go to Playlists→On-The-Go. Under On-The-Go, you see the number of songs you just compiled. Press the Select button to see the song titles.

❺ If you like what you see, scroll up to Save Playlist and click the center button. If you don't like the collection, choose Clear Playlist to dump the songs and start over. If you like some, but not all, of the songs, you can remove individual tunes by selecting one, holding down the center button, and choosing "Remove from On-The-Go."

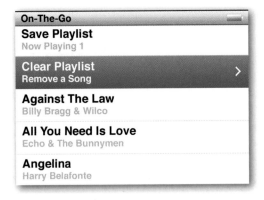

Your freshly inspired playlist now appears in your Playlists menu as On-The-Go 1. The next one you make and save will be On-The-Go 2, and so on. When you reconnect your iPod to iTunes, you can click these names and change them to something peppier—or more descriptive.

TIP You can also add a whole album to your On-The-Go inspiration. Just select the LP title in your Albums list, hold down the center button, and choose Add to On-The-Go.

Make a Genius Playlist in iTunes

PLAYLISTS ARE FUN TO make, but occasionally you just don't have the time or energy. If that's the case, call in an expert—the iTunes Genius. With the Genius feature, you click any song you're in the mood for and iTunes crafts a playlist of 25 to 100 songs that it thinks go well with the one you picked.

The first time you use it, Genius asks permission to go through your music collection and gather song information. Then it uploads that data to Apple. When your information has been analyzed (by software) and anonymously added to a big giant database of everybody else's song info (to improve the Genius's suggestions), the Genius is ready for duty. Here's the procedure:

❶ Click a song title in your library.

❷ Click the Genius button (✳) at the bottom right of iTunes. (If you're playing the song, click the Genius icon in the iTunes display window.)

❸ iTunes presents you with your new playlist in a flash.

❹ Use the buttons at the top of the Genius window to adjust the number of songs in the playlist, refresh it with new songs if you want a different mix, and—best of all—save the list permanently.

The Genius doesn't work if it doesn't have enough information about a song—or if there aren't enough similar songs for it to draw from. In that case, pick another tune. If you frequently add new music to your library and want to get it in the mix, inform the Genius at Store→Update Genius.

And if you happen to have the Genius Sidebar panel open in your iTunes window (Chapter 4), the Genius cheerfully presents you with a list of other songs that you can buy right there to round out your listening experience.

> **NOTE** If you declined iTunes' initial offer to activate the Genius, you can summon it again by choosing Store→Turn On Genius. And if you're regretting your choice to invite the Genius into your iTunes home, kick it out by visiting the same menu and choosing Turn Off Genius.

Make a Genius Playlist on the iPod

YOU MAY GET SO hooked on making Genius playlists in iTunes that you never want to leave your computer. Before you end up on a neighborhood "Lost" flier, consider this: You can also make Genius playlists on the iPod itself. You just need to have a recent Touch, Nano, or Classic.

To use your portable pocket Genius, though, you first have to set it up and upload your information from iTunes to Apple, as described on the previous page. But you've probably already done that by now, so here's how to make the Genius do your bidding when you're away from your computer.

❶ On the Touch, tap Music→ Playlists→Genius Playlist and then tap the song you want Genius to use as a starting point. If you're currently *listening* to that song, tap the screen to summon the playback controls (Chapter 3), and then tap the ❋ icon.

On the Nano, play the song you want to start with and tap the album cover on the Now Playing screen. Swipe the screen to the left and tap the ❋ icon.

On a Classic, select a song and hold down the iPod's center button for a few seconds, until a menu appears; choose Start Genius. If you're already playing the song you want to use, press the center button until you see the Genius option appear, and then flick the click wheel over to Start.

❷ If you don't like the resulting mix, select or tap the Refresh option atop the screen to get new tunes.

❸ If you love the work of the Genius, select or tap the Save option at the top of the screen.

As in iTunes, Genius playlists are titled with the name of the song you originally chose as the foundation for your mix. When you sync the iPod with iTunes, the traveling Genius playlists get copied back to iTunes, where you can edit the title.

Genius Mixes in iTunes

YES, THE ITUNES GENIUS feature takes almost all the effort out of making a playlist—all you do is click the Genius button. But if even a one-button click seems like too much effort, iTunes makes playlist creation even *easier*. Welcome to Genius Mixes.

The Genius Mix feature works like this: iTunes takes it upon itself to search your entire music library and then automatically compose (depending on the size of your library) up to 12 different types of song collections. Unlike a Genius playlist of songs calculated to go well together, a Genius Mix is more like a radio station or cable-TV music channel, with the music based on *genre*. Depending on what's in your iTunes library, the Genius could present you with a hip-hop mix, a country mix, a classical mix, and so on. In addition, the Genius Mix creates up to 12 playlists at once, all saved and ready to play, unlike the Genius's single mix that you have to save to preserve.

If you don't already see a square Genius Mix icon in your iTunes Source list, choose Store→Update Genius. Once activated, the Genius quietly stirs up its sonic concoctions from your music library.

To play a Genius Mix, click the Genius Mix icon in the Source list. The iTunes window reverts to Grid view and displays the different mixes it's created. It represents each by a quartet of album covers from tracks in the mix. Pass your mouse over the album squares to see the name of the mix, or click the squares to start playing the songs.

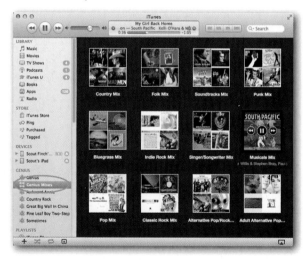

Like more traditional radio stations, you don't get to see a playlist of what's actually *in* a particular Genius Mix—it's all a surprise. If you don't care for a particular song the Genius has included, you can always hit the forward button or tap the right arrow key on the computer's keyboard to skip to the next track.

Genius Mixes can be another great way to effortlessly toss on some background music at a party, and you may even hear songs you haven't played in forever. Want to take the Genius Mix with you? Turn the page.

Genius Mixes on the iPod

AS WITH MOST PLAYLISTS (except for those mobile made-on-the-iPod kind), you need to copy Genius Mixes over to the iPod by way of iTunes. But there's one other little requirement: You have to copy the Genius Mixes over by *syncing* them through iTunes.

People who autosync their entire libraries don't have to do anything to get the Genius Mixes onboard their iPods. People who manually manage music by dragging tracks from the iTunes library onto the iPod can't physically drag a Genius Mix onto the player—for now, anyway. For those who selectively sync, copying a Genius Mix takes just a few steps:

❶ Connect your iPod to your computer and click its icon when it appears in the Source list.

❷ Click the Music tab in the middle of the iTunes window.

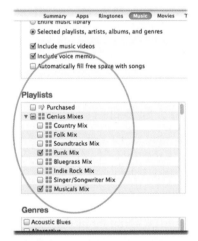

❸ If you haven't done so, turn on the checkbox for Sync Music and click the button for "Selected playlists, artists, and genres." (If you selectively sync anyway, you've already done this step.)

❹ Turn on the checkboxes next to the Genius Mixes you want to copy to your iPod. Click the Apply and/or Sync button to transfer them to the player.

❺ To play a mix on your iPod Touch, tap Home→Music→Genius. Swipe your finger across the screen until you get to the mix you want, and then tap the Play triangle to fire it up. (The dots at the bottom of the screen tell you how many mixes you have.) On a Nano, tap the Genius icon and swipe the screen to browse the mixes. On a Classic, choose iPod→Music→Genius Mixes. Use the click wheel's Next or Previous buttons to get to the right mix. Press the center button or Play/Pause to listen it.

Publish Your Own Playlists

IF YOU HAVE A playlist you consider a masterwork of mixing, you can share it with other iTunes Store shoppers or with your pals on Ping, Apple's music social-networking service (page 170). You can name it, write your own liner notes explaining your inspiration, and put it out there for everyone to see. (You're not actually copying songs up to the Store; you're just showing off your cool taste, which Apple hopes will lead others to buy those songs.) Here's how to share:

❶ Start by signing into your Store account.

❷ In the iTunes Source list, select the playlist you want to publish. (If it contains any songs that Apple doesn't sell or copy-protected songs you bought elsewhere, they'll get knocked off the list—which may ruin your carefully constructed mix.)

❸ In the Store menu, choose Share Playlist.

❹ In the box that appears (shown here), click the Publish button; you also have the option to "gift" the playlist, which means you buy every song on it and have them delivered to a lucky friend.

❺ On the "Create a Playlist on iTunes" or "Create a Ping Playlist" screen (you get the latter if you're logged into Ping), write a short description of the playlist. Ping users can even turn on the option to let others add to the mix. Once you click the Publish button, iTunes releases your playlist into the wild. Now other people can see it, rate it, be inspired by it, or—and let's face it, here's the key thing from Apple's perspective—buy the songs on it.

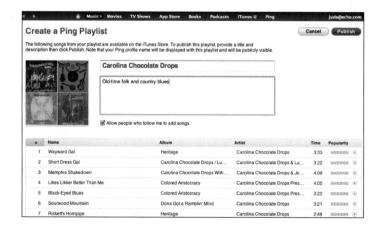

Smart Playlists: Another Way for iTunes to Assemble Your Songs

AS COOL AS THE Genius is, sometimes you want a little more control over what goes into your automatically generated mixes. That's where iTunes' Smart Playlists rise to the occasion.

Once you give it some guidelines, a *Smart Playlist* can go sniffing through your music library and come up with its own music mix. A Smart Playlist even keeps tabs on the music that comes and goes to and from your library and adjusts itself based on that.

You might tell one Smart Playlist to assemble 45 minutes' worth of songs that you've rated higher than four stars but rarely listen to, and another to play your most-often-played songs from the 1980s. The Smart Playlists you create are limited only by your imagination.

❶ **To start a Smart Playlist, press Ctrl+Alt+N (Option-⌘-N) or choose File→New Smart Playlist in iTunes**. A Smart Playlist box opens: It sports a gear-shaped icon next to its name in the Source list (a regular playlist has a music-staff icon with a music note on it).

❷ Give iTunes detailed instructions about what you want to hear. You can select a few artists you like and have iTunes leave off the ones you're not in the mood for, pluck songs that fall within a certain genre or year, and so on. To add multiple, cumulative criteria, click the plus (**+**) button on each line.

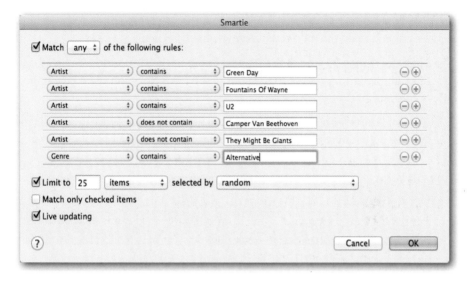

❸ Turn on the "Live updating" checkbox. This tells iTunes to keep the playlist updated as your collection, ratings, and play count change. (The play count tells iTunes how often you play a track, a good indicator of how much you like a song.)

❹ To edit an existing Smart Playlist, right-click (Control-click) the playlist's name. Then choose Edit Smart Playlist.

A Smart Playlist is a dialogue between you and iTunes: You tell it what you want in as much detail as you want, and the program whips up a playlist according to your instructions.

You can even instruct a Smart Playlist to pull tracks from your current Genius playlist. Just click the **+** button to add a preference, choose Playlist as another criteria, and select Genius from the list of available playlists.

TIP When you press Shift (Option), the **+** button at the bottom of the iTunes window turns into a gear icon. Click this button to quickly launch the Smart Playlist creation box.

iTunes DJ: Get the Party Started

THE STANDARD ITUNES SONG-SHUFFLE feature can be inspiring or embarrassing, depending on which songs the program happens to play. The iTunes DJ feature, on the other hand, lets *you* control which songs iTunes selects when it shuffles at your next shindig. It also shows you what's already been played and what's coming up in the mix, so you know what to expect.

❶ **Click the iTunes DJ icon in the Playlists area of the iTunes Source list**. Click through the intro screen if this is your first DJ list. Now you see a new pane at the very bottom of iTunes.

❷ **Use the Source pop-up menu to select a music source for the mix**. You can use either an existing playlist, a Genius playlist, or your whole library.

❸ **If you don't like the song list that iTunes proposes, click the Refresh button at the bottom-right of the iTunes window**. iTunes generates a new list of songs for your consideration.

❹ **Click the Settings button at the bottom of the window**. In the Settings box, you can change the number of recently played and upcoming songs that iTunes displays.

If iTunes is DJing your interactive music party, the Settings box also has a place to add a welcome message for guests changing up your music with the Remote program on their iPhones and iPod Touches (see page 267 for more on the Remote app).

❺ **Arrange the songs if you feel like it**. Back on the playlist, you can manually add songs, delete them from the playlist, or rearrange the playing order. To add songs, click the Source list's Music icon and then drag your selected tunes onto the iTunes DJ icon.

❻ **Click the Play button**. And let the music play on.

Three Kinds of Discs You Can Create with iTunes

IF YOU WANT TO record a certain playlist on a CD for posterity—or for the Mr. Shower CD player in the bathroom—iTunes gives you power to burn. In fact, it can create three kinds of discs:

- **Standard audio CDs**. This is the best option. If your computer has a CD burner, it can serve as your own private record label. iTunes can record selected sets of songs, no matter what their original source (except for non-iTunes Store tunes that have copy protection), onto a blank CD. When it's all

over, you can play the burned CD on any standard CD player, just like the albums you get from Best Buy—but this time, you hear only the songs you like, in the order you like. Turn the page for playlist-burning instructions.

- **MP3 CDs**. A standard audio CD contains high-quality, enormous song files in the AIFF format. An *MP3* compact disc, however, is a data CD that contains music files in the MP3 format. Because MP3 songs are much smaller than AIFF files, many more of them fit in the standard 650 or 700 MB of space on a recordable CD. The bottom line? Instead of 74 or 80 minutes of music, a CD full of MP3 files can store *10 to 12 hours* of tunes. The downside? Older CD players may not be able to play these discs.

- **Backup CDs or DVDs**. If your computer can play and record CDs and/or DVDs, you have another option: iTunes can back up all the song files on a playlist by copying them to a CD or DVD. (The disc won't play in any kind of player; it's just a glorified backup disk for restoration when something goes wrong with your hard drive.) You can back up all the songs in your library to disc by selecting them all and choosing File→New Playlist From Selection—and then burning *that* monster playlist to a set of data discs.

To see if your disc drive is compatible with iTunes, select a playlist and click the Burn Disc button on the iTunes window to get the Burn Settings box. If your drive is listed next to "CD Burner," iTunes recognizes it.

> **NOTE** Even if you've got a DVD drive, you still see it listed next to the label "CD Burner."

Burn a Playlist to a CD

MAKING A CD OUT of your favorite playlist takes just a few steps with iTunes, so get your blank disc ready and click along.

❶ **Select the playlist you want to burn**. Check to make sure your songs are in the order you want them; drag any tune up or down to reorder.

❷ **When you're ready to roll, choose File→Burn Playlist to Disc or right-click (Control-click) the playlist in the Source list and choose Burn Playlist to Disc**. When the Burn Settings box pops up, pick the type of disc you want to create (see the previous page for your choices).

❸ **Insert a blank disc into your drive when prompted**. If your computer has a CD platter that slides out, push it back in. Then sit back as iTunes handles things.

iTunes prepares to record the disc, which may take a few minutes. In addition to prepping the disc for recording, iTunes has to convert the files (if you're burning an audio CD) to the industry-standard format for CDs.

Once iTunes has taken care of business, it lets you know that it's burning the disc. Again, depending on the speed of your computer and disc burner, as well as the size of your playlist, the recording process could take several minutes. When the disc is done, iTunes pipes up with a musical flourish. Eject the disc and off you go. But if you want to make a nice-looking CD cover...

Print Playlists and Snazzy CD Covers

YOU USED TO HAVE to do a lot of gymnastics just to print a nice-looking song list that would fit into a CD case. But with iTunes, all you need to do is choose File→Print, select a preformatted option, and then click the Print button.

The Print dialog box is *full* of choices.

- **CD jewel case insert**. You can print out a perfectly sized insert for a CD jewel case, complete with a song list on the left and a miniature mosaic of all your album artwork on the right—or just a plain list of songs on a solid-color background. Your resulting printout even comes with handy crop marks to guide your scissors when you trim it down to size.

- **Song listing**. If you want something simpler, you can opt for a straightforward list of all the songs on the playlist. This option is also great for printing out a list of all the podcasts you currently have in your iTunes library—just click the Podcasts icon in the Source list, click the "Song listing" option, and print away.

- **Album listing**. You can print a list of all the albums that contributed songs to your playlist, complete with the album title, artist name, and the songs' titles and play times for each track culled from that album.

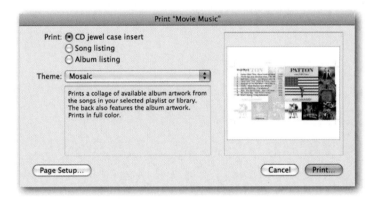

Want to use one of your own photos for the cover of your CD case? Start by adding the artwork of your choice to a track (Chapter 5). When you're ready to print, select that track on the playlist and then choose File→Print→CD jewel case insert→Theme: Single Cover to place your photo front and center. This method also works great if you're looking to create jewel-case inserts that look just like the ones that come with commercial CDs.

CHAPTER 7

Shop the iTunes Store

MUSIC FANS HAVE BEEN DOWNLOADING SONGS FROM THE INTERNET since the 1990s, from sites that were legal and others that were, well, not so much. People loved the convenience, but record companies saw potential profits slipping down millions of modem lines. They fought back by suing file-sharing services and other software companies for aiding and abetting copyright infringement.

The need for a legal music-download site was obvious, but most early efforts resulted in skimpy song catalogs and confusing usage rights. Things changed dramatically in April 2003, when Apple opened its online iTunes Music Store, selling legal, iPod-ready digital versions of popular songs for 99 cents a pop. In January 2009, Apple even did away with the restrictive copy protections built into most Store songs. This liberating act gave consumers unfettered use of their songs and even the ability to play them on (gasp!) non-Apple players.

Now simply called the iTunes Store, the media emporium's virtual shelves stock millions of songs, plus full-length movies, TV shows, iPod Touch programs, audio books, eBooks, podcasts, music videos, and more. It's all custom-tailored for the iPod, and best of all, once you buy a title, it's yours to keep (rentals, of course, come with a time limit). This chapter shows you how to find and use the media you're looking for, and how to get the most out of the Store.

Get to the iTunes Store

COMPARED WITH BUYING GAS, fighting traffic, and finding a parking spot at the mall, getting to the iTunes Store is easy. All you need is an Internet connection and a copy of iTunes running on your computer. Then you can either:

① Click the Store icon in iTunes' Source list. You land squarely on the Store's home page, where you can start wandering around, clicking on what looks good.

② Click the icon in the lower-right corner of the iTunes window (circled) to slide open the iTunes/Ping sidebar. You'll see one of three things here: If you haven't turned on iTunes' Genius feature (page 143) or Ping (page 170), you'll see a pitch for Ping. If you've got the Genius working for you, you'll see all the albums and songs it thinks you should buy. If you're logged into Ping, you can check out the tunes your Ping friends like. (And once *you* buy something, it shows up in your friends' Ping sidebars, starting the cycle anew.) The sidebar can be a great way to learn about new music; click the Buy button or a music title to get swept into the Store.

Once you land in the iTunes Store, you can preview suggested songs by clicking the music-note icon in front of a track's title. The Buy button is there waiting for your impulse purchase, making it extremely easy to run up your credit card tab.

If you have an iPod Touch and are in range of a wireless network, you can get to the Store a third way: over the airwaves, as explained on the next page.

TIP Longtime iTunes Store customers—especially those still stuck on dial-up modems—may be deeply dismayed to see the loss of the Shopping Cart feature from earlier versions of iTunes. The Shopping Cart, which let you pile up songs and then download them simultaneously at the end of your shopping session, has been loosely replaced with the Wish List feature, described on page 173.

Shop the iTunes Store via WiFi

OWNERS OF THE IPOD Touch don't even *need* a computer to shop the iTunes Store—those lucky souls can tap their way right into the Store over a wireless Internet connection. Many WiFi-enabled Starbucks coffee shops also let you hook into the iTunes Store for free to browse and buy music, including whatever track is playing *at* Starbucks.

Now, to buy stuff when you're out and about—and in the mood to shop:

❶ Tap the purple iTunes icon on the Touch's Home screen. Make sure you have a WiFi connection; see Chapter 11 for guidance on making that happen.

❷ The Store appears onscreen. Tap your way through categories like "New Releases" until you find an album or song that interests you. (Tap an album to see all its songs.)

❸ Tap a song title for a 90-second preview.

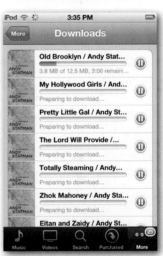

❹ Tap the Music, Videos, or Search buttons at the bottom of the window for targeted shopping, or type in search terms from the Touch keyboard.

❺ To buy and download music or videos, tap the price button, and then tap the Buy button.

❻ Type in your iTunes Store password and let the download begin. You can check the status of your purchase-in-progress by tapping the Downloads button, which also lets you pause a download if you need to. (If you don't have an iTunes Store account, tap the Create New Account button on the Sign In screen and follow the steps. You sign in and out of your account with a link at the bottom of the media listings.) Tap the Purchased icon to see all the things you've ever bought on iTunes on any computer or iOS device—and download them again here.

When the download is done, you have some brand-new media ready to play on your Touch—the new acquisitions land on your media app's Purchased page. To get those freshly harvested songs or videos back into the iTunes library on your computer, sync up the Touch. The tracks pop up in the iTunes playlist creatively titled "Purchased."

The iTunes Store Layout

THE ITUNES STORE IS jam-packed with digital merchandise, all neatly filed by category in links across the top of the main window: Music, Movies, TV Shows, and so on. Click a link to go to an "aisle" of the Store. You can also hover your mouse over a link and click the triangle that appears; a pop-up menu lets you jump to a subcategory within that category (Blues, Pop, and so on in Music, for example).

The main part of the iTunes Store window—that big piece of real estate smack in the center of your browser—highlights iTunes' latest audio and video releases and specials. It's usually stuffed full of digital goodies, so scroll down the page to see featured movies, TV shows, and apps. Free song downloads and other offers appear down below, too.

If you're looking for a specific item, use the search box in the upper-right corner to hunt your quarry; enter titles, artist names, and other searchable info.

The Quick Links box on the right side of the window has shortcuts to iTunes gift certificates (see page 172), iTunes Match (page 113), Genius suggestions, an advanced search feature, your account settings, tech support, and more.

As you scroll, you also see Top Ten lists along the right side of the screen, showing you the hottest-selling items in the Store at that very moment.

Navigate the Aisles of the iTunes Store

YOU NAVIGATE THE ITUNES Store aisles just as you'd navigate a website—by using links on the Store's page. Most artist and album names, for example, have links—click on a performer's name or an album cover to see a list of associated tracks.

Click the button with the small house on it (circled below) to jump to the Store's home page, or click iTunes' Back button in the upper-left corner (to the left of the house) to return to a previous page.

When you find the name of an album or performer you're interested in, click it to jump to a page with more information. You'll see a list of all the tracks on an album, other albums by the same artist, reviews from other iTunes users, and a list of similar albums to buy. Double-click a track title to hear a 90-second snippet. If you're shopping for videos or audiobooks, you can preview them, too.

If you get excited by something you find and want to share it with friends—or want to drop a not-so-subtle hint for your birthday—click the black triangle next to any Buy button to get a pop-up menu that lets you post your discovery on your Facebook or Twitter page.

Set Up an iTunes Store Account

BEFORE YOU CAN BUY any of the cool stuff in the iTunes Store, you need to set up an account with Apple, also known as an Apple ID. To do so, click the Sign In button on the upper-right corner of the iTunes window.

If you've ever bought or registered an Apple product on the company's website, signed up for an AppleCare tech-support plan (page 283), ordered prints, books, or calendars from iPhoto, or used another Apple service, you probably already have the requisite Apple login info. All you have to do is remember the ID (usually your email address) and password.

If you've never had an Apple ID, click Create New Account. The iTunes Store Welcome screen presents you with three steps you need to follow:

❶ Agree to the terms for using the Store and buying music.

❷ Type in a user name and password.

❸ Supply a credit card or PayPal account number and billing address.

As your first step in creating an Apple ID, you must read and agree to the long, scrolling legal agreement on the first screen. The multipage statement informs you of your rights and responsibilities as an iTunes Store and App Store customer. It boils down to this: *Thou shalt not download an album, burn it to CD, and then sell bootleg copies of it at your local convenience store* and *Third-party crashware apps are not our fault*.

Click the Agree button to move on to step 2. Here you create an Apple user name, password, and secret question and answer. If you later have to click the "Forgot Password?" button in the Store sign-in box, this is the question you'll have to answer to prove that you're you. Apple also requests that you type in your birthday to help verify your identity—and to make sure you're old enough to use the service (iTunes account holders have to be 13 or older).

On the third and final screen, tell Apple how you want to pay for purchases: provide a valid credit card number and a billing address, or type in your PayPal account info.

Click Done. You've got yourself an Apple ID. From now on, you can log into the iTunes Store by clicking the Sign In button in the upper-right corner of the iTunes window.

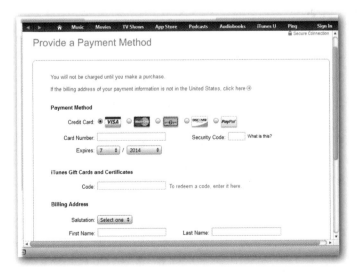

Change the Information in Your Apple Account

YOU CAN CHANGE YOUR billing address, switch the credit card you have on file for Store purchases, and edit other information in your Apple account without calling Apple. Just launch iTunes and click the Store icon in the Source list. In the Quick Links area on the right side of the Store window, click Account and then sign into your account in the box that appears.

Once you do, you'll see your account name (email address) in the main Store window. Click it. In the box that pops up, re-enter your password and click View Account. If you want to change your password or secret identity-proving question, click Edit Account Info. To change your billing address or credit card information, click Edit Payment Information. You can also deauthorize all the computers that can play songs purchased with this account (more on why and when you'd want to do that on page 179).

You can change other account settings here, too, like the information in your Ping profile (page 170) or the nickname that appears when you post a customer review in the Store. You can also see how many of your five-possible-computers you have looped into the automatic downloads feature of iTunes in the Cloud (page 112) and control the alerts the iTunes Store sends you when it thinks you should spend more money inside its electronic walls.

> **NOTE** By the way, any changes you make to your Apple ID through iTunes affect other programs or services you use with your account, like ordering pictures with iPhoto (Mac owners only).

Find Music by Genre

THE MAIN PAGE OF the iTunes Store can be a bit overwhelming, especially if you just want to slip in and buy a few Gregorian-chant tracks or browse the latest additions to the Classical section. To quickly find music by genre, hover your cursor over the Music link at the top of the Store window until a down-arrow appears. Click it to reveal a detailed drop-down menu (right).

More than 20 genres await you, from Alternative to World, with Hip-Hop/Rap, Latino, Jazz, Reggae, and Rock in between. You'll also find sections for Music Videos and Children's Music, too.

Select one of the genres, and the middle section of the Store window displays the latest additions in that category, including the newest records, music videos, and other content recently added to iTunes' ever-growing catalog. At the same time, the Top Sellers list in the right-hand column changes to reflect the most popular downloads for that genre.

Buy a Song or Album

CLICK ANY ALBUM NAME to see a list of its songs. To purchase any of the tunes, click the Buy button in the Price column. As of 2011, tracks cost 69 cents, 99 cents, or $1.29, depending on the age and popularity of the song. In most cases, you also have the option to buy a whole album (use the Buy Album button). Album prices vary as well, but tend to range from $8 to $12.

When you download an album, or even a song, you get a color picture of the album cover, which appears in iTunes when you play the song, or on the color screen of your iPod. Albums designated as "iTunes LPs" include multimedia extras, like music videos and liner notes.

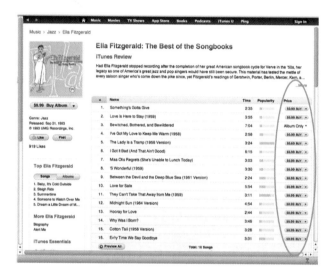

Once you click that Buy Song button, iTunes pops up an alert box, asking if you really want to buy the item you just clicked. Click the glowing Buy button to confirm your purchase, or click Cancel if you suddenly remember that your credit card is close to its limit this month. Once you click Buy, your download begins, and you soon have a new bit of music in your iTunes library.

TIP Buy three songs off an album and wish later you'd just bought the whole thing? If it's within six months of your original purchase, click the Complete My Album link on the main Store page. You get whisked to a screen that lets you download the rest of the tracks—all for a price that's less than paying for each remaining song.

Buy or Rent Movies and TV Shows

TO BUY MOVIES OR television shows, click the appropriate link at the top of the Store's main page. Apple's full-length movie library is small but growing. You'll see titles like *Bridesmaids, Captain America*, and a handful of Pixar classics like *WALL-E* and *Monsters, Inc.* Compared to little ol' song files, movies take up a ton of hard drive space—up to a full gigabyte or more—so be prepared for a download time of 30 minutes or so, depending on your Internet connection.

If you want to watch a movie but not own it, check the flick's Store page to see if it's available as a rental. Rentals cost less than $5, download just like regular Store-purchased movies, and play on your iPod, computer, or Apple TV (see page 267). You have 30 days to start watching a rental, and 24 hours to finish it.

Dozens of old and new TV shows, like *Mad Men, The Daily Show*, and *The Office*, are available by episode or for an entire season. If you sign up for a Season Pass, iTunes automatically downloads each new show as it's released. But even half-hour TV shows are big files: One 30-minute episode of *30 Rock* in standard definition, for instance, runs close to 300 megabytes.

Once you find a movie or TV show you like, click the Buy or Rent button next to the title. The downloaded video lands in your iTunes library.

Many videos in the iTunes Store come in your choice of high-definition or standard-definition format. The HD versions look great on a computer or an Apple TV, and include a standard-definition version, too—perfect for your iPod. (See Chapter 8 if you want to 'Pod-view video.)

Buy iPod Touch Apps

THE APP STORE HOSTS more than 500,000 little programs you can add to your iPod Touch to make it a tiny pocket computer as well as a stylish media machine. Currency converters, 3-D video games, newsreaders, eBooks, blogging tools, guitar-chord programs, and mobile versions of popular sites like Facebook and eBay are among the many offerings.

Click the App Store link on the main Store window to see program categories like Sports and Finance. Many apps are free (each category's page has a list of freebies), and most for-pay programs cost less than $10.

You purchase apps just as you do music and movies: see, click, buy. Your libraries sync up when you connect the Touch with iTunes. (You can also buy apps right on the Touch, as Chapter 3 explains.) Note that some apps are intended for the iPhone and its hardware, so, as with any software, check the system requirements before you buy.

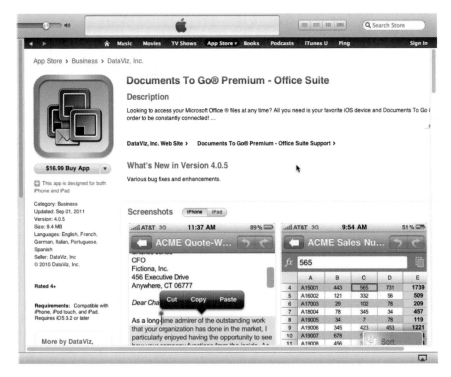

Buy Audiobooks and Books

SOME PEOPLE JUST LIKE the *sound* of a good book, and any iPod, even the tiny Shuffle, can play an audiobook.

iTunes has plenty to offer in its Audiobooks area, including verbal versions of everything from the latest best-sellers to classic literature. Prices depend on the title, but they're usually cheaper than buying a hardback copy—which would be four times the size of your iPod, anyway. Click any title's name and then the Buy Book button; the rest of the process works just like buying songs or albums.

If you have an iPod Touch, you can both hear *and* read eBooks. The Touch works with digital tomes from all the big eBookstores: Amazon, Barnes & Noble, and, of course, Apple's own iBooks emporium. You just need to download Amazon's Kindle app, Barnes & Noble's Nook app, or Apple's iBooks app (all free) from the App Store. You also need to set up an account with Amazon (*www.amazon.com*) or Barnes & Noble (*www.bn.com*). Buy the books on those sites with Safari on the Touch and then open the relevant app to sync them up with your account. With iBooks, you can buy books from within the app itself, since Apple runs that store. Have an iPod Classic? See page 231 for using electronic books there.

> **NOTE** If audiobooks are your thing, you can find even more iTunes- and iPod-friendly books—along with radio shows and recorded periodicals like the *New York Times*—at Audible.com (*www.audible. com*). To purchase Audible's wares, though, you need to go to the site and create an Audible account. The site has all the details, plus a selection of subscription plans to choose from. If you use Windows, you need to download a small piece of software from Audible called Audible Download Manager; details and instructions for the past several versions of Windows are at *http://tinyurl.com/lm2963*. Mac fans don't need to worry about that, as the Audible files land directly in iTunes when you buy them.

Download and Subscribe to Podcasts

THE ITUNES STORE HOSTS thousands upon thousands of *podcasts*, those free audio (and video!) programs put out by everyone from big television networks to a guy in his basement with a microphone.

To see what podcasts are available, click the Podcasts link at the top of the Store's main page. If you click the menu under the Podcasts list, you can jump to just audio or video podcasts, or to podcasts on a specific topic. On the main Podcasts page, you can browse shows by category, search for podcast names by keyword (use the iTunes Store's search box), or click around until you find something that sounds good.

Many podcasters produce regular installments of their shows, releasing new episodes as they're ready. You can have iTunes keep a lookout for fresh editions and automatically download them; all you have to do is *subscribe* to the podcast. Click the podcast you want, and then click the Subscribe Now button underneath the artwork. If you want to try out a single podcast, click the Free link near its title to download just that one show.

Tired of a podcast and want to stop the automatic downloads? In the Source list, click Podcasts and, in the middle of the window, click the unwanted show. Then click the Unsubscribe button at the bottom of the window.

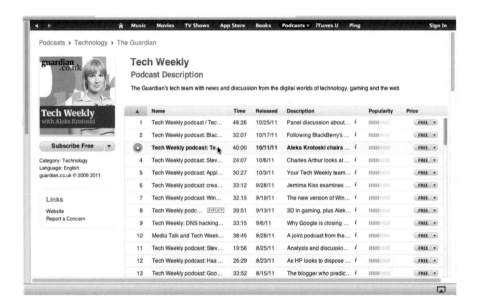

What to Do if Your Download Gets Interrupted

IT'S BOUND TO HAPPEN sometime: You're breathlessly downloading a hot new album or movie from iTunes, and your computer freezes or your Internet connection goes on the fritz. Or you and your iPod Touch were in the middle of snagging an album when the rest of the gang decided it was time to leave the coffee shop.

If this happens, don't worry. Even if your computer crashes or you get knocked offline while you're downloading your purchases, iTunes is designed to pick up where it left off. Just restart the program and reconnect to the Internet.

If, for some reason, iTunes doesn't go back to whatever it was downloading, choose Store→Check for Available Downloads to resume your downloading business.

You can use this same command to check for available purchases any time you think you might have something waiting, like a new episode from a TV show Season Pass. You'll also find any digital booklets that come with albums you bought here—those don't download to your Touch from the WiFi Store because they're PDF files meant to be viewed on your computer.

TIP If you need help from a human at Apple, you can either call them at (800) 275-2273 or drop them an email. To email them, click the Support link on the iTunes Store's main page. You'll see the main iTunes service and support page; click any link in the Customer Service area and then, at the bottom of the page that appears, fill out the Email Support form. Live online chat is also available for some issues.

Ping Your Way to New Music

FACEBOOK, TWITTER, TUMBLR, FLICKR—if there's anything the top social-networking sites have proved, it's that people like to share stuff with their friends. And now there's Ping, Apple's very own social network designed to connect people who have a mutual love of music.

When Apple introduced Ping in September 2010, it was described as "Facebook and Twitter meet iTunes," which gives you a good idea of Apple's vision for the service. Ping was originally supposed to hook into Facebook so you could include your Ping activities in Facebook updates, but a case of "unfriending" between Apple and Facebook prevented the partnership. So far, anyway. For now, you can at least link Ping to your Twitter account.

As with any social network, the first thing you have to do on Ping is set up a profile page, your own little part of the network where you can list your favorite bands and artists, keep track of upcoming events, exchange notes with other music-minded pals, and listen to samples of what your friends are listening to on iTunes.

To set up your Ping profile:

❶ **Click the Ping link in the Source list**. Apple doesn't force all iTunes users to join, so you have to click a button that says Turn On Ping and agree to the legal disclaimer about using the service and privacy.

> Turn On Ping

❷ **Fill in your personal details**. As you do on most social-networking sites, you fill in your name, the city where you live, and other information. You can also add a photo to your profile page. Since this is a music-themed service, you can announce your three favorite genres of music on your page, too. You can tell as much or as little about yourself as you want, and even select up to eight iTunes tracks (complete with audio samples) to display on your page. People who follow you see your Ping status updates and iTunes purchases as you make them, and, in return, you can see theirs if you follow them.

❸ **Adjust privacy settings**. As part of the Ping profile setup, you're asked how public you want to be so other members can find you. You have three choices: You can let everyone else on the service look at and "follow" your profile page—whether you know them or not, which is a good way to find new friends (and sometimes stalkers). You can also make your basic profile visible to others only after you give them permission to see it. And lastly, you can hide your page from everyone and just use it as a personal place to track concert listings.

❹ **Find friends**. Once you set up your profile page and privacy settings, Ping encourages you to find other media lovers on the service. You can search for the email addresses of people you know and invite them to be your Ping friends. At the same time, your friends' updates—and links to their Ping pages—appear on your own patch of Ping real estate.

Once you get Ping set up, it works just like any other social network. You can post your thoughts on the current state of music and read those of your Ping friends. You can sign up to follow bands and musicians who use Ping—to see what Lady Gaga, Yo-Yo Ma, and others are up to, for example. You can write your own album reviews, comment on friends' pages, browse music news, and check concert listings for your favorite groups. You can click the Like button next to albums or tracks to publicly post your approval.

Items you buy in the iTunes Store get listed on your Ping page, so everyone knows what you're into these days. If you'd rather keep your '80s synth-pop addiction a secret, hide your purchases by clicking the Remove button next to the item on your Recent Activity feed.

If you're an iPod Touch owner and use iTunes' handy Ping sidebar to see what your pals are listening to, you're not chained to the desktop for updates. On the Touch's Home page, tap iTunes→Ping to call up a mini version of the service (right) so you can keep up with Ping things while you're out.

If you decide that Ping isn't for you, click the Account link on the main Store page and log into your iTunes account. On the Account Settings page, click Turn Off in the Ping section (you can edit your profile here, too—or from a link on your Ping page itself).

Give the Gift of iTunes

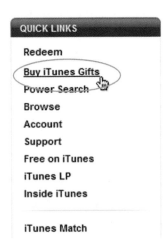

QUICK LINKS

Redeem

Buy iTunes Gifts

Power Search

Browse

Account

Support

Free on iTunes

iTunes LP

Inside iTunes

iTunes Match

IF YOU'RE STUMPED TRYING to find something for The Person Who Has Everything, consider a gift of iTunes Store credit or music. Apple conveniently gives you several ways to send the gift that keeps on giving—or at least the gift that keeps on rocking out.

- **Gift certificates**. To buy one, click Buy iTunes Gifts in the Quick Links box on the Store's main page, and then select a gift denomination ($10 to $50). You can have the certificate emailed to the recipient, or you can print it out so you can deliver it yourself. The rest of the process is like buying anything else on the Web: fill in your address, add a message, and so on. You need an Apple ID to send and use gift certificates.

  To redeem an electronic gift certificate, go to the iTunes Store and click the Redeem link in the main window. Copy the Redeem Code from your email and paste it into the box provided. (If you got a printed certificate, type in the gift code.) Click Redeem, and then start shopping.

- **Gift cards**. The brightly colored prepaid iTunes Music Card is a fun spin on the gift certificate concept. Available in dollar amounts ranging from $15 to $100, givers can find cards at places like Amazon.com, Target, and Apple's own stores. You can also buy them in the iTunes Store (and have them mailed out by the Postal Service) by clicking the Buy iTunes Gifts link. Recipients can spend it all in one place—the iTunes Store—by clicking the Redeem link on the Store's main page.

- **Gift content**. In a daring feat of bending a noun into a verb, the iTunes Store also lets you "gift" selections of music, videos, or apps. Your recipient can download your thoughtful picks right from the Store onto their own computers. You can send iTunes goodies to any pal with an email address. Click the triangle next to an item's Buy button and choose "Gift This..." from the menu.

- **Gift playlists**. If you're proud of a certain iTunes playlist you made yourself, you can send all the songs on it—if they're available in the iTunes Store—to a friend with a couple of clicks. Select the playlist in the iTunes Source list and choose Store→Share Playlist. A box pops up asking if you'd like to send the list as a gift or publish it. Click the Gift button, which takes you back to the iTunes Store to make it all happen over the Internet.

Plan Ahead: Wish Lists

WITH NO PAPER MONEY flying about to remind you of reality, it's easy to rack up hefty credit card charges at the iTunes Store. Consider, then, making an iTunes *Wish List* to keep track of songs you want to buy...when your budget allows.

For iTunes customers still using dial-up Internet connections, the Wish List replaces the old Shopping Cart feature as a place to park your stuff before you're ready to download all your purchases at the end of your shopping session. (The 1-Click instant download of iTunes purchases can overwhelm a poor dial-up modem if you aren't done shopping.)

Adding items to your Wish List is easy: When you see something you want, click the triangle next to the Buy button and choose Add to Wish List from the pop-up menu.

To see all the items that have piled up in your list, visit the Quick Links box on the Store's home page and click My Wish List. If your wishes have changed since you added an item to the list, select the item and click the circled **x** that appears next to it to remove it. When you're ready to buy something on the Wish List, click the item's Buy button. The file begins downloading to your computer.

If you've been using the Wish List as a substitute Shopping Cart to hold your songs until you're ready to download them all, there's a special button just for you. It's the Buy All button up in the top-right corner of the Wish List. Click it and let your dial-up modem have a few hours to itself to download your purchases.

Total: 2 Items $11.28 Buy All

> **NOTE** The iTunes Store sends out invoices by email, but they don't arrive right after you buy a song. You usually get an invoice that groups together all the songs you purchased within a 12-hour period, or for every $20 worth of media you buy.

iTunes Allowance Accounts

ALLOWANCE ACCOUNTS ARE A lot like iTunes gift certificates. You, the parent (or other financial authority), decide how many dollars' worth of Store goods you want to give a family member or friend (from $10 to $50). Unlike gift certificates, however, allowance accounts automatically replenish themselves on the first day of each month—an excellent way to keep music-loving kids out of your wallet while teaching them to budget their money.

Both you and the recipient need to have Apple IDs, but you can create an ID for the recipient during the set-up process. To set up an allowance, from the iTunes Store's main page, click the Buy iTunes Gifts link, scroll down to the Allowances section and click "Set up an allowance now." Fill out the form. After you select the amount you want to deposit each month, fill in your recipient's Apple ID.

Once the giftee logs into the designated Apple account, she can begin spending—no credit card required. When she exhausts her allowance, she can't buy anything else until the following month. (Of course, if the recipient has a credit card on file, she can always put the difference on her card.) If you need to cancel an allowance account, click the Account link on the Store's main page to take care of the matter.

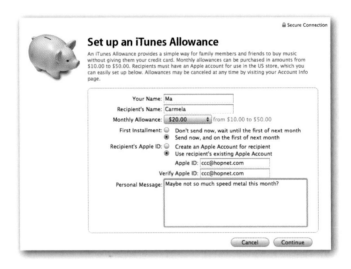

TIP One thing you students don't have to pay for: an iTunes education. The iTunes U link on the main Store page leads to audio or video content from hundreds of schools around the country. Presentations, video tours, lectures, and more are all available at iTunes U—yay, rah, Fightin' Downloaders!

Set Up Parental Controls for the Store

IF YOU HAVE CHILDREN with their own allowance accounts, you may not want them wandering around the iTunes Store buying just *anything*. With the Parental Controls feature, you can give your children the freedom to spend and discover, but restrict the types of things they can buy—without having to helicopter over them every time they click a Store link.

❶ In the iTunes Preferences box (Ctrl+comma [⌘-comma]), click the Parental Control tab.

❷ A box unfurls with all the media you can limit. For Store material, you can block songs and other items tagged with the Explicit label, restrict movie purchases to a maximum rating (G, PG, PG-13, or R), and choose one of the TV show content ratings geared to kids (TV-Y, TV-Y7, TV-G, TV-PG, TV-14, or TV-MA). You can also limit app purchases, including games, to age restrictions of 4+, 9+, 12+, and 17 years and older.

❸ Click the lock to password-protect the settings so the kids can't change them themselves.

You can also block certain icons from appearing in the iTunes Source list, including those for podcasts, Internet radio, shared libraries, and even the entire iTunes Store itself. You can, however, make an exception for educational content from iTunes U to keep your kids learning.

Adjust Your Store Preferences

THE ITUNES STORE AIMS to be a one-stop-shopping hub for all your digital entertainment: music, movies, TV shows, audio lectures on universal themes in the *Harry Potter* novels, and so on. In fact, some people have even canceled their cable TV subscriptions, preferring instead to go à la carte with iTunes.

If you use iTunes' Season Pass feature, which lets you buy a whole season of a TV show in advance, or if you preorder an album before it's released, you may never know when iTunes will decide to jump up and start downloading your pre-purchased content. This could be a little inconvenient if, say, your weekly Season Pass episode of *Gossip Girl* starts downloading on your big computer monitor while iTunes DJs your holiday party.

To control how iTunes behaves around your Internet connection, visit the Store tab of the iTunes Preferences box (Ctrl+comma [⌘-comma]). Here you can decide if you want iTunes to automatically download the music, apps, and books you buy on iOS devices (like an iPhone or iPad) to your iTunes library via Apple's iTunes in the Cloud service (see page 112 for details). The lower part of the Store preferences has your options to make iTunes check for downloads and to download pre-purchased content.

NOTE   Music, videos, and other content you download from the iTunes Store lands in its respective Source list library—songs in the Music library, *Glee* episodes in TV Shows, and so on. Those paid-for music and videos also live on the Purchased playlist in the Source list, a one-click trip to see where all your spare cash went.

Usage Rights: What You Can Do with Your Purchases

THE STUFF YOU BUY at the iTunes Store is yours to keep (unless you rented it). Apple doesn't charge you a monthly fee, and your digitally protected downloads don't go *poof!* after a certain amount of time.

You do have to cope with restrictions on some iTunes purchases, namely anything that's copy-protected. Copy-protected media include movies, TV shows, music videos, and songs you bought before April 2009, when Apple still copy-protected its music files (it no longer does; see below). For those types of files, you're bound by the iTunes Store usage agreement:

- You can play protected songs on up to five different iTunes-equipped Windows PCs or Macs (in any combination)and on as many iPods as you like, and you can burn playlists with protected songs in them to CD up to seven times.

- You can watch movies, videos, and TV shows on any five computers, on as many iPods as you own, or piped over to your TV with an AV cable or via an Apple TV box (page 267).

- You can download music to a single iPod from up to five separate iTunes accounts, but the 'Pod won't accept files from a sixth account—a restriction designed to prevent someone from filling up their player with copyrighted content from the accounts of, say, their entire sophomore class.

You can burn backup CDs and DVDs of your purchases, but you can't burn an iTunes movie or TV show to disc and watch it on your DVD player. (On the flip side, some newer DVDs come with an "iTunes Digital Copy" that you can add to your iTunes library; instructions are in the package.)

So how does Apple keep track of how many devices you play protected media on? Easy: You have to authorize your computer or iPod through Apple, which maintains a giant tote board of registered devices. Turn the page to learn how to authorize.

Now, about those unprotected (post-April 2009) music files. The good news is, you can play them on any player that supports the AAC song format, and you can burn copies to CD for personal use and play them in commercial CD players. The bad news? To do most anything else with these copy-free songs, like playing or copying them via Home Sharing and re-downloading them if you accidentally erase them, the devices involved have to be authorized with Apple.

Authorize Your Computer to Play iTunes Purchases

WHEN YOU BUY A song, movie, TV show, or other media from the iTunes Store, the computer you use to make the purchase is automatically authorized to play it. As mentioned on the previous page, you can authorize a total of five computers using the same Apple ID. To authorize a second computer (say, a desktop machine you sometimes use when you don't feel like hunching over the laptop), open iTunes on the machine and choose Store→Authorize Computer. Type in your Apple user name and password on the computer. Repeat for up to three more computers.

Each computer you authorize must have an Internet connection to relay the information back to Store headquarters. (You don't have to authorize each and every purchase you make in the Store, you just authorize the computers themselves.)

Deauthorize Your Computer

IF YOU HAVE PROTECTED music, movies, TV shows, books, or other purchased content and you try to play them on a sixth computer, Apple's authorization system will see five other computers already on its "authorized" list and deny your request. That's a drag, but a user agreement is a user agreement.

To play protected files on computer #6, you have to deauthorize another computer. From the computer about to get the boot, choose Store→ Deauthorize Computer, and then type in your Apple ID. The updated information zips back to Apple.

Are you thinking of putting that older computer up for sale? Before wiping the drive clean and sending it on its way, be sure to deauthorize it, so your new machine will be able to play copy-protected files. Erasing a hard drive, by itself, doesn't deauthorize a computer.

If you forget to deauthorize a machine before getting rid of it, you can still knock it off your List of Five, but you have to reauthorize every machine in your iTunes arsenal all over again. To make it so, in the iTunes Store, click the Account link. On the Account Information page, click the Deauthorize All button.

TIP Do you have a ton of tracks from the early days of the iTunes Store (before 2009) and would prefer the hassle-free life of an iTunes Plus library? Go to the iTunes Store and click the iTunes Plus link on the main page. You can upgrade your older tracks to iTunes Plus versions for 30 cents a pop—instead of having to buy them all over again at full price. And the cherry on top: iTunes Plus tracks have higher audio quality (a bit rate of 256 kilobits per second, if you want to get technical) than old regular iTunes songs, which used the much lower (and lower fidelity) 128 kbps setting.

Use Your iPod to Copy Purchases to Other Computers

YOU MAY LOVE THE convenience of buying music and movies from any Internet-connected Windows PC or Mac—whether it's your regular computer or not. But what do you do if you buy iTunes Store stuff on one computer (at work, say) and need an easy way to move it to another (like your machine at home)?

Sure, you can snag a copy via iTunes in the Cloud (page 112), but if you have an iPod set to manually manage songs and playlists (page 128), you can use that 'Pod to ferry Store purchases back to your day-to-day computer. Both computers need to be authorized with the same iTunes account, but if you're just toting tunes around between your work and home PCs, that shouldn't be a problem. Here's what you do:

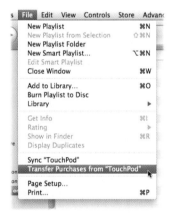

❶ Connect your iPod to computer #1 and load it up with the Store files you want to transfer.

❷ Eject the iPod from computer #1 and connect it to computer #2.

❸ In iTunes, choose File→Transfer Purchases from iPod.

This painless transfer technique works only on Store-bought items, so you can't use it to, say, copy a mix-and-match library borne of Store songs and your own ripped tracks.

You do have ways to move your non-Store purchases between machines, however. For one, you can use the method described on the next page. Second, you can use a third-party program to pluck songs off the iPod and deposit them into your iTunes library; page 130 has more on doing it that way.

NOTE If you purchased music or video at the iTunes WiFi Store with your iPod Touch, iTunes automatically syncs the new content from the Touch to your computer's iTunes library when you connect the two. If for some reason it doesn't, choose File→Transfer Purchases from iPod.

Moving iTunes Files the Long Way

The Home Sharing feature of iTunes, described in Chapter 5, makes shuttling iTunes purchases among home computers easier than ever before. But not every computer you want to tap into is part of your Home Sharing network—maybe you downloaded Season One of *House* on your office's fast fiber-optic network instead of your pokey residential DSL line. Yes, iTunes in the Cloud (page 112) is great for re-downloading, but it can hog up your home network's bandwidth.

So without using Home Sharing *or* iTunes in the Cloud *or* the iPod's wonderful purchase-transferring powers, here's yet another way to move a bunch of iTunes files from Computer A on one network to Computer B on another:

❶ **On the computer you used to purchase an iTunes Store item, grab any file you bought from iTunes**. You can drag the files right out of your iTunes window and onto your desktop, or you can find the song and video files in your iTunes Media (or iTunes Music) folder: Music→iTunes→iTunes Media (Home→Music→iTunes→iTunes Media). Copy-protected Store files are easily recognizable by their *.m4p* or *.m4v* file extensions. Movies are stored in a folder called Movies, and so on.

❷ **Move the file to the second computer**. Copy the file onto a CD or USB drive, email it to yourself, or use whatever method you prefer for schlepping files between machines.

❸ **Deposit the file in the iTunes Media folder on the second computer. Then import the copied file into iTunes on the second computer**. To import the file, you can either choose File→Add to Library (and then select and open the file), or drag the file right into the iTunes window.

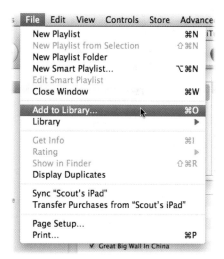

❹ **In your iTunes list, select a transferred file, and then click the Play button**. For protected content, iTunes asks for your Apple ID name and password.

❺ **Type in your Apple ID and then click OK**. This second computer is now authorized to play that file—and any other copy-protected songs or videos you bought using the same Apple ID.

See Your iTunes Purchase History and Get iTunes Store Help

THE ITUNES STORE KEEPS track of what you buy and when you buy it. If you think your credit card was wrongly charged, or if you suspect that one of the kids knows your password and is sneaking in forbidden downloads, you can contact the Store or check your account's purchase history page to see what's been downloaded in your name.

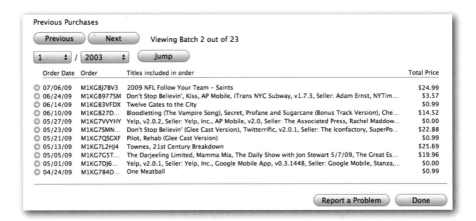

To do the latter, on the iTunes Store's main page, click the Account link, type in your password, and then click Purchase History. Your latest purchase appears at the top of the page, and you can scroll down to see a list of previous acquisitions. You'll see everything billed to your account over the months and years, including gift-certificate purchases. If you see something wrong, click the "Report a Problem" link and say something.

If you have other issues with your account or want to submit a specific query or comment, the online help center awaits. From the iTunes Store's main page, click the Support link. Your browser presents you with the main iTunes service and support page; click the link that best describes what you want to learn or complain about. For billing or credit card issues, check out the iTunes Account and Billing Support link on that same page.

> **NOTE** Want to get way more bang for slightly more buck on your album purchase? Visit the main Music page and click the iTunes LP link. Certain albums, available as iTunes LPs, offer more than just songs—you get extra features like bonus tracks, digital liner notes booklets, artist interviews, video documentaries, and more. An iTunes LP averages $13 to $15—not that much more for all the extra perks that can take you behind the scenes of that new album.

Buy Songs from Other Music Stores

THERE ARE MANY ONLINE music services out there, and every one of 'em wants to sell you a song. But due to copy protection, some of these merchants' songs don't work on the iPod. Some of them do, though. Thanks to recent moves by many stores to strip out the digital rights management (DRM) protection on song files, their music has been liberated into the friendly MP3 play-anywhere format. Vive la musique!

Buying songs from somewhere other than the iTunes Store is as easy as supplying a credit card number and downloading the file using a web browser. Once you have the file on your computer, use iTunes' File→Add to Library command to add it to your collection. Here are some of the online music services that now work with the iPod:

- **eMusic**. Geared toward indie bands, eMusic offers several subscription plans based on quantity: For 16 bucks a month, for example, you can download 35 songs of your choice. (*www.emusic.com*)

- **The Internet Archive**. Thousands of live concert recordings, old-time radio shows, historic audio gems rescued from old 78 rpm discs and wax cylinders, and much more await you here. And it's all free. (*www.archive.org*)

- **Amazon MP3 Downloads**. From the main page, click Digital Downloads and then choose MP3 Downloads. Amazon has a free piece of software called the Amazon MP3 Downloader that takes half a minute to install and automatically tosses your purchases into iTunes for you. Click the link (circled below) at the top of the Amazon MP3 page to snag the Downloader program. (*www.amazon.com*)

CHAPTER 8

It's Showtime: Video on the iPod

VIDEO-PLAYING IPODS HAVE BEEN AROUND SINCE OCTOBER 2005, when Apple introduced that year's 'Pod with a video chip on the inside and a video screen on the outside. Among the 2011 iPods, just the Touch and the faithful old Classic still play moving pictures.

The iPod Touch, with its high-resolution, 3.5-inch screen, has become the premier video iPod on all levels. Although previous iPod Nanos before 2010 played—and even recorded—video, Apple removed the video features from the current, tiny Nano to recast it as the iPod that focused on music and fitness.

Touch or Classic—no matter which iPod you use, you're not stuck watching just 2- or 3-minute music videos. As explained in the previous chapter, the iTunes Store has all kinds of cinematic goodies you can buy: full-length Hollywood movies and episodes (or entire seasons) of TV shows. Some videos even come in super-sharp, high-definition format, which looks great on both your TV and your computer screen. And yes, if you want music videos, like the kind MTV used to play back when it, uh, played music, you can choose from thousands of them.

This chapter shows you how to get videos from computer to iPod—and how to enjoy them on your own shirt-pocket cinema.

Add Your Own Videos to iTunes

THE ITUNES STORE IS full of videos you can buy or rent (Chapter 7 shows you how), but sometimes you want to add your own flicks to your iTunes library. No problem; you can do that in four ways. One is to drag the files from your desktop and drop them anywhere in iTunes' main window. The second is to choose File→Add to Library, and then locate and import your files.

Additionally, you can add video files (and music files, for that matter) by dragging them into the folder labeled Automatically Add to iTunes. New since iTunes 9, this folder checks a file's extension and, based on that, shelves it in the right media library for you. You find the auto-folder not through iTunes itself, but by navigating your hard drive. In Windows, it's usually at C:/Music→iTunes→ iTunes Media→Automatically Add to iTunes; for Macs, it's at Home→Music→ iTunes→iTunes Media→Automatically Add to iTunes.

If iTunes doesn't recognize a file extension, it dumps the file into a Not Added subfolder.

If you copy over a lot of videos from your camcorder, make it easy to get to the auto-folder by creating a desktop shortcut for it. That way, you can drag files directly to the shortcut without having to root around your hard drive.

Once you add videos to your iTunes library, you can play them back right there in iTunes (see opposite page), copy them to your iPod for on-the-go viewing (page 190), or watch them on a big TV screen (page 196).

If you bought a TV show from the iTunes Store on another iOS device, like an iPad or iPhone, and never synced the file back to iTunes on your computer, you can re-download that show with iTunes and sync it to your iPod. Page 112 explains how to do that with Apple's magical iTunes In the Cloud feature.

> **TIP** Movies and TV shows go into separate libraries, each with their own icon in the iTunes Source list. If you import a video and it's in the wrong place, you may need to tweak the file's labeling info. Open the file's Get Info box (Ctrl+I [⌘-I]), click the Options tab, and then assign it a video format from the Video Kind drop-down menu choices: Music Video, Movie, TV Show, Podcast, or iTunes U file.

Play Videos in iTunes

CRANKING UP YOUR ITUNES movie theater is a lot like playing a song: Double-click a video's title, and iTunes starts playing it. When you click either the Grid or Cover Flow (circled) view buttons, you see the videos represented by either a movie-poster-type picture or a frame from the video (top). (Like album covers, videos you buy from the iTunes Store come with nice artwork.)

You can play the video in iTunes' main window; in a separate, floating window as shown below; in iTunes' artwork window (the small pane that also displays album art at the bottom of the Source list); or full-screen on your computer. Slide your mouse cursor over the screen to get to the video playback controls.

To pick your preferred window size for the video you have onscreen, choose View→Video Playback. In the submenu that appears (shown at left), you can pick the

window that suits your needs at the moment. For example, while the Full Screen view is very nice for turning your computer into a movie theater, it may not be the best choice if, say, you're at work and trying to catch up on your favorite video podcast or sports highlight reel. In situations like those, the Artwork Viewer window might work better.

Transfer Videos to Your iPod

CHAPTER 1 GIVES YOU the lowdown on syncing all kinds of files between iTunes and your trusty iPod. If you don't feel like flipping back there, here's a quick summary:

- **Synchronization**. Connect your iPod to your computer and click its Source list icon in iTunes. Click the Movies tab and turn on the Sync Movies checkbox. You can choose to sync only certain movies to save space on your iPod. If you have TV programs in your iTunes library, click the TV Shows tab and adjust your syncing preferences there.

- **Manual management**. Click the appropriate library in the Source list (Movies, TV Shows, Podcasts, and so on), and then drag the files you want from the main iTunes window onto your connected iPod's icon.

If you made any video playlists in iTunes, you can copy those over to your iPod, just as you would a music playlist (see page 139). If you haven't tried making a video playlist, it's just like making a music playlist; see page 136 for details.

Video Formats That Work on the iPod

AS DESCRIBED IN CHAPTER 7, the iTunes Store now sells and rents movies, TV shows, and music videos. You can also import your own home movies, downloaded movie trailers, and other videos into iTunes, as long as the files have one of these extensions at the end of their names: *.mov, .m4v,* or *.mp4*. Once you can sync these files to your iPod, you can play them when you're out and about.

Other common video formats, like *.avi* and Windows Media video (*.wmv*), won't play in iTunes (or on your iPod), but you can convert them with Apple's $30 QuickTime Pro software or any of the dozens of video-conversion programs floating around the Web. (If you find you have an incompatible file type, first try dragging the file into iTunes' main window and then choosing Advanced→Create iPod or iPhone Version. That converts some, but not all, files, and Apple doesn't specify which ones.)

Here are a few popular video-conversion tools:

- **PQ DVD to iPod Video Converter Suite**. This $40 program for Windows converts TiVo recordings, DVD video, DivX movies, Windows Media Video, RealMedia files, and AVI files to the iPod's video format (*www.pqdvd.com*).

- **Videora iPod Converter**. With this free software, you can gather up all those *.avi* and *.mpg* video clips stashed away on your PC and turn them into iPod clips. Find it at *www.videora.com*.

- **UltiConvert**. Something of a work in progress—but free—this program lets Mac OS X owners convert several video formats, even *.avi* files, into iTunes-friendly versions (*http://mac.softpedia.com/get/Video/UltiConvert.shtml*).

- **HandBrake**. Now available in versions for Windows and Mac OS X, this easy-to-use bit of freeware converts DVD movies and other files for your iPod. You can get it at *http://handbrake.fr*.

Play Videos on the iPod Touch

WATCHING VIDEO ON THE Touch is a breeze. Just tap open the Videos icon on the Home screen, flick to the movie, TV show, or video podcast you want to watch, and then tap the title to start the show.

Want to fast-forward, jump back, pause, and perform other video-playback moves? Just tap the screen to call up the touch-based controls. Want to dismiss the control panel? Tap the screen again so you can watch your show without the clutter. Apple has crammed a lot of buttons into a small space, so here's what each one does:

- **Done** When you finish watching a video, tap this button (in the top-left corner) to stop the show and return to the Videos menu.

- **Scroll slider**. The bar at the top of the screen shows you how much time has elapsed in your current video—and how much more you have to go. Stuck in a boring part or want to see something again? Drag the white dot forward or backward to move through the clip.

- **Zoom/Unzoom**. Full-screen or widescreen playback? Tap the ▣ or ▣ icons in the top-right corner of the screen to zoom in or out of the picture. The next page explains a bit more about the zoom levels.

- ▣ Some videos have alternate audio tracks for other languages or subtitles. Tap here to see your options.

- **Play/Pause (▶/II)**. These buttons start the show—and pause it when you need to take a break.

- **Previous, Next (◄◄, ►►)**. Press down to zip through the video in the chosen direction; the longer you hold down the button, the faster you rewind or fast-forward.

  You can jump around the film between major scenes in iTunes Store–bought movies or in any other video that has DVD-like chapter markers embedded in them; just quickly tap the ◄◄ or ►► buttons.

- **AirPlay.** You can stream the Touch's video to a television screen with a second-generation Apple TV and a WiFi network. Just tap the ◰ icon and choose Apple TV from the menu. Page 266 has more on using AirPlay.

- **Volume**. If you don't feel like using the volume buttons on the side of the Touch, tap the screen and drag the white dot in the volume slider at the bottom of the screen forward or backward in the scroll bar to raise or lower the sound level.

Zoom/Unzoom

The 2011 iPod Touch has a bright, razor-sharp screen—Apple's high-resolution Retina Display packs 960 x 640 pixels into the 3.5-inch screen. That's 326 pixels per inch, four times as many as earlier Touch models.

The screen, however, is still rectangular. That means that older TV shows in the squarish standard-definition format (also known as the 4:3 aspect ratio) don't fill the screen from side to side, so the Touch fills in the gap with black letterbox bars. Conversely, TV shows and movies in the high-definition widescreen standard are a bit *too* wide, which means you get black letterbox bars on the top and bottom of the screen.

Some movie lovers are used to this and ignore the letterboxing, because they want to see the film as the director originally envisioned it. But other people want their video to fill the screen in all directions, even if it means cutting off the edges. The Touch tries to satisfy both groups. With the playback controls onscreen, tap the ▣ or ▣ buttons to expand the video to full screen or shrink it to its original size.

If you don't want to hunt around for the buttons, there's an even quicker way to zoom in and out: double-tap the video while it's playing. If you decide you hate the way the picture looks, double-tap again to reverse course.

> **TIP** Want your video to remember where you paused or stopped it? Easy. In iTunes, select the video and then press Ctrl+I (⌘-I). Click the Options tab and turn on the checkbox next to "Remember playback position."

YouTube Videos on the Touch

SINCE IT FIRST GRACED the Web in 2005, YouTube has become a huge online vault of video from around the world. From news clips to movie parodies to cats playing the piano, YouTube (now owned by Google) offers some of the best—and worst—of the human experience caught on video. And you can see it all on your iPod Touch with its built-in YouTube app.

Well, most of it, anyway. While many YouTube movies come in a format called Adobe Flash that the Touch doesn't play, many of its finest clips have already been converted to what's called the H.264 standard, which happens to play quite nicely on the Touch.

Find and Play Videos

The Touch loves to present you with lists of things to choose from, and its YouTube app is no exception. Tap the YouTube icon on the Home screen and here's what you'll see:

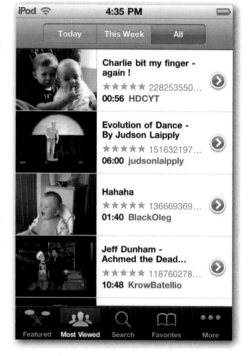

- **Featured**. Selected by YouTube staffers, this list shows you newsworthy clips of the moment and other videos of interest. Flick your way down the list and tap a tile to play the video.

- **Most Viewed**. Tap here to see what The People are watching. You can view the most popular videos *Today*, *This Week*, or *All* (as in "of all time," to be precise). When you get to the end of the list, tap "Load 25 More" to see the next batch.

- **Search**. Keywords make everything easier to find, and YouTube's videos are tagged with bits of info like titles, descriptions, names, and other explanatory text. When you tap Search, the Touch's keyboard slides up, ready for action.

- **Favorites**. If you have a YouTube account (it's free, and it also means you can upload your own clips), you can mark videos as your faves so you can find them easily in the Favorites list.

Tap YouTube's More button to see six additional menu options:

- **Most Recent**. Tap here to see videos *just* posted to YouTube.

- **Top Rated**. As with App Store apps and songs, everyone's a critic and can apply star ratings to express an opinion of a particular clip. Here you can see what's earned the most stars. (When you sign into your YouTube account, you can rate videos yourself.)

- **History**. Like a web browser, the YouTube app keeps track of what you've looked at. And also like a browser, you can wipe out the evidence that you checked out those skateboarding dogs videos again with a tap of the Clear button.

- **My Videos**. Tap here to see a list of the clips you've uploaded to YouTube (you need to be logged into your YouTube account to do so).

- **Subscriptions**. Many organizations and celebrities have their own YouTube "channels" that you can subscribe to. Once you sign up, tap here to see the latest video dispatches from Oprah or the Queen of England.

- **Playlists**. As with music, you can create video playlists of favorite clips so you can watch them in a certain order.

So how do you add videos to Playlists or your Favorites lists? Just tap the ⊙ button (shown on the opposite page) on any video in a list to open a page of video details. The Details page has buttons so you can add the video to a Playlist or Favorites list, or share it by email. You also get info like the length of the clip, its rating, who uploaded it, its keyword tags, related videos, and more.

YouTube Video controls

To start playing a video, just tap its name and flip the Touch to its horizontal position it. The clip begins as soon as YouTube downloads enough if it from its servers to start the stream.

Although you do need to be online to use YouTube, the video playback controls work just like they do on regular videos on the Touch (flip back to page 190). However, the YouTube app includes three new icons in the control bar: the ▥ button, which adds the video to your Favorites list, the AirPlay wireless streaming icon (▨) and the ➦ button, which lets you share a link to the clip by email or Twitter (page 68) or mark it as a personal YouTube favorite.

Play Videos on the iPod Classic

VIDEOS YOU BUY OR rent from the iTunes Store (as well as other iTunes-friendly videos) appear in your iPod's Videos menu after you copy them onto your Classic. To watch a movie, TV show, or music video, scroll through the various Video submenus (Movies, TV Shows, and so on) until you find something.

Say you want to watch a TV show. Select TV Shows from the main Videos menu. The next screen lists all your iPod's TV shows by title. Scroll to the show you want and click the center button. The resulting menu lists all the *episodes* you have for that series. Scroll to the one you want and press the Play/Pause button to start the show.

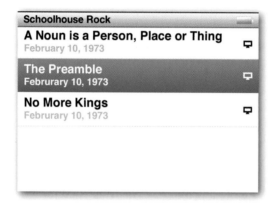

Here's a quick tour of the iPod Classic's main video playback controls:

- **Press the Play/Pause button again to pause the program**. Pausing on the iPod works just like hitting Pause on a DVD player or TiVo so you can get more Doritos. Press the button again to pick up where you left off.

- **To increase or decrease a video's volume, run your finger along the scroll wheel**. Adjusting the volume of a video on the Classic works the same way as controlling the volume of a song.

- **To fast-forward or rewind through part of a video, tap the Select button twice**. A time-code bar appears along the bottom of the screen. Use the scroll wheel to advance or retreat through a big chunk of the video. For moving forward and backward in smaller increments, hold down the Fast-Forward and Rewind buttons on the click wheel (see page 21).

When your video ends, the iPod flips you back to the menu you were on before you started watching the show. If you want to bail out before the movie is over, press the Menu button.

Some videos come in letterbox format, which leaves a strip of black above and below your video window. If you're not into widescreen HamsterVision, visit the Settings area of the Videos menu and turn on the Fit to Screen option.

TIP Both iTunes and the iPod Touch and Classic can play videos that have closed-captioned text onscreen for the hearing impaired. To turn it on in iTunes, open the Preferences box (Ctrl+comma [⌘-comma]), click the Playback tab, and then put a checkmark in the box next to "Show closed captioning when available." On the iPod Touch, tap your way to Home→Settings→Video to get to the controls. On the Classic, choose iPod→Videos→Settings→Captions.

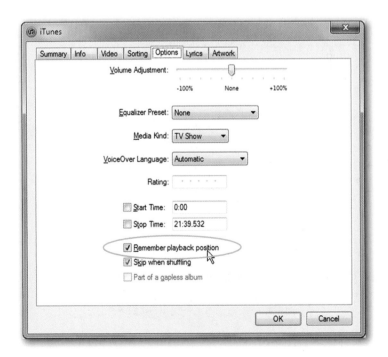

Play iTunes and iPod Videos on Your TV

MOVIES ON THE IPOD and computer screen are great, but watching them on a bigger screen is often even more gratifying. In case you were wondering, you *can* watch all those videos on your TV—you just need to connect your computer or iPod to your television. *What* you connect them with depends on what you start with.

If you're connecting your computer to the TV, here are your best options:

- Connect computers that have S-video connections with an S-video cable; that pipes high-quality video to your TV. For the audio side of things, a $10 Y-shaped cable with a stereo mini-plug on one end and the standard red and white RCA plugs on the other provide the sound.

- If you have a computer-friendly television (the kind that doubles as a computer monitor thanks to VGA or DVI ports), you can plug your laptop right into the TV using one of the cables described below.

To mate your iPod with your TV, your options depend on which generation iPod you have:

- **Early video iPods (the ones that came out before Apple dubbed the model the "Classic")**. You can connect these iPods to your TV with a special cable, like the Apple iPod AV Cable, available at *http://store.apple.com* and other places. This $19 cord has a stereo mini-plug on one end (for the iPod's headphones jack) and red, white, and yellow RCA plugs on the other end that link to the audio and video ports on your TV. Some similar camcorder cables may work, as do third-party cables from Belkin and Monster Cable, and special iPod video docks from Apple and others.

- **The iPod Touch or Classic (or older video-friendly Nanos).** You need a different cable—one that can unlock the chip that controls the iPod's ability to pipe video to your TV. (Older iPod cables and many third-party offerings won't work with these models, unless you use them with one of Apple's Universal Docks for iPods.)

  The easiest place to find these cables is the Apple Store (*www.apple.com/ipodstore*). Here, you can get the Apple Composite AV Cable for TVs with older video inputs. You can also find the Apple Component AV Cable, made for high-end TVs and widescreen sets that can handle higher-quality video and audio connections. Both versions of the cable cost about $50, but that includes an integrated AC adapter to make sure your 'Pod is powered for a whole-weekend movie marathon.

  Several third-party companies also make video docks and cables for the iPod; see Chapter 12 to get an idea of who's selling what. If you go with a non-Apple product, make sure it's rated to work with your particular iPod make and model.

Once you connect your iPod to your TV, set it up so the video appears on the big screen. The iPod Touch automatically senses the connection in most cases and is ready to play. On the Classic and older Nanos, choose iPod→Videos→Settings and set TV Out to On. While you are in this settings area of the older iPods, you can also choose the TV signal (pick NTSC if you live in the U.S.) and if the video should play in widescreen format. And the Settings area here is where you can also turn on closed captioning for videos that support the onscreen titles.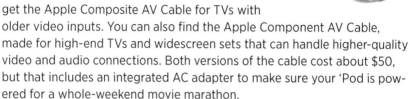

Once you get the iPod or computer hooked up to play movies, be sure to select the alternate video source or display input on your TV set, just as you would to play a DVD or game.

If you have an iPod Touch, a home wireless network, and a second-generation Apple TV box (the little black model) connected to your television set, you can stream your video files to the big screen *wirelessly* with Apple's AirPlay feature. Page 266 has the details on watching big video without wires.

TIP Not sure which iPod you have? Apple has an illustrated chart of almost every pre-2010 'Pod that ever scrolled the Earth at *http://support.apple.com/kb/HT1353*. And if you're not sure which ones support TV Out, see *http://support.apple.com/kb/HT1454*.

CHAPTER 9

Picture Your Photos On the iPod

WHO WANTS TO SHARE TREASURED PHOTOS WITH FRIENDS WHEN they're in the cracked plastic picture sleeves of an overstuffed wallet? If you have an iPod Touch, Nano, or Classic, you can transfer your prized shots from your computer to your 'Pod and display them on a glossy color screen wherever you happen to be.

And if you have an iPod Touch running Apple's iOS 5 software, you can share photos in more ways than ever: You can tweet them out to your Twitter followers, zip them to other iOS 5 users as iMessages, or go retro and send them as good old-fashioned email attachments.

The picture-perfect fun doesn't stop there, either. This trio of 'Pods can create slideshows of your images right there in the palm of your hand. And as with many previous iPod models, you can plug any of the 2011 iPods (save the Shuffle) into a TV set so you can see your stills on a big living-room screen. This chapter shows you how to do everything but microwave the popcorn.

Set Up: Get Ready to Put Photos on Your iPod

TO MOVE PICTURES TO your 'Pod, you need a computer loaded with iTunes and an iPod outfitted with a screen—sorry, Shuffle owners, the photos thing is just not happening for you.

Even with a photos-compatible iPod in tow, you need a couple of other things to make your pictures portable:

- **Compatible photo software for your Windows PC or Mac, or a folder of photos on your hard drive**. iPods can sync with several popular photo-management programs that you may already use. Windows mavens can grab pictures from Adobe Photoshop Elements 3.0 or later. On the Mac, there's Aperture or iPhoto 6 or later. You can also transfer pictures from a folder on your computer, like the Pictures (or My Pictures) folder on a Windows system, the Mac's iPhoto Library folder (for those who haven't upgraded past iPhoto 6), and even the Mac OS X Pictures folder.

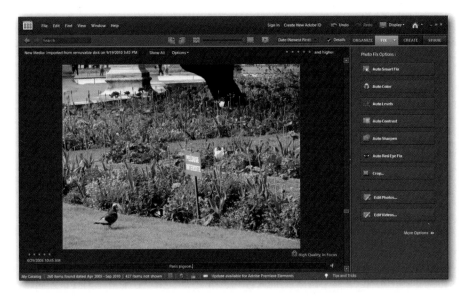

- **Digital photographs in the proper format**. iTunes plays well with the photo formats used by most digital cameras, web pages, and email programs, as well as a few other file types. Windows users can display JPEG, GIF, TIF, BMP, PSD, SGI, and PNG pics on your iPod. On the Mac, JPEG and GIF files, along with images in the PICT, TIFF, BMP, PNG, JPEG 2000, SGI, and PSD formats work just fine. (If you have iPhoto 5 or later, you can also sync MPEG-4 videos over to your iPod Touch.)

There are a couple of other things to remember when you add images to your iPod. For one, you can't import pictures from one of those photo CDs from the drugstore or from a backup disc you made yourself. Photos you store on DVDs or CDs won't cut it, either. iTunes needs to pull photos directly from your hard drive. The solution in both cases? Transfer your pics from the disc to your computer so they're ready for your iPod.

When it comes to photos, the iPod allies itself with just a single computer. That means that, unlike manual music management, where you can grab songs from several different computers, you can synchronize pictures only between one

iPod and one computer. If you ignore the warning box (pictured here) and try to load photos from a different computer, iTunes replaces all your iPod's existing photos with the pictures from that new machine. Ouch.

You also can't dump photos directly into the iPod from your digital camera—you need to go through iTunes. (There used to be a handy gadget called the iPod Camera Connector that siphoned photos from your camera's memory card to the iPod's hard drive, but it doesn't work on modern iPods, nor does Apple's *iPad* Camera Connection Kit. One can only hope that a variation of this device comes out for the iPod Touch/iPhone one of these days....)

Get Pictures onto Your iPod

OKAY, SO YOU'VE GOT your screen-outfitted iPod and a bunch of pictures in an iTunes-friendly format on your hard drive. How do you get those photos from your drive to your iPod? The same way you transfer music—through iTunes. First, you need to set your preferences in iTunes and on the iPod so they can sync the photos you want to carry around, like so:

➊ Connect your iPod to your Windows PC or Mac with the iPod's USB cable (or use iTunes Wi-Fi Sync on the iPod Touch, as page 16 explains).

➋ Once your iPod shows up in the iTunes Source list, click its icon to select it.

➌ In the iTunes tabs for your iPod, click the one for Photos.

➍ Turn on the checkbox next to "Sync photos from" and then choose your photo-storage folder or photo-management program; that lets iTunes know where to find your pics. You can copy over every image or just the *albums* (sets of pictures) you select.

➎ Click Sync (or Apply, if this is your first time syncing photos).

TIP If you own a Touch and use the Places feature in iPhoto '09 or later to embed GPS location data into your photos (also known as *geotagging*), you can see your pictures represented by pins on a map by tapping Photos→Places; tap a pin to see the pic.

If you don't use a photo-management program and you just want to copy a folder of photos from your hard drive to your iPod, select "Choose folder" from the menu and navigate to the desired folder. Then select whether you want to sync just the photos in that folder, or include the photos tucked away in folders *inside* your chosen folder.

If you use a photo-management program, select it, and then select the "All photos and albums" option to have iTunes haul every single image in your photo program's library over to your iPod. If you don't want to copy over those bachelorette-party snaps, opt for "Selected albums" and choose only the folders you want from your photo program. (Of course, you need to make sure those party pics aren't *in* any of those folders.)

If you use a Mac with iPhoto '09 or later and take advantage of the program's face-recognition feature, you can also sync photos according to who's in the pictures. Just scroll down the photo-sync preferences page to the Faces area and turn on the checkboxes next to the names of your favorite people. You can sync iPhoto *Events* (typically, photos taken on the same day) here as well.

Whenever you connect your iPod to your computer, iTunes syncs the photo groups you designate, adding any new pictures you stored in the groups since you last connected. During the process, iTunes displays an "Optimizing..." message in its status window, like the one shown here.

Don't let the term "optimizing" scare you: iTunes hasn't taken it upon itself to touch up your photographic efforts. The program simply creates versions of your pictures that look good on anything from your tiny iPod screen to your big TV screen (in case you want to connect your iPod to it). Then it tucks all those copies away on your hard drive before adding them to your iPod.

Want to get certain albums or photos *off* of your iPod? Reconnect it to iTunes, go back to the Photos tab, deselect the albums you no longer want, and then sync up. If you want to banish individual pictures, remove them from your desktop album and sync. On the iPod Touch, you can delete photos in the Camera Roll album by tapping 🖿, selecting the images to go, and then tapping Delete.

TIP Want to take a snap of some cool thing you see on your Touch's screen? Hold down the Home button and then press the Sleep/Wake button as though it were a camera shutter. The resulting screenshot lands in Photos→Camera Roll. You can transfer the pic back to your computer the next time you sync. In fact, if your computer has a photo-organizing program that senses a connected digital camera, it will likely leap up and offer to pull in the Touch's shots, just as it would digicam photos.

View Photos on the iPod Touch

WITH ITS BIG COLOR screen, the iPod Touch shows off your photos better than other iPods—and lets you have more fun viewing them because it's literally a hands-on experience.

To see the pictures synced from your computer, tap the Photos icon on the Home screen. Tap the buttons in the bottom row to see photos grouped by Albums, Events, Faces, or Places. Tap an album title, name, or place to see thumbnails of those photos. To get back to your library, tap the Albums (or whatever) button at the top-left of the screen.

To see a full-screen version of a picture, tap its thumbnail image. The Touch displays photo controls for a few seconds; tap the photo to make them go away (tap it again to make them reappear). Double-tap a photo to magnify it. You can also rotate the Touch so that horizontal photos fill the width of the screen instead of getting letterboxed. (When you tap the Edit button in the top-right corner of a photo, you can also make basic fixes to your pics, like cropping out unwanted parts or taming red-eye in your subjects. Page 79 has the details.)

Here are some other things you can do with your photos on the Touch:

❶ Tap the triangle icon at the bottom of a full-frame photo to start a slideshow. You can pick a transition style and music track here, and tap Start Slideshow to begin. Page 208 has more on the settings.

❷ To set a photo as the wallpaper for your Touch (you know, that background picture you see when you wake the Touch from a nap), tap ➦ in the lower-left corner. Then tap Use As Wallpaper. This ➦ icon also calls up buttons that let you email photos or send them as iMessages (page 66) over the Touch's WiFi connection, share pictures with your Twitter followers (page 68), and assign a photo to someone in your Touch contacts list.

And, if you have a printer that works with Apple's AirPrint technology (page 258), you can even make a color print of the photo.

❸ Spread and pinch your fingers onscreen (one of those fancy Touch moves described in Chapter 3) to zoom in and out of a photo. Drag your finger around the screen to pan across a zoomed-in photo.

❹ Flick your finger horizontally across the screen in either direction to scroll through your pictures at whizzy speeds. You can show off your vacation photos *really* fast this way (your friends will thank you).

As mentioned earlier, tapping ☛ with a single photo onscreen attaches that image to an email message; tapping the same icon from the *thumbnails* screen lets you attach multiple photos to a message. Tap the thumbnails of all the pics you want to send, address your email, type a note if you like, and then tap Send.

TIP To make a new photo album on the Touch, tap the Albums icon at the bottom of the screen, and then tap the Edit button in the top-right corner. Tap Add to create and name the new album. On the next screen, tap the photos you want to add to it and tap Done when finished.

View Photos on the iPod Nano or Classic

ONCE YOU GET YOUR photos freed from the confines of your computer and onto your Nano or Classic, you probably want to show them off to friends and relatives—or admire them yourself when you're stuck on a train or traveling far away from home. Here's how to get a palm-sized picture show:

- **iPod Nano**. Tap the Photos icon on the Nano's Home screen to call up a list of your photo albums, along with an "All Photos" option. Select an album and flick up or down to see all the thumbnails in it. Tap a thumbnail to see a pic full-screen (well, as full-screen as you can get on a 1.5-inch-square screen where your photos will be letterboxed unless you zoom in on  them). Flick your finger on the screen from right to left to glide through the images. Double-tap a picture to zoom in and out of it; if you loaded Faces on your Nano through iPhoto '09 or later, the zoom centers on the face. To see more of a photo while you're zoomed in, drag your finger on the screen to pull a different part of the picture to the center.

  You can tap the screen once to call up the navigation controls, which give you a ▶ button that starts an automatic slideshow (page 208), and ◀ and ➡ arrows so you can advance through an album at your own pace. The control bar also has a small square grid icon in the top-left corner; tap it to go back to your list of albums.

- **iPod Classic**. Choose Photos→All Photos (or select an album) from your Classic's main menu to see a screen of thumbnail images. Use the scroll wheel to maneuver the little yellow highlight box, and then zoom along the rows until you get to the pic you want. If you have hundreds of pee-wee pics, tap the Previous and Next buttons to advance or retreat through the thumbnails by the screenful. Highlight a photo and press the center button to call up a large version of it.

  Press the Previous and Next buttons—or scroll the click wheel—to move through pics one by one. Press Menu to return to the full album.

Digital Photographer Alert: Store Full-Quality Photos on Your iPod

WHEN ITUNES OPTIMIZES YOUR photos for iPodification, it streamlines the images a bit instead of transferring the big, full-resolution files. But if you want the high-res photos, you can copy them over to your Nano or Classic—good news if you're an avid photographer and want to haul a big, print-ready photo collection from one machine to another. (But not so good news if you're a Touch owner, because you can't use your iPod as an external drive unless you get a third-party program like TouchCopy, as mentioned on page 130.)

Nano and Classic users can follow these steps:

❶ Connect your Nano or Classic and select it in the iTunes Source list. Make sure you've set up your iPod as a portable hard drive (see page 228 for details). The short version: In your iPod's Settings page in iTunes, click the Summary tab and then turn on the "Enable disk use" checkbox.

❷ Click the Photos tab in the iTunes window.

❸ Turn on the "Include full-resolution photos" checkbox.

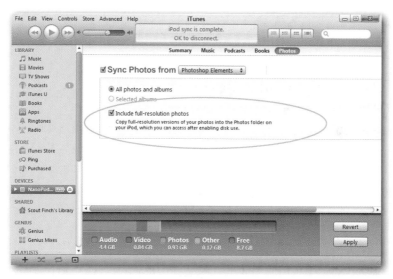

After you sync, full-resolution copies of your photos sit happily in the Photos folder on your iPod's hard drive. (The Photos folder also includes a subfolder called Thumbs that's full of iPod-optimized images in special *.ithmb* format; you can safely ignore these.) Since your iPod is now pulling double duty as a flash drive, you just need to connect it to another computer, open its icon, and copy the full-res photos over to the second computer.

Play Slideshows on Your iPod

A PHOTO SLIDESHOW TAKES all the click-and-tap work out of showcasing your images, freeing you up to admire your pictures without distraction. To run a slideshow on an iPod, you need to set up a few things, like how long each photo appears onscreen and what music accompanies your trip to Disneyland.

Slideshow Settings on an iPod Touch or Nano

To customize the way photos slide by on your Touch, press the Home button and then tap Settings→Photos. The Nano has similar menu items, but in a different order. On either iPod, you have these options:

- **How long each picture stays onscreen.** Tap the time shown to get a menu of choices, which includes 2, 3, 5, 10, or 20 seconds per shot.

- **The transition between photos.** The Nano gives you a choice of animated effects, like a folding-paper Origami transition and the "Ken Burns" setting that slowly pans across a photo (a technique the documentary director popularized in his films). As mentioned on page 204, the Touch keeps its choice of Hollywood-style dissolves, wipes, and ripples ready to select when you tap the ▶ button on a selected photo in the album.

You can also choose to have the iPod shuffle your photos in random order, or repeat a slideshow when it ends, so that it loops until you manually stop it.

The iPod Touch photo settings, shown here, also hold a switch you can flip to turn on the Photo Stream feature of Apple's iCloud service. Jump ahead to page 212 to learn more.

TIP If you wrangle your picture collection in iPhoto '09 or later on the Mac, you can export your intricately crafted and scored iPhoto slideshows as little movies sized up just for the iPod—and put them right into iTunes. Select a slideshow in iPhoto and click the Export button. In the "Export your slideshow" box, turn on the checkbox for Mobile or Medium (the preferred settings for iPod Touch and Classic viewing, respectively) and make sure you turn on the checkbox next to "Automatically send slideshow to iTunes." Click the Export button. To actually complete the transfer, connect your iPod to your computer and then click the Movies tab on the iPod's Preferences screen in iTunes. Select the slideshow and sync away.

Slideshow Settings on the iPod Classic

YOU SET SLIDESHOW OPTIONS on the Classic by choosing Photos→Settings. You'll see a slew of options ready to shape your slideshow experience.

- Use the Time Per Slide menu to set how much time (from 2 to 20 seconds) each photo stays onscreen. (During the show, you can also go to the next image with a tap of the click wheel.)

- Use the Music menu to pick a song from your iPod's playlists to serve as the soundtrack for your show (assuming you want one). You may even want to create a playlist in iTunes to use with a particular slideshow.

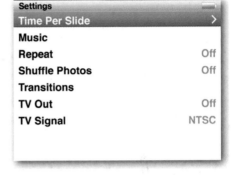

- As with music tracks, you can shuffle the order of your photos and repeat the slideshow. You can also add fancy transitions by choosing Photos→Settings→Transitions. You get to pick from several dramatic photo-changing styles, including effects that let you zoom out and fade to black.

- To make sure your slideshow plays on your iPod's screen, turn the TV Out setting to Off, which will direct the video signal to your iPod. (Turn the page if you want to project your slideshow on a TV.) Alternatively, you can select Ask, so that each time you start a slideshow, the iPod inquires whether you intend to display it on the big or small screen.

Once you get your settings just the way you want them, select the album or photo you want to begin with, and then press the Play/Pause button on the click wheel to start the show. Press the Play/Pause button during playback to temporarily stop the show, and press it again to continue.

The show's time per slide, music, and transitions should all match the settings you chose. All you have to do now is sit back, relax, and enjoy your handiwork, not only in taking great photos, but in picking great slideshow effects as well.

> **NOTE** The tiny iPod Nano doesn't include a slideshow music option in its Settings menu. To get a soundtrack going for Nano Theater, go to the Home screen, tap the Music icon, and then tap up a song or playlist. When the music starts, jump back to Photos and start your slideshow. It's a little clunky, but then again, you're watching a slideshow on a screen that's about the size of four postage stamps, so your viewing experience is not exactly immersive theater. But if you want to share that slideshow on the big screen, turn the page. Comparatively, it'll feel like watching the show on an IMAX screen.

Play Slideshows on Your TV

TO SEE YOUR DIGITAL goodies on the big screen, you first need to connect your iPod to your TV. Flip back to the previous chapter if you need help doing that (you need a special AV cable, for example). Once you make the iPod-TV link, you need to adjust a few more things on your iPod.

For the iPod Touch and 2010/2011 Nano

❶ **Connect your iPod to the TV with an AV cable**. When you connect an AV cable to the Touch or Nano, your slideshow automatically appears on your TV instead of on your iPod. Touch owners who also have a second-generation Apple TV can ditch the cable and connect with AirPlay (page 267).

❷ **On the Nano, choose Settings→Photos→TV Signal and select your local television broadcast standard**. If you're in North America or Japan, choose NTSC. If you're in Europe or Australia, choose PAL. (The Touch takes care of this on its own.)

❸ **Turn on your TV and select your iPod as the video source**. You tell your TV to use the iPod as the input signal the same way you tell it to display the signal from a DVD player or game console. Typically, you press the Input or Display button on your TV's remote to change from the live TV signal to a new video source.

❹ **On the iPod, navigate to the album you want**. Tap the photo you want to start with, and then tap the Play triangle at the bottom of the screen to begin your show.

For the iPod Classic and Older Video Nanos

❶ **Choose Photos→Settings→TV Out→On**. The On option tells your iPod to send the slideshow *out* to a TV screen instead of playing it on its own screen. (You can change your iPod's Ask setting so that it always asks you which screen you want to use; see page 209.) If you have a Classic or older Nano and use one of Apple's AV cables, TV Out gets set to On automatically.

❷ **Select your local television broadcast standard**. If you're in North America or Japan, choose Photos→Settings→TV Signal→NTSC. If you're in Europe or Australia, choose Photos→Settings→TV Signal→PAL. If you're in an area not listed above, check your television's manual to see what standard it uses or search the Web for "world television standards."

❸ **Turn on your TV and select your iPod as the video source**. You select the input for the iPod's signal the same way you tell your TV to display a signal from a DVD player or game console. Typically, you press the Input or Display button on your TV's remote to change from a live TV signal to a new video source.

Now, cue up a slideshow on the iPod and press the Play/Pause button. Your glorious photographs—scored to the sounds of your selected music, if you wish—appear on your television screen. (Because television screens are horizontal displays, vertical shots end up with black bars along the sides.)

Your pre-selected slideshow settings control the show, though you can advance through it manually with your thumb on the click wheel. If you have the iPod Universal Dock, you can also pop through shots with a click of its tiny white remote control. Although just one photo appears at a time on the TV, if you're driving the iPod Classic, your *iPod* displays not only the current picture, but the one before and after it as well, letting you narrate your show with professional smoothness: "OK, this is Shalimar *before* we got her fur shaved off after the syrup incident...and here she is later."

NOTE As explained in the previous chapter, the type of iPod you have dictates the equipment you need so you can display photos and videos on your TV. First-generation video iPods that came out between 2005 and 2006 can use the older iPod AV cable that connects through the headphone port or Line Out jack on an iPod dock. Newer Touches, Nanos, and Classics connect through the Apple Universal Dock, the Apple Composite AV Cable, the Apple Component AV Cable, or a compatible third-party offering. In any case, it's going to cost you a few bucks.

Share and Stream Photos With iCloud

Just think about all the possible ways to take digital photos, especially if you have an iPod Touch, an iPhone, and an iPad. You might have a digital camera, too. Luckily, iCloud's Photo Stream feature ensures that you'll always have a copy of all your pictures on all your iOS devices and on your computer. Now you don't have to be embarrassed when you pull out your Touch to show the girls in the book club a picture of your new niece, only to remember you actually took the photo with your iPad, which is sitting on the desk at home.

With Photo Stream in action, iCloud stores the last 1,000 pictures you've taken for 30 days, which should give you plenty of time to sync your pics across all your devices and, most importantly, to your desktop computer, which serves as the archive for your gallery. So, while iCloud holds only your last thousand shots up in the sky, all your pictures are permanently stored on your Windows PC or Mac—which probably has a bit more storage space than your iPod Touch.

To use Photo Stream, you have to activate it on your Touch, on your other iOS devices, and on your desktop computer. If you didn't turn on Photo Stream when you set up your Touch (page 14), go to the Home screen and tap Settings→iCloud→Photo Stream→On. Repeat this step on all the iOS 5 devices that you want to paddle along in the Stream. (You can also turn Photo Stream on by tapping Settings→Photos→Photo Stream→On.)

Once your iOS devices are ready, you need to bring your computer into the Photo Stream mix so it can serve as the archive.

Photo Stream for Windows Users

If you use a Windows PC, you first need to install the iCloud software for Windows (page 256). Once you do, choose Start→Control Panel→Network and Internet→iCloud. When the box opens, type in your iCloud user name and password. Next, turn on the checkbox next to Photo Stream and click Options.

In the box that appears (shown right), you need to designate two folders on your computer for Photo Stream's personal use. The first is a folder for downloads—iCloud stores the photos you snap or save to your iPod's Camera Roll here. Next, you need to pick an  upload folder—photos you put here get pulled up to iCloud and copied around to the Photo Stream album on your Touch and other iOS 5 devices (which get smaller JPG copies of the photos).

By default, iCloud sets up a Photo Stream folder in your Windows Pictures library, in a subfolder called My Photo Stream (for downloads) and one called Uploads. You can click the Change button next to either folder to pick a different name. Click OK when you're done and ready to start streaming photos.

Photo Stream for Mac OS X Users

Apple makes things a bit easier for its own operating system and computers. You just need to use the most recent version (and update) of its iPhoto '11 or Aperture programs for organizing and editing pictures. To turn on Photo Stream in either Mac program, click the Photo Stream icon in the left panel and then click the Turn On Photo Stream button that appears in the window.

To see the Photo Stream preferences in iPhoto (and adjust them if needed), choose iPhoto→Preferences→Photo Stream. In the Preferences box, like the one below, turn on the checkbox next to Enable Photo Stream. You can also turn on checkboxes next to Automatic Import (which lets iPhoto include Photo Stream images in its Events, Photos, Faces, and Places albums) and Automatic Upload (which pushes the photos you import from your camera's memory card up to iCloud; the iCloud server then sends smaller JPG versions of your camera's big chunky files to all your waiting iOS 5 devices).

IPhoto Stream on the Apple TV

If you've fully stocked your house with Apple hardware, you probably have an Apple TV connected to your television set so you can take advantage of AirPlay (page 267). Like AirPlay, Photo Stream only works on second-generation Apple TVs (the one that looks like a thick black drink coaster). And if you've had the box for a while, you may need to update its software. From the main screen, use the remote and surf to Setttings→General→Update Software, then download and install any updates available.

To see your streamed photos on your TV set, switch over to your Apple TV. On the main menu screen, use the remote control to slide along to Internet→Photo Stream, log in if asked, and enjoy the show on your HDTV.

CHAPTER 10

The iPod as Personal Assistant

THE EARLY CHAPTERS IN THIS BOOK WERE ALL ABOUT SHOWING you how your iPod works and how you can fill it up with music, movies, photos, eBooks, and more. But if you think that's *all* the iPod can do, think again. For instance, that gorgeous color screen on the Touch is happy to display your address book and calendar. The Classic can list your contacts and show you your schedule.

And that's just for starters. If you're looking for a handsome timepiece, your iPod can function as a world clock when you're on the road, and as a stopwatch when you're on the track. The Nano can even automatically count your steps, track your workouts, and mark your progress—and when you're done exercising, you can unclip it from your running clothes and snap it into an optional watchband.

If you've got an iPod Nano, Classic, or Shuffle, you can use it as an external hard drive for hauling around monster files, like PowerPoint presentations and quarterly reports. And most iPods can record your thoughts when you dictate them into the microphone.

So if you've mastered the iPod's AV Club talents and you're looking for even more ways to use your 'Pod, this chapter is for you.

The iPod as Address Book

PUTTING A COPY OF your contacts file—also known as your computer's address book—on your iPod is easy with the help of iTunes. (iPod Touch owners using iCloud to sync contacts and calendars [page 254] can skip to page 220.)

Windows users need to store their contacts in Outlook Express, Outlook 2003 or later, Windows Contacts, or the Windows Address Book (used by Outlook Express and some other email programs).

Mac folks need to have at least Mac OS X 10.5 (Leopard) and the Mac OS X Address Book (shown below), which Apple's Mail program uses to stash names and numbers. You can also use Entourage 2004 or later and Outlook 2011, but you have to *link* before you *sync*: In the mail program, choose Preferences, and then click Sync Services. Turn on the checkboxes for sharing contacts and calendars with Address Book and iCal (Apple's calendar program) to have the shared info synced up with Address Book and iCal.

You need one other thing for an on-the-go contacts list: the right type of iPod. That means a Touch or Classic, or an older click-wheel Nano. Sadly, the small, square touchscreen Nano can't display contacts, calendars, or notes.

To turn your iPod into a little black book, follow these steps:

❶ Connect your iPod to your computer and click its icon in iTunes' Source list. (If you use Outlook or Outlook Express, launch that now, too.)

❷ In the main part of the iTunes window, click the Info tab.

❸ Windows owners: Turn on the checkbox next to "Sync contacts from" and use the drop-down menu to choose the program that holds your contacts. Mac owners: Turn on the "Sync Address Book contacts" checkbox. If you want to sync contact *groups*, select them from the "Selected groups" box. You can also choose to import the photos in your contacts files.

❹ Click the Apply button in the lower-right corner of the iTunes window.

iTunes updates your iPod with the contact information stored in your address book. If you add new contacts while you have your iPod plugged in, choose File→Update iPod or click the Sync button in iTunes to move the new data over to your pocket player. When you decide someone doesn't deserve to be in your contacts list anymore, delete her from your computer's address book, and she'll disappear from your iPod the next time you sync up.

To look up a pal on an iPod Touch, tap the Contacts icon on the Home screen and flick your way to the person's name. Tap that name to see his contact info. Tap Send Message or FaceTime (Chapter 6) to directly contact your contact; tap the Share Contact button to email the info. On the Classic (and older click-wheel Nanos), choose iPod→Extras→Contacts and scroll to the name of the person. Press the center button, and you'll see his address card pop up onscreen.

TIP If you have an iPod Touch, you get a few extra sync options for your contact info. First, you can sync contacts from your Google Gmail and Yahoo Mail address books. To do that, go into iTunes' Info tab and click the Configure button next to your mail account name. Enter your Gmail or Yahoo user name and password (you need an Internet connection to sync). Second, because you can enter contacts directly on the Touch by tapping the ✚ button and filling in the boxes, the Info settings give you the option to pull the contacts you create on the Touch and add them to your online Google or Yahoo address book the next time you sync.

The iPod as Calendar

JUST AS ITUNES CAN pluck contacts out of your computer's address book, it can also snag and sync a copy of your desktop's daily or monthly schedule to your iPod Touch, Classic, or older click-wheel Nano—*if* you use Outlook on your PC or iCal on your Mac. (You can also use Entourage 2004 or later by choosing, in Entourage, Preferences→Sync Services and turning on the option to have Entourage share events with iCal; Outlook 2011 for the Mac works the same way.)

To get your calendar connected, fire up iTunes and follow these steps:

❶ Connect your iPod to your computer and click the iPod's icon when it shows up in the Source list.

❷ In the main part of the iTunes window, click the Info tab. Scroll down past Contacts to Calendars.

❸ Turn on the checkbox next to "Sync calendars from Microsoft Outlook" (Windows) or "Sync iCal calendars" (Mac). If you have multiple calendars, select the ones you want to copy.

❹ In the lower-right corner of the iTunes window, click the Apply button.

❺ If iTunes doesn't automatically start updating your iPod with your date-book, choose File→Sync iPod. If you haven't changed any sync settings and you're just *updating* contact info, iTunes' Apply button turns into a Sync button, and you can click that instead of going up to Menuville.

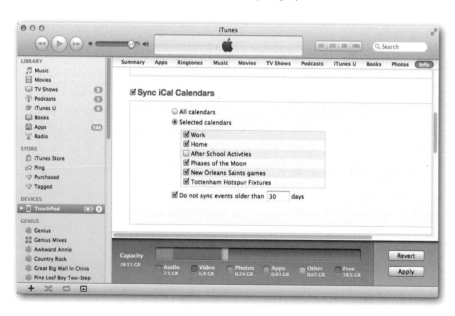

After the sync, it's time to check your dates. On the iPod Touch, tap the Calendar icon on the Home screen. Tap List, Day, or Month to see your schedule for the short or long term, or tap Today to see the current day's events. List view shows all your upcoming appointments one after the other. In Month view, your Touch represents events with black dots and lists them by day below the calendar. Tap the black triangles on either side of the month name to advance forward or backward through the months. Tap the **+** button to add an event.

To look up your busy schedule on an iPod Classic or pre-2010 Nano, choose iPod→Extras→Calendars. Select the name of the calendar you want to examine and press the round center button. On the Classic, you get a blue-and-gray grid with tiny red flags planted on the days you have something scheduled; older Nanos list the day's events under the calendar. Use the scroll wheel to navigate to a particular day, and press the center button to see the details.

A few other calendar-keeping tips:

- If you use the To Do list function in your calendar program, your action items appear in their own place on the Classic and older Nano. Choose iPod→Extras→Calendars→To Do's.

- On the Touch, tap the 📥 icon to see the meeting and event invites you've received and add them to your calendar with a tap.

- You can have your iPod remind you of upcoming events. The Touch flashes a beeping onscreen alert keyed to the event reminders in your synced calendar. You can set your own alert by selecting an event and tapping the Edit button. Tap the Alert screen and pick a suitable amount of advance warning. To turn on Nag Alerts on the Classic and older Nano, choose iPod→Extras→Calendars→Alarms. You have your choice of Off, Beep, or None (the last displays a silent message onscreen).

Track Time: The iPod as Stopwatch

THE IPOD TOUCH, NANO, and Classic all have a Stopwatch feature riding alongside their great music and video capabilities. Using the iPod stopwatch is like using a regular stopwatch, except that the iPod can be a very expensive timer.

iPod Touch and Nano

To get to the Touch's stylish full-screen stopwatch, tap Home→Clock→Stopwatch. On the newest Nano (and the 2010 edition), tap the Clock icon on the Home screen and flick from right to left past the standard clock to get to the stopwatch.

To start timing yourself on either the Touch or Nano, tap the green Start button. The timer starts counting, and the Start button turns into a red Stop button. (Tap that when you're done timing.) If you're running a series of laps, tap the gray Lap button each time you finish a turn on the track. The iPod records your time for that lap and then starts timing your next one.

The iPod displays the time for the lap-in-progress above the overall session timer. It lists the time for completed laps below the timer, so you can track your workout. The timer keeps ticking even if you tap your way to another program to, say, play some jogging music. When you return to the stopwatch, it's still going.

If you need to pause the timer, tap the Stop button; to pick up where you left off counting, tap Start again. When you're finally done with your exercise, tap the Stop button to halt the clock. To clear the times from the screen, hit the gray Reset button. The Touch doesn't store your performance history, but the Nano displays your last session's results when you tap the ≡ button in the top-right corner of the screen.

TIP Depending on your gym's equipment, you may be able to find iPod-compatible cardio machines to make your workouts more entertaining. Some treadmills, ellipticals, and stationary bikes include iPod docks that let you enjoy your music and video through the machine's AV system. And some gym equipment even taps right into the Touch and Nano's Nike + iPod software (page 222) so you can track your workouts precisely. Visit *http://www.apple.com/ipod/nike/workout.html* to learn more.

---

iPod Classic and Click-Wheel Nano

The Stopwatch feature on these iPods not only clocks your time around the track, it *keeps track* of your running sessions. To turn your Classic or older Nano into a timer, choose Extras→Stopwatch. Here's what you do from there:

- Press the Play/Pause button to begin. The iPod begins to clock you by hours, minutes, seconds, and milliseconds.

- After each lap, tap the iPod's center button to record that time; the iPod lists the lap time underneath the overall session time. The screen displays up to three lap times.

- Press Play/Pause to stop the clock. When you're done timing, press the Menu button. That takes you back to the Stopwatch menu. Here you can click Resume to start up the clock again.

- If you want a new session with the stopwatch, select New Timer.

The iPod stores logs of your last several workouts. To review your progress, scroll to Extras→Stopwatch, where you see previous sessions listed by date and time of day. Scroll and select a session to see a list of your lap times, with the shortest, longest, and average time noted on top. Press the iPod's center button to delete a log.

- If you have a lot of old logs cluttering up the screen, select Extras→Stopwatch→Clear Logs to wipe them all out.

- If you're in the middle of a run, go to Extras→Stopwatch→Current Log to see your current state of progress.

Stopwatch Log	
Oct 30 2011	**6:30 AM**
Total	**00:17:05.8**
Shortest	**00:02:57.1**
Longest	**00:05:01.2**
Average	**00:04:16.4**
Lap 1	00:04:32.2
Lap 2	00:05:01.2
Lap 3	00:02:57.1
Lap 4	00:04:35.0

TIP The Touch and Nano also have a Timer feature, which is great for cooking. Nestled right next to the Stopwatch, the Touch Timer works just as you'd expect: Pick your countdown time using the virtual spinwheels and press Start. On the Nano, flick to the screen after the Stopwatch screen, set your time wheels, and press Start.

The iPod as Personal Trainer

IN ADDITION TO THE Stopwatch feature, the iPod Touch and Nano include the Nike + iPod software for fitness buffs. With this built-in iTrainer beside you at the gym, you can record your workout statistics, pick your favorite exercise music, and upload your daily results to *www.nikeplus.com* to track your progress over time; you need to register for a free account at the Nike site to store your workout data. Each iPod handles your routine in its own way, so here's what you need to know about using the Nike software on either player.

Nike + the iPod Touch

To use this fitness feature on the iPod Touch, you need to purchase a special set of Nike gym shoes that contain a small compartment to stick in an iPod-compatible shoe sensor. The Nike shoes can be found at most stores that sell athletic footwear. The sensor costs $19 and can be found online at *www.apple.com/ipod/nike*. The sensor transmits your steps to the iPod Touch, which dutifully records the information.

That information lives in the Nike + iPod app. If you don't see a red Nike icon on your Touch, Tap Home→Settings→Nike + iPod→On.

Tap the Workouts screen to pick an exercise session that suits your needs. You can choose:

- A Basic workout with no set goals.

- A Time workout based on 20 to 90 minutes (or a custom amount) of activity.

- A Distance goal to cover a specific amount of ground (like 3K or 5 miles).

- A Calorie workout that lets you target the fat you want to burn off after last night's pizza-and-cookies binge.

Once you choose a workout, the Touch asks you to pick some music. The first time you work out, you're also prompted to link the iPod to the shoe sensor so the two can communicate. Tap Settings→Nike + iPod to further personalize your workout with a power song, spoken feedback, your weight, and more.

To create your own routines, tap the My Workouts icon at the bottom of the screen. Tap ✚ and compile a new workout by selecting the Basic, Time, Distance, or Calorie options. (To calibrate the Touch to your own stride, when you finish a workout, tap the End Workout button, and then tap Calibrate.) And to send all this info to your online Nike+ account via WiFi, tap History→Send to Nike+.

Nike + the iPod Nano

On the iPod Nano, just swipe along the Home screen until you get to the Fitness icon and tap it open. Unlike the iPod Touch or older Nanos, you don't need to buy special shoes or a sensor, because the 2011 Nano does it all for you.

On the Fitness screen, you have three options: Walk, Run, and History. When you tap Walk, the Nano turns into a clip-on musical pedometer as described below. If you tap Run, you get the same choice of workout options (Basic, Time, Distance, and Calorie) as described for Touch owners on the previous page. When you tap History, you see a menu of your past personal bests and overall workout statistics.

To upload your info to the Nike+ website, connect your Nano to iTunes. A box pops up asking if you'd like to send your data to Nike; if you do, you're taken to the site to set up a Nike+ account. To have your stats automatically uploaded to the site each time you connect your Nano to iTunes, click the Nike + iPod tab in the iTunes window and select "Automatically send workout data to Nike+."

Counting Steps With the iPod Nano

The Nano has another fitness tool tucked inside its small square case: a colorful pedometer that tells you how many steps you've taken since you turned it on.

To set up the pedometer for the first time:

❶ On the Home screen, tap Fitness→Walk.

❷ Use the onscreen wheels to spin up your weight. (If you need to change your weight later, go to Settings→Fitness→Weight.)

❸ Tap the Start button to begin counting your steps, Nano-style (this also turns the Start button into a Stop button). A little shoe icon in the Nano's menu bar tells you that the pedometer is on and counting away.

❹ Tap the Stop button when you're done so you can see the total number of steps you took (plus distance and calories burned) for the day.

As the most fitness-oriented iPod in the bunch, the latest Nano lets you set a goal for how much walking you want to do in a day. From the Home screen, tap Settings→Fitness→Walk→Daily Step Goal. Tap the Off button to On, use the spinny wheels to dial up a goal, and then tap Done. The Nano displays your progress on the pedometer's main screen so you can see how you're doing. And while you're in Settings→Fitness, you can further customize your Nike experience with a motivational "power song," spoken feedback as you work out, your preferred units of measure, and more.

Tick Tock: The iPod as a World Clock

AS DISCUSSED EARLIER IN this book, all iPods (except for the screenless Shuffle) have built-in clocks with a simple alarm feature. The Touch and the Classic, however, let you set multiple clocks for different time zones, each with its own alarm. If you travel frequently, you can create a clock for each destination instead of constantly fiddling with time zone settings. Cool.

The iPod should already have one clock—the one you created when you first set up your player and selected your time zone.

Add a Clock on Your iPod Touch

❶ Tap Home→Utilities→Clock→World Clock.

❷ Tap the **+** button in the upper-right corner of the screen.

❸ When the keyboard pops up, start typing in the name of any large city.

❹ Tap the name of the city to add its clock to your list.

If you want to rearrange your list of clocks, tap the Edit button and use the three-stripe gripstrip (≡) to drag them into the order you want.

To delete a clock, tap the Edit button, tap the ⊖ icon next to the clock's name, and then tap the Delete button.

Add a Clock to Your iPod Classic or Click Wheel Nano

❶ Go to iPod→Extras→Clocks and then press the iPod's center button.

❷ You'll see your local clock. Press the center button again to select Add. (Choose Edit if you have just one clock but want to change it.)

❸ On the next screen, select a world region, like North America, Europe, Africa, or Asia. Some categories on the Region menu are less obvious: Select Atlantic if you live in Iceland or the Azores; choose Pacific if you live in Hawaii, Guam, or Pago Pago.

❹ Once you select a region, a new screen displays a list of major cities and the current time in that part of the world. Scroll and select the city of your choice. Once you do, the iPod creates a clock named after the city and showing the local time. It adds the clock to your Clock menu.

If you want to change a clock, select it and press the iPod's center button to bring up the Edit and Delete options. Choose Edit, which takes you back through the whole "pick a region, pick a city" exercise.

If you decide you have too many clocks and don't need that Bora Bora time-keeper after all, select the unwanted clock from the list. Press the center button on the iPod, scroll down to Delete, and then press the center button again to erase time.

NOTE To make adjustments to your personal time stream, like changing to daylight saving time or switching the iPod's current time zone, tap Settings→General→Date & Time to get to the time controls for the Touch and Nano. On a Classic, choose iPod→Settings→Date & Time.

Make Time Fly With the iPod Nano

AS MENTIONED BACK IN Chapter 2, the iPod Nano comes with a clock you can use to check the time. In fact, it almost feels like checking an old-fashioned pocket watch, especially if you have the Nano clipped to a vest or belt.

But if you find it cumbersome to wake up the Nano from its slumber and fumble around for the Clock icon just to check the time, you can fix things up so that the Nano displays the clock face as soon as you press the Sleep/Wake button. To do that, tap Settings→General→Date & Time→Time On Wake→On.

If you find the default iPod Nano clock a bit on the dull side, tap Settings→ General→Date & Time→Clock Face. On this screen, you'll see all the different clock faces you can choose for your Nano. To pick one, first tap the preview to see how you like it. If you do, tap the Set button to make this your new clock face. If not, tap Cancel to get back to the click face preview screen.

The 16 clock faces include serious gold watch hands on a black background, a clock that looks like a lighted scoreboard from a high-school football game, and several cartoon characters. Yes, if you've never owned a Mickey Mouse watch, you do now. You can also display the time with Minnie Mouse, Kermit the Frog, or Animal, the hard-pounding Muppet drummer.

Want to go all the way and turn your Nano into a wristwatch? Thanks to a number of accessory makers, you can. Just pick up a compatible wristwatch band and snap the player into place. Prices depend on watchband style and material—metal, leather, and rubber are all available—but typically start at $25.

Companies that sell Nano bands include LunaTik (*lunatik.com*), iWatchz (*iwatchz. com*), and Griffin Technology (*griffintechnology.com*), maker of the colorful $25 Slap silicone watchbands (shown here). The benefits of using the Nano as a watch? You always know the time and you always know where your iPod is.

Voice Memos: The iPod as Audio Recorder

THE TOUCH, NANO, AND 160-gigabyte iPod Classic don't just *play* sound, they *record* it, too, thanks to their Voice Memos feature. If you have an older, microphone-free version of the Touch (new Touches have a built-in mic), a Nano, or a Classic, you need to invest in Apple's optional Earphones with Remote and Mic, (available for $29 at *www.apple.com/ipodstore*) or a compatible third-party microphone.

Once you have your microphone in place, you can start your recording session:

❶ On the Touch, tap the Voice Memos icon on the Home screen; it's inside the Utilities folder on new models. On the Nano, tap the Voice Memos icon that appears when you plug in the mic. On the Classic, choose iPod→Voice Memos.

❷ To start recording, tap the red dot on the Touch or Nano screen. On the Classic, choose Voice Memos→Start Recording. You can pause your recording by tapping the Touch or Nano's onscreen Pause icon, or by pressing the Play/Pause button on the Classic's click wheel. Tap the pause icon on the Touch or Nano to re-start recording; on the Classic, choose Resume.

❸ On the Touch or Nano, tap the black square on the right side of the screen to stop recording. On the Classic, choose Stop and Save. To play back a recording, tap the ≡ icon on the Touch or Nano; on the Classic, select the recording from the Voice Memos menu.

To delete a recording on the Touch, select it on the Voice Memos menu and then press the Delete button. The Touch has a Share button on the same screen that lets you send the recording as an email attachment. If you tap the recording's ◉ icon, you get a Trim Memo button that lets you edit the clip. On this same screen, tap the recording's name to assign it a predefined label, like "Interview" or "Lecture."

To delete a clip from the Nano, tap the ≡ icon. Tap the Edit button on the next screen, and then hit the ⊖ icon before you confirm the deletion. Just as on the Touch, you can label a clip by tapping its name and then tapping Label.

To erase a recording from the Classic, press the center button to select it and then choose Delete from the menu. If your iPod is set to sync, iTunes copies your recordings to its Voice Memos playlist. You can find the audio files on Nanos and Classics enabled for disk use (page 228) in the iPod's Recordings folder.

The iPod as Portable Hard Drive

AS IF BEING A portable entertainment system and organizer isn't enough, your iPod Nano, Shuffle, or Classic can also serve as a portable hard drive to shuttle documents, presentations, and other files from one computer to another. (The Touch doesn't naturally work as an external drive; to get it to do that, you have to use a utility program like TouchCopy, mentioned back in Chapter 5.)

To give your iPod these file-toting powers:

❶ Plug your 'Pod into your computer.

❷ When its icon shows up in iTunes' Source list, select it, and then click the Summary tab in the main iTunes window.

❸ Turn on the checkbox next to "Enable disk use" in the Options area of the Summary screen. To set a limit for non-music storage on the storage-shy Shuffle, spin its triangle open, click the Music icon, and then click the Autofill settings button (page 24). Drag the slider to the desired amount of space.

❹ In the lower-right corner of the iTunes window, click the Apply button. If you forget and try to move on to something else, iTunes reminds you that you modified an iPod setting and prompts you to OK the change.

Your iPod now shows up as an icon in the My Computer area of Windows or on the Mac desktop. You can drag files on and off the icon just as you would files for any other drive connected to your computer. You can also double-click the iPod icon to create folders for your files. Delete files by dragging them to the Recycle Bin or the Trash. Steer clear of the folders labeled Photos (and, on the Classic, the folders tagged Calendars, Contacts, and Notes); the iPod uses those folders to store the eponymous items. (Turn the page to see what you can do with the Classic's Notes folder.)

Keep in mind that once you turn your iPod into an external hard drive, you have to treat it like one by formally ejecting the drive from iTunes before disconnecting your 'Pod. (Do so by clicking the Eject icon next to the iPod's name in the iTunes Source list and you'll avoid huffy alert boxes from your operating system about improper device removal.)

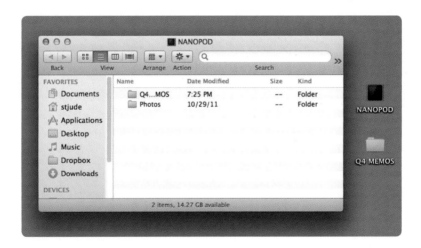

Your iPod keeps music, movies, and other iTunes stuff in a special, invisible area of the player, so you can use all those features even when you use your 'Pod as a file courier. (And syncing your music with a PC or Mac doesn't affect the computer files, either.) But remember that the more you fill up your iPod with data files, the less room you have for entertainment—and vice versa.

NOTE Windows can't read the Mac disk format, but a Mac can read a Windows-formatted iPod Classic or Nano. If you want to use your iPod with both systems, plug it into the PC first and let iTunes format your 'Pod for Windows. The Shuffle and the Touch work with both Windows PCs and Macs right out of the gate.

The iPod as eBook and Text Reader

WANT TO READ A great book or review notes on your iPod Touch or Classic? Both of these iPods can work as pocket-size eReaders.

Read PDF Files and Other eBooks on the iPod Touch

Even before the App Store came into being, the iPod Touch offered ways to read chunks of text onscreen, whether it was from notes synced from Outlook or Apple's OS X Mail program, or documents stashed in Safari-friendly online lockers, like Google Docs.

The arrival of the App Store a few years ago made reading on the Touch even easier, with plenty of 99-cent books and even a free Shakespeare app, which puts the complete works of the Bard (sonnets, too!) within reach of your fingertip. The App Store is also well-stocked with interactive children's books to entertain the bambinos.

But if it's current bestsellers, general titles, and free books you seek, a well-stocked eBookstore is your best bet for browsing—and downloading samples. Apple, or course, has its own iBooks and Newsstand apps (described on page 70) that bills your purchases to the credit card associated with your Apple ID. And even if you don't want to buy books from Apple, installing the free iBooks app gives you a great place to download and stash PDF files you get via email (see top-right).

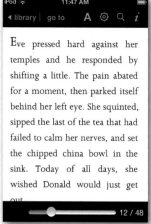

iBooks also lets you read PDF files that you copy over from your computer (by dragging them into iTunes and syncing your 'Pod). To find the files, tap the PDFs button on iBooks' bookshelf.

Amazon's Kindle app and Barnes & Noble's Nook app (shown above) are your link to the other two major online bookstores out there. Once you sign up for an account at either *www.amazon.com* or *www.bn.com* and supply your payment information, you can buy your electronic books right there on the Web. When you're ready for some Touch reading, just open the store's app and tap to download your purchases to the iPod. Both apps make eBooks easy to read, with adjustable font sizes, tinted backgrounds, and instant bookmarks. Your purchased titles are kept safely online, where you can always snag them again.

Read Text Files on the iPod Classic and Click-Wheel Nano

It's a little-known feature, but the iPod Classic and older click-wheel Nanos can also display basic text files onscreen. You create these iPod notes from plain text files (those with a *.txt* extension), like those from Windows Notepad or TextEdit on a Mac. (You can't read full-fledged word-processing documents from Microsoft Word or AppleWorks unless you save them as plain text files.)

To use the iPod's Notes feature:

❶ Connect your iPod to your computer as an external drive (flip back two pages to find out how).

❷ Once you save your text files in the proper plain-text format, open your iPod by double-clicking its icon in the Computer window in Windows (the My Computer window for Windows XP) or on the Mac desktop.

❸ Drag the files into the Notes folder on your iPod.

❹ After you copy your files, eject the iPod from iTunes by clicking the Eject button next to its name in the Source list, or use the Eject button in the corner of the iTunes window.

❺ When you're ready to start reading, choose Extras→Notes. You'll see the names of your text files listed in the Notes menu. Scroll to the one you want, and then press the iPod's center button to bring it up onscreen.

As you read, you can use the scroll wheel to page up and down through the file. Press the Menu button to close the file and return to the list of Notes files.

Using the iPod as a text reader is a handy way to bring your grocery list with you so you can rock while you shop. But to browse prose more challenging than "Buy Pampers," swing by Project Gutenberg's website at *www.gutenberg.us*. Here you can download thousands of public-domain literary works as plain text files and transfer them to your iPod's Notes folder. (The iPod can display files up to only 4 kilobytes in size; to see a list of shareware programs that let you read longer files that go beyond that measly 4K, visit *www.missingmanuals.com/cds/ipodtmm10/*.)

> **Boswell's Life of Johnson highlights.txt**
>
> Mr. Cambridge, upon this, politely said, 'Dr. Johnson, I am going, with your pardon, to accuse myself, for I have the same custom which I perceive you have. But it seems odd that one should have such a desire to look at the backs of books.' Johnson, ever ready for contest, instantly started from his reverie, wheeled about, and answered, 'Sir, the reason is very plain. Knowledge is of two kinds. We know a subject ourselves, or we know where we can find information upon it. When we enquire into any subject, the first thing we have to do is to know what books have treated of it. This leads us to look at catalogues, and the backs of books in libraries.'

CHAPTER 11

Surf the Web and More with the iPod Touch

IF YOU HAVE AN IPOD TOUCH, YOU KNOW THAT IT CAN DOWNLOAD and run apps from the App Store (Chapter 3). But your Touch also comes with a preinstalled app that, in terms of cool factor, is the equal of anything you can find in Apple's online emporium: Safari, Apple's versatile web browser, scaled down and redesigned for your Touch. Safari lets you comfortably surf the World Wide Web from wherever you can hop onto a WiFi connection.

You may already use Safari on your Mac or Windows PC—why yes, there *is* a Windows version—so using it on your Touch will feel familiar. But browsing on the Touch is a little different from surfing on a full-size computer screen, with *little* being the operative word here. Never fear— this chapter shows you the techniques, tips, and tricks you need to get big results out of that small window to the Web.

Surfing with Safari isn't the only advantage of a WiFi-enabled Touch. You can use Apple's new (and free!) online storage locker, iCloud, to keep your contacts, calendars, and other personal information in sync across all your computers and iOS 5 devices. And to get the most bang for your Touch buck, you can print documents, photos, and web pages wirelessly, too.

Get Your WiFi Connection

TO JUMP ONTO THE Web with your Touch, you first need to *get connected* to the Internet. That's pretty easy, thanks to the sheer abundance of wireless networks these days—in homes, coffee shops, airports, hotels, college campuses, libraries, and more. WiFi, like love, is all around.

WiFi is geekspeak for *wireless fidelity*, a networking technology that lets you connect to the Internet over radio waves instead of wires. Also known as 802.11, it's the same technology that lets desktop PCs, laptops, game consoles, and other devices connect to the Web over the air. When you come across a network you can tap into, you've found what's called a *WiFi hotspot*.

Odds are you jumped on your home WiFi network when you activated your brand-new Touch (page 14). If you didn't, here's what to do:

❶ Fire up a Net-needy app like Safari or Mail. Your iPod scans the airwaves for a WiFi signal and presents you with a list of available networks. If you don't get one, tap Home→Settings→Wi-Fi→On.

❷ In the "Select a Wi-Fi Network" box, tap the name of the network you want to join.

❸ If you select one with a small lock icon (🔒) next to its name, you'll need a password to join it. Type in the password when the Touch prompts you (on the next screen), and you're ready to start surfing. The 📶 icon at the top of the Touch means you're network-connected.

Thankfully, the Touch remembers your network name and password. So if it detects a previously used network that's up, running, and in range, it jumps back onto that network without fuss, and the 📶 icon at the top of your screen confirms your connection.

If the Touch can't find a previous network, it pops up the "Select a Wi-Fi Network" screen again, listing nearby hotspots, and you start the first-time connection dance all over again. See the next page for directions.

At home and confused about why your own network didn't link your Touch (review your typing) or isn't showing up in the list of hotspots? Check your network's modem and wireless router (the box with the blinking lights that broadcasts the network signal from your modem) to make sure everything's working.

Find More Hotspots

The Touch is great at suggesting nearby networks and you may quickly find one you can join. But you'll see only a couple of them in the "Select a Wi-Fi Network" box, usually the ones with the strongest signal and no password requirement— the iPod tries to provide a solid, simple connection.

While that keeps the list short and tidy (especially in big cities with lots of networks), it's not the full list of nearby nets. And the list also doesn't show *hidden* networks, where the owner has decided to not publicly broadcast the network's name for security reasons.

To see a list of *all* nearby *visible* networks, go to the iPod's Home screen and tap Settings→Wi-Fi. On the list that comes up, tap the name of the network you want to join.

Don't see the network you want in the list? Odds are, it's one of those "hidden" ones. Tap Other and move on to the next screen. In the box, type in the exact name of the network. You also need to know the type of security the network uses (like WPA2 or WEP; you may have to ask the owner if it's not you) and its password so you can join your pal's network for gaming or other WiFi fun.

Use Commercial Hotspots

Although your home and office WiFi networks are free, that's not always the case when you're on the go. Airports, hotels, and other places offer *commercial* hotspots. When you try to join of one these pay-to-play networks, you get a screen requesting your billing information before you can do anything online. (Before you start typing, make sure you're in a legitimate hotspot by checking the network name posted in the hotel room or airport waiting area. Fake hotspots are out there, so be careful.)

If you travel a lot, getting a long-term, discounted account with a hotspot vendor like Boingo, T-Mobile, or AT&T may save you money in the long run.

> **TIP** Tired of the Touch bugging you to join hotspots when you don't need to—or even want to? From the Home screen, tap Settings→Wi-Fi. At the bottom of the screen, tap the Off button next to "Ask to Join Networks." You can reverse this process later if you decide you do want to be Net-connected.

Take a Safari Tour

READY TO SURF? ON the Touch, Safari is your on-ramp to the Web. By default, it occupies the third icon on the Home screen's bottom row (below left), but you can put it anywhere (page 53). The first time you tap the Safari icon, a blank browser window appears (below middle). Tap its address bar to summon the Touch keyboard (below right) so you can type in a web address. Once you do, hit the keyboard's blue Go button to jump to that site.

So how do you use Safari once you get out on the Web? Here's a guided tour of the program's bars and buttons, starting from the upper-left:

- **Address bar**. As shown in action on the right-most screen above, this narrow strip of typeable turf is where you enter a page's web address (also known as its *URL* or Uniform Resource Locator—a term that dates back to the early days of the Web, when researchers, programmers, and scientists were its big users.)

- **✕, ↻ (Stop, Reload)**. See a typo after you enter an address, or change your mind about going to a site? Click the ✕ button in the address bar to stop loading the page-in-progress.

> **NOTE** The iPod Touch runs pretty much the same operating system (OS) as the iPhone, and Apple usually releases OS updates a few times a year. While some updates are simply security fixes, the company does occasionally make bigger overhauls, like redesigning the Safari interface. If your copy of Safari doesn't look exactly like the one pictured here, odds are you're running a version of the Touch's OS released before or after iPhone/iPod Touch OS 5.0.1. You can see what flavor OS you have by tapping Home→Settings→General→About→Version.

After you tap Go, a Blue Progress Bar of Loading displays the page's download status. Once the page appears onscreen, Safari converts that ✖ button to a ↻. Tap this circular-arrow icon to reload the page if, say, you're checking sports scores or election results and want the absolute latest news—or if the page doesn't look right and you want to download it again.

- **Search box**. The lilliput search box in the upper-right corner of the screen is now a staple of most desktop browsers, and mini-Safari follows suit. Tap the box and type in your keywords, and then tap the blue Search button that appears in the bottom-right corner. (See page 249 to select a search engine—you have your choice of Google, Yahoo Search, or Microsoft Bing these days.)

- ◀, ▶ **(Back, Forward)**. The first two icons on Safari's bottom toolbar let you navigate backward and forward through the pages you visit during an Internet session. Tap the ◀ button to go back to the page you were just on. When you do that, you now have the option to return to the page you just left with a tap of the ▶ button.

- ☞ **(Action menu)**. Tap here to do one of six things. You can bookmark the current page, add the page to your Reading List for later consumption (see page 251), or add a shortcut to that page on your Home screen. If you're in a sharing mood, you can also send a link to the page in an email message (which brings up the Touch's mail app with the link already embedded), share it with your Twitter followers (page 68), or print out a copy with your AirPrint-compatible printer (page 258).

- ☐ **(Bookmarks)**. By tapping this icon, you can see all the bookmarks you've added to the Touch (page 242), along with any you synced over from your desktop or laptop computer (page 244).

- ☐, ☐ **(Pages)**. You're not stuck with just one active web page at a time, and this icon (in the bottom-right corner) tells you how many pages you currently have open. See page 252 for more on multiple web pages.

Zoom and Scroll Web Pages

WHEN THE IPHONE AND iPod Touch first appeared in 2007, many new owners spent hours zooming and scrolling through web pages because it was cool, fun, and novel. It was also useful, because a lot of websites hadn't yet developed easy-to-read mobile versions of their sites, with type and graphics designed to maximize readability on the small screen (see page 247).

Thanks to the global invasion of smartphones, many sites have jumped on the mobile bandwagon, so the problem isn't so bad anymore. But even when a site offers a mobile edition, you sometimes need to see the full-size version. Happily, when you type in the address of a "desktop" website today, the Touch scrunches down the site's pages into palm-size replicas.

So now you can see a whole web page at once, but can you read it? Probably not, unless you have extremely good (even microscopic) vision. Here's where Safari on the Touch shows its versatility, because it offers multiple ways to make that page readable:

- **Rotate the Touch**. Need just a bit of a size boost? Turn the Touch 90 degrees to the left or the right so you get a wider viewing window, which is known by its formal name, *landscape mode*.

- **Zoom and pinch**. Place your thumb and forefinger (or whichever fingers you prefer) together on the screen and slowly spread them apart to zoom in on (enlarge) the part of the page between your fingers. To go in the opposite direction and *reduce* the size of the selected area, move your spread fingers closer together in a pinch formation (the same way you harassed your siblings in the back of the car on family vacations).

- **Double-tap**. Web pages are made up of different sections, and Safari can isolate each one and magnify just that part. Find the section of a page you want to read and double-tap it to expand it to the width of the Touch's screen. Double-tap the area again to reduce the section to its original size.

Double-tap

When you zoom in on a page and want to read a part that's out of view, simply drag your finger on the glass to pull that section to the center. You can also scroll around a page quickly by flicking your finger. As your finger flies around, you'll pass over links, but Safari knows you're in transit and doesn't open them. To actually click a link, stop scrolling and tap the link with your finger.

TIP Ever hit one of those page-within-a-page situations (also known as a *frame*), where the inner window has its own scroll bar but you can't scroll inside it without scrolling the outer page? Don't you just hate that? Never fear, Safari Touch can handle it. Just place *two* fingers on the frame and gently drag them up or down to scroll through just that part of the page.

Surf with Safari

USING SAFARI ON YOUR Touch, you can freely roam around the Web in several ways:

- **Typing**. As mentioned earlier, you can go to just about any page on the Web as long as you can type in its address correctly.

- **Bookmarks**. These shortcuts to favorite sites work like they do on desktop and laptop PCs, except that you tap them instead of clicking them.

- **History**. Yes, Safari for the Touch keeps a record of your page-browsing activity. It's in the History folder under the Bookmarks icon, and you can easily tap your way to a page from your recent past.

- **Links**. It wouldn't be the Web without links. And all you need to do is tap.

The next few pages look into each of these surfing moves in detail, but first consider the address bar—and its handy shortcuts:

- **Jump back to the top**. No matter how many miles down a page you've scrolled, you can quickly bop back up to the top by tapping the Touch's black status bar, the one with the clock and battery icon. That brings you to the top of the page *and* to Safari's address bar, where you can type in a fresh address to surf to another site.

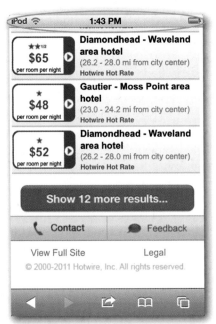
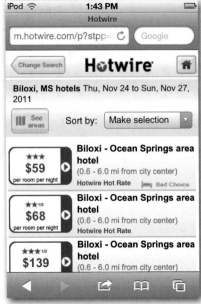

- **Delete an address all at once**. You don't have to hold down the delete key to whack a web address so you can type in a fresh one—just tap the ⊗ button at the right end of the bar to obliterate the address. To get to the ⊗ icon (and pull up the keyboard), tap inside the address bar.

  In recent versions of the iPod Touch software, tapping the URL inside the address bar also brings up the Select and Select All buttons so you can copy a web address to the Touch's clipboard (Chapter 3). If you already did that, you'll see a Paste button.

- **Don't over-type**. As with most modern browsers, you can skip pecking out *http://* and *.com* in web addresses, since Safari is savvy enough to stick those on for you. So, instead of typing *http://www.ama-zon.com*, just type *amazon* and hit Go. (If you need the suffix *.net, .edu, .org*, or *.us*, press and hold the *.com* button and slide across to the suffix you need, as shown at right.)

If you jumped right to this chapter because you wanted to start using Safari to roam the Web immediately, flip back to Chapter 3 for more on using the Touch keyboard.

Create and Use Safari Bookmarks

YOU CAN ADD BROWSER bookmarks to Safari for the Touch two ways: right from the Touch as you search, surf, and discover new places around the Web, or by syncing your desktop bookmarks with the Touch (flip ahead to page 244 to do that).

No matter how you save 'em, you find your Touch's bookmarks in the same place: tap ⚏ at the bottom of the Safari screen.

Depending on how you organize your web addresses, you may see a collection of single bookmarks (as shown at right), or you may see them grouped into folders, just as you had them in your desktop browser. Tap a folder to open it, and then tap a bookmark inside to visit the corresponding site.

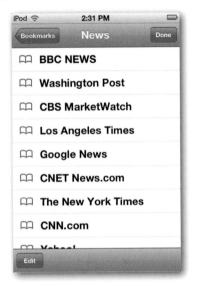

Add a New Bookmark

To add a cool new site to your Bookmarks list, tap the **+** icon at the bottom of the screen and then tap Add Bookmark. On the Add Bookmark screen, you have these choices:

- **Rename it**. Some websites have hideously long names, like "Uncle Earl's Good-Time Five-String Finger-Pickin' Jam Session," but you can change that. Tap the top box on the Add Bookmark screen and rename the site to something shorter, like "Banjos."

  The box right below that—which you can't mess with—displays the site's official web address.

- **File it**. The third box down lets you file a bookmark in a folder (see opposite page). Tap the Bookmarks link to open Safari's list of bookmark folders. When you find the one you want, tap the folder's name to deposit your bookmark there.

Edit and Organize Bookmarks and Folders

SAFARI LISTS BOOKMARKS IN the order in which you save them, and that may not be the easiest way to find them. Touch Safari is ready for this inevitability, as well as the probability that you'd like to delete old bookmarks every once in a while.

Editing your bookmarks and bookmark folders is quick and efficient on the Touch. To do either, tap the ⊞ button and then tap Edit. To edit bookmarks *inside* a folder, tap ⊞, tap open the target folder, and then tap Edit. Here's what you can do with the bookmarks and folders:

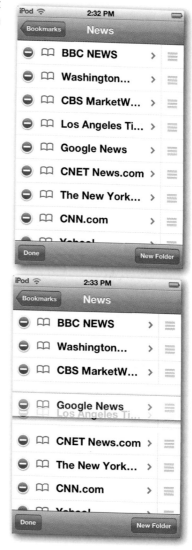

- **Delete them**. When it's time for that bookmark or folder to go, tap the ⊖ button and then tap Delete to confirm. (You can't delete the History folder, however.)

- **Edit them**. Need to rename a bookmark or folder? To edit a bookmark, tap it to get to the Edit Bookmark screen, where you can change its name and address. Tap a folder to get to the Edit Folder screen so you can change the folder's name. Tap the Bookmarks button in the upper-left corner when you're done.

- **File/refile them**. To make, name, and file a new folder, tap the New Folder button in the upper-left corner of the Edit screen, then name the folder and tap Bookmarks to file it. You move an existing folder by tapping it, tapping Bookmarks on the Edit Folder screen, and then choosing a new location.

- **Rearrange them**. Need a new order for your bookmarks or folders? As shown at right, drag the grip strip (≡) up or down the list to move them to a new place. (You can't move the History folder, however.)

Tap Done when you're finished.

Sync Bookmarks with iTunes

OVER THE YEARS, YOU'VE probably built up a considerable collection of book-marks on your desktop and laptop computers. In fact, you're probably very attached to some of those links. The good news is you *can* take them with you—at least on the iPod Touch.

To copy your entire Internet Explorer or Safari bookmark library from your computer to your Touch, all you need to do is turn on a checkbox in iTunes. Connect your iPod, click its icon in the iTunes window, and click the Info button at the top of the screen. Scroll down past things you can sync, like contacts, calendars, and mail accounts, until you get to the section called Other. Now, do the following, depending on the type of computer you have:

- **Windows PCs**: Turn on "Sync bookmarks with" and then choose either Safari or Internet Explorer from the menu. Click Apply or Sync.

- **Macs**: Turn on "Sync Safari bookmarks" and then click Apply or Sync.

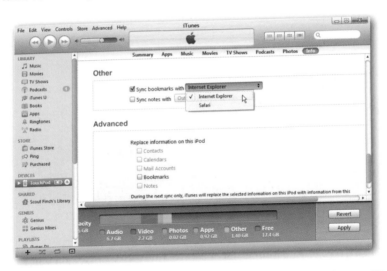

If you use Mozilla's Firefox browser, drop into the App Store (Chapter 3) and search for "Firefox." You can find mini-programs, like Firefox Home, Mozilla's own free app, to port your Firefox faves over to the Touch.

Any bookmarks you create on your iPod can make the trip *back* to your computer when you sync, too. But if things start to get too messy on the Touch, you can wipe out all its bookmarks and start over. In iTunes, scroll down to the Info screen's Advanced area (under "Replace information on this iPod") and turn on the checkbox next to Bookmarks. Click Apply or Sync to have iTunes replace all the bookmarks on the Touch with those from your computer.

The Safari History List

THE HISTORY BUTTON ON desktop browsers has saved many a soul who can't remember the name of that really informative site from the other day. Safari on the Touch doesn't let you forget your history, either (well, not without some work), and it, too, keeps a list of the sites you've surfed recently.

To see your web trail, tap 🕮 and then tap the History folder, where Safari collects your past sites in tidy subfolders with names like "Yesterday." Tap a bookmark within one of the subfolders to go back in time—or at least back to that site. The link won't be in the History folder forever (time does march on, and so does the History list), so you may want to bookmark it for real before it slips away.

Erase the History List

Don't want to leave a record of your browsing history in case someone picks up your Touch? One way to prevent that is to set up a Passcode Lock. Then, anyone who wants to get into your Touch will need a four-digit code to unlock the screen; see page 58 for more.

Another way to clean up after yourself is to erase your whole History list. To do that, open the History folder (below left), tap the Clear button in the bottom-left corner (below middle), and then tap the Clear History button (below right). You've just wiped away History. Many politicians are probably envious.

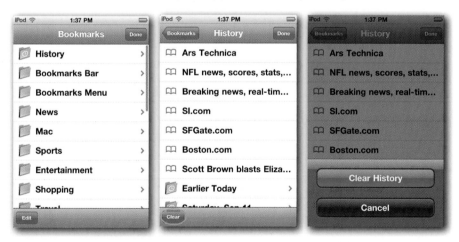

> **TIP** Proud of a bookmark and want to plant it on your Home screen? Tap the **+** button at the bottom of your browser and choose Add to Home Screen. The site's icon now sits right on the Touch's main screen. And don't worry about filling up your Home screen pages—you can have up to 11 of 'em and flick between them.

Tap Links

LINKS ON THE TOUCH work just like links on any other computer, except that on the Touch, you tap a link with your finger instead of clicking it with your mouse. While websites traditionally display links in blue, that's not always the case—you can find links of just about any color online, and oftentimes pictures, logos, and other graphics turn out to be links as well.

If you want to know where a link points to before you click it (not a bad idea in these days of rampant bad behavior and evildoing on the Web), hold your finger on the link for a second or two. A box like the one below-right slides up, offering you four options: to open the page right away, to open the page in a new window ("Open in New Page") so you can switch back and forth among pages, to add the page to your Reading List (see page 251), and to copy the link.

If you prefer to keep your original pages onscreen when you click links, you can tell Safari to open new pages in the background, where you can find them later by tapping the ⬚ icon. To do that, tap Settings→Safari→Open Links→In Background. When you do, the pop-up menu options change accordingly.

Want to stash the linked page away for later? Tap Add to Reading List (page 251). The Copy option lets you paste the link into a Notes document so you can save it (page 74 or into an email message so you can share it. Speaking of email, when you tap a link in a Touch mail message (page 89), Mail closes and Safari opens to take you the site. Yes, these hyperlinks are a pretty nifty invention.

RSS Feeds and Mobile-Friendly Sites

AS COOL AS TOUCH Safari is about showing you full websites on a tiny screen (well, except for sites that use Adobe Flash, an interactive technology the Touch doesn't support), they can sometimes be a lot of work to read. That's especially true if you just want to get a quick look at the news, or find out the basics of a story. That's where two really wonderful parts of the Web come in: RSS feeds and mobile-friendly sites. Here's how to use both:

RSS Feeds

Depending on which nerd you're taking to, RSS stands for Rich Site Summary or Really Simple Syndication. No matter what you call it, RSS is a fabulous technology for your Touch (or any mobile device with a browser). It lets you subscribe to short text dispatches called *feeds* sent out by thousands of sites and news sources around the world.

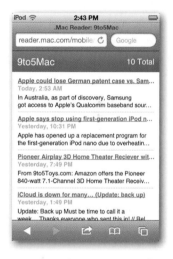

Feeds, like the one shown at right, provide a linked headline and a short summary of the related story. You can see (and bookmark) a site's feed on your Touch by tapping the RSS Feed link on its home page, or by typing the feed's own URL into the Safari address bar (hint: It often starts with the prefix *feed://*). Once you get to the feed's home page, there are no ads, flashing banners, or dancing hamsters clogging up the works—just straightforward text. When you want to read more about a story, tap its link.

Mobile-Friendly Sites

Many major news organizations and other companies have noticed that this whole smartphone/mobile browser thing has caught on with the public, and they offer versions of their sites optimized for the small screen, using smaller graphics and bigger type.

When you surf on the Touch, you'll likely get served up the mobile edition of a site automatically. If that doesn't happen, try exchanging the *www* in the URL with an *m*, as in *m.cnn.com*. (The *m* stands for *mobile*.) When you land on a mobile site, your eyes will be much happier.

Search the Web

IMAGINE TRYING TO FIND anything on the Web *without* search. At more than 11 billion indexed pages and counting (according to *www.worldwidewebsize. com*), the Web would be a pretty hard place to pinpoint information unless you knew exactly where to find it. And how many of us can lay claim to that sort of confidence?

Fortunately, the Web offers search engines. And fortunately for iPod Touch owners, three of them are built right into Safari. You can use any one as your Sherlock of the 'Net.

The next page explains how to set your default search engine, but no matter which one you use, they work the same way. To search the Web, tap the search box on the upper-right side of the Safari window and then, when the keyboard appears, type in your keywords. Tap the blue Search button in the bottom-right corner to start the hunt.

Mobile web search has come a long way since 2007, when the original iPhone and iPod Touch hit the scene; back then, their browsers didn't even have a search box. Nowadays, many search engines come in mobile-friendly versions that round up not just general results, but news stories, video clips, and images. As you can see below, Google and Bing let you tap different tabs on the search results page (or under the ◦ menu on the Yahoo screen) to see the various types of information the search engine has thoughtfully rounded up.

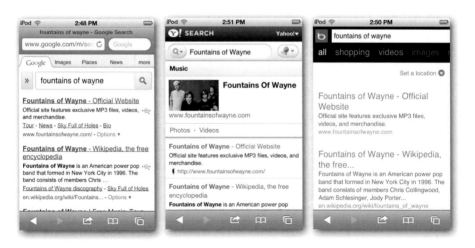

Change Your Default Search Engine

Google is the default search engine for many people, both at the desk and on the go, but it's not like you *have* to use it. Yahoo and Microsoft also offer smooth-running engines that can bring back slightly different results from what the Big Goog might give you. In the case of search, the more choices, the better, and you can change things up any time you want by switching Safari's default search engine.

To try Yahoo Search or Microsoft Bing (or to go back to Google if you switched before), visit the Home screen and tap Settings→Safari→Search Engine. On the Search Engine screen (shown bottom-right), tap the name of the service you'd like to use.

Tap the Safari button in the top-left corner to go back to the previous screen to adjust other settings (like turning on the Autofill feature that lets Safari automatically fill in your contact info and user name and password on web forms), or press the Home button to bail out of the Settings area and get back to searching and surfing.

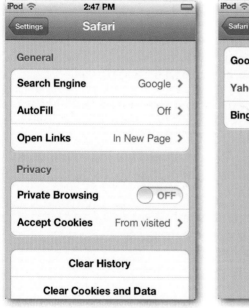

TIP Search engines do more than find web pages—they can also act as electronic crib sheets for quick data points. Need the weather forecast for Boston? Type *weather 02114* into the search box. Movies in Manhattan? Type *movies 10018*. You can also get stock quotes by typing in a company's ticker symbol, unit conversions (*kilometers in 6 miles*), and dictionary definitions (*define bildungsroman*).

Play Online Audio and Video

IN THE EARLY DAYS of the Touch, streaming audio and video from the Internet was an exercise in frustration, mainly because many sites used media formats, like RealPlayer and Flash, that the Touch couldn't play. While there are still plenty of sites that don't work with mobile Safari, more and more do. And on its own, the Touch can play MP3, WAV, and QuickTime audio files right off the Web. It also plays QuickTime movies in certain formats, like H.264.

Here are a few audio news sites that play well with Safari on the Touch:

- **BBC News**. The Beeb's podcasts stream nicely, and you can search shows by radio station, genre, or get an A-to-Zed list. *www.bbc.co.uk/podcasts/*

- **National Public Radio**. This is a whole page of news shows and podcasts that start streaming when you tap the Listen link; you can also get NPR's official apps as well. *www.npr.org*

But you're not just stuck with Safari—you can stream audio or video through apps like the ones below, all available in the App Store (Chapter 3):

- **Last.fm**. With a free account and the free Last.fm app from the App Store, you can build your own streaming radio station. *www.last.fm/*

- **Pandora Radio**. Another option for personalized radio, also with its own desktop site and App Store offering, Pandora analyzes your music taste and streams similar, but new, tracks. *www.pandora.com*

- **Netflix**. Stream high-quality movies and TV shows to your Touch. All you need is an unlimited plan from Netflix ($8 and up) and the Netflix app, available free in the App Store. *www.netflix.com*

- **Hulu Plus**. A mere $8 a month in subscription fees and the free Hulu Plus app from the App Store sets you up with thousands of TV episodes from old and new series. *www.hulu.com/plus*

Don't want to pay for streaming video? You can always visit Home→YouTube for something truly entertaining (or weird). And Apple, in addition to all its iHardware offerings, hosts a huge collection of current movie trailers at *www.apple.com/ trailers*. Tap a movie poster to get started.

Use Safari Reader and Reading List

APPLE'S IOS 5 SOFTWARE brings a couple of treats to Safari for serious browsers of the Web: Reader and Reading list. Here's what each one does:

Reader

Hate web pages full of distracting graphics and ads? iOS 5 now has a wonderful feature called Safari Reader that works with many sites (but not all) around the Web. Like its cousin-in-code for the desktop, Safari Reader strips away all the distracting and nonessential graphics and other elements on a page, and presents that article in a nice, easy-to-read format. It's like a pair of comfy slippers for your eyes.

To tell if a web page supports Safari Reader, look up in the address bar for a Reader icon. If you see one, tap it. Like magic, the distracting ads melt away, and only the essential text and images appear front-and-center on the page. You can even adjust the font size within the Reader version of a page by tapping the ₐA icon until you're satisfied with the way things look. Under the ☞ menu, you find options for mailing and printing the page in the sleek, streamlined Reader format. Tap Done to return to the regular page.

Reading List

No time (at the time) to read? When you're browsing around in Safari and find an article that you just don't have time to fully explore, tap the ☞ icon and choose Add to Reading List from the menu. That article is now saved to your personal reading list within the browser, where it waits for you.

Later, when you have time to read, tap the ⌂ icon and choose Reading List from the menu. Now you can see a tidy set of all your saved articles. To read one, tap its entry. Safari divides the Reading List into two parts, All and Unread. All, as you may have guessed, shows every article you've added to the list. The Unread list shows just the stories you haven't opened yet. As you open, read, and move on with each saved article, the link for it automatically moves from the Unread list to the All list—saving you the trouble of remembering what you have and haven't read.

Use Multiple Web Pages

TABBED BROWSERS, LIKE INTERNET Explorer and Firefox, have changed the way people surf. If you need to compare two pages or flip back and forth between them, you no longer have to open them in two separate windows. Tabs let you easily click back and forth between pages in the *same* window, making your own personal space-time continuum much more efficient.

Safari on the iPod Touch lets you do a variation on that concept. You can push older pages off to the side when you need to open a new one, but still have both within a finger's reach. Here's what you can do:

- **Open a new page**. Need to check something on another site? Tap the ⎙ button in the lower-right corner of Safari. Your current page shrinks into the background. Tap the New Page button in the lower-left corner to get a fresh blank page to address. You can open up to eight pages this way. To see how many pages you have open at once, check the ⎙ icon, which now has a tiny number inside it. If you see ⎙, for example, you have three pages open.

- **Switch to another open page**. Go back and tap ⎙ again. See those dots (• • •) underneath the mini-page (circled)? The number of dots equals the number of web pages you have open, with the white dot highlighting the current page. Flick through and tap a mini-page to expand it full-screen.

- **Close a page**. Tap that useful ⎙ icon again and flick to the mini-page you're ready to close. Tap the ⊗ button in the top-left corner to do so.

Use Safari Security

THE WEB IS FULL of wonders—it's like the collective consciousness and accumulated knowledge of everyone who's ever used it, right there for you to explore. The Web is also full of jerks, criminals, and general-purpose evildoers, so you have to take care to keep your *personal* information safe in this Playground of Information. To see how Safari can help protect you, go to the Touch's Home screen and tap Settings→Safari. Your defenses include these:

- **Private Browsing**. Tap this setting to On, and you can surf incognito because Safari won't store browser history, searches, and other web evidence. The Safari window changes from gray to black during a private session.

- **Accept Cookies**. A cookie is a file that helps a website recognize you. This can be good—you get a personal greeting from sites you revisit, for example—or bad, because some cookies track and report (to paying third parties) the ads you respond to. Here, you can choose to have Safari take a cookie Never, Always, or only from sites you actually visit.

- **Fraud Warning**. Some websites aren't what they appear to be; their main purpose is *phishing*—using a masquerade to get you to enter personal information, like bank account and Social Security numbers. Make sure this setting is on so Safari can warn you when a site stinks like bad phish.

- **JavaScript**. Developers use this coding tool to run little programs within web pages. Many are innocent, and most people leave JavaScript turned on, but some are not, and JavaScript can also slow down page loads a bit. Turn it off or on here.

- **Block Pop-ups**. Once a web surfer's lament, these unwanted extra windows (usually filled with ads) have largely been shattered by pop-up blocking controls in most browsers. Still, you may *need* a pop-up window here and there to order concert tickets or to fill in web forms. You can block or unblock pop-ups here, but it's a universal setting for all sites.

- **Clear History**. Tap this button to erase your Safari history (page 245).

- **Clear Cookies and Data**. This info cache is where your Touch stores cookies, downloaded graphics, and other web-page parts to speed your surfing. You can jettison these files by tapping the Clear button here.

- **Advanced**. Tap Website Data to see and delete info that websites store on your 'Pod, or to turn on Debug Console to track programming errors.

Set Up an iCloud Account

BACK BEFORE ICLOUD FLOATED into view, if your iPod Touch got broken or lost—and you hadn't backed up its files to your desktop computer—you were out of luck.

But Apple's free iCloud service backs up all your stuff, including music, apps, personal info, and more, to a great big server in the sky. Providing, that is, that you have iCloud turned on and actually set to back up your data. You also need iOS 5 installed on your iPod and any other iOS devices you want to keep synced up with each other. If you didn't create an iCloud account when you first set up your iPod (page 14), here's what to do:

❶ Go to the Home screen and tap Settings→iCloud.

❷ Create an iCloud account. Tap the Account button and fill in your Apple ID (page 160) and other requested info. Along with an iCloud account, you get a free email account on Apple's me.com servers to add to your address collection.

❸ Now it's time to tell iCloud what you want it to back up and sync. The first batch of apps in the list are iOS 5's personal information and organizer programs: Mail, Contacts, Calendars, Reminders, Bookmarks, and Notes. Tap the button to On for each one you want iCloud to sync for you. You also get online versions of the Mail, Contacts, and Calendars apps that you can tap into, read, and edit using any web browser (see page 256).

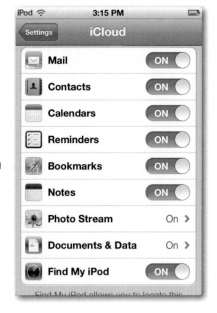

❹ Once you have these files secure, it's time to get your photo stream flowing. If you want iCloud to automatically transfer photos you take with your Touch to your computer, Apple TV, and other iOS devices (like your iPhone or iPad), tap Photo Stream settings to On. Page 212 has more on using Photo Stream.

❺ Thanks to the iWork apps for iPhone, iPod Touch, and the iPad, you can edit and review documents, spreadsheets, and presentations on your various iOS 5 devices, and iCloud can keep those files in sync across your gadgets—and backed up to the Web as well. To make sure that happens, go to the iCloud settings page, tap Documents & Data, and then tap the On button. Flipping this setting to On also syncs up your Safari Reading List (page 251) between your iOS 5 gadgets and any computers running Safari.

⑥ Another benefit of iCloud is its Find My iPod feature. You can use it to track down a missing Touch, whether it's just lost in the house somewhere, back at the office, or hijacked by an evildoer. Tap the On button here if you want to Find Your iPod. Later, when you need to locate the errant 'Pod, go to *www. icloud.com/find* and log into your account. If your iPod is still on a WiFi network somewhere, you see it on a map—with commands to send a sound alert or message to display on its screen, like "Yo, this is my lost iPod" along with your contact info. To protect personal data, you can also lock the screen or erase the iPod's contents from afar.

⑦ Although your iTunes Store purchases and your Photo Stream pictures don't count against iCloud's free 5 gigabytes of storage, you may need more room if you have a lot of documents and other data to back up. If you suspect things are getting tight, tap the Storage & Backup button on the iCloud settings screen to see how much space your stuff currently takes up. If you don't want to delete anything, tap the Buy More Storage button. On the next screen, you can tap to sign up for an additional 10 GB ($20 a year), 20 GB ($40 a year), or 50 GB ($100 a year) of space. All of this is on top of your free 5 GB. The extra gigs get billed to your iTunes Store account.

⑧ Finally, if you want to back up your iPod's system settings, app settings, and Camera Roll photos, pop down to the "Back Up to iCloud" line on the Settings screen and tap it to On. iCloud now copies your Touch's house-keeping settings and pics daily via your WiFi connection. You can trigger a backup session right away by tapping Back Up Now. (Remember, all your other data—iTunes purchases, personal info, and documents—are taken care of by other parts of the iCloud service.)

iCloud does its deep-in-the-background backup thing when you have your iPod connected to a WiFi network, plugged in to a power source, and locked. (You can perform a similar backup through iTunes on your computer, as page 278 describes.) When setting up a new Touch (or one you restored to its factory set-tings), you get the option to restore all that backed up data.

If you ever need to adjust your backup settings, add more online storage, or even delete your account, just return to Home→iCloud→Settings.

Use iCloud on Your Computer

SOME PEOPLE WILL NEVER sync their iPod Touches to a computer, and for them, the iCloud setup process concluded on the previous page. But what if you want to bring the power of the cloud down to earth, namely your desktop or laptop computer? When you loop your computer into iCloud, it can download content from your account, like permanent copies of pics from your Photo Stream.

You can also update the iPod's address book and calendar by typing new information into your computer's programs, like Microsoft Outlook or iCal. Once you make a change on the computer, iCloud pushes it out to your iPod Touch and other iCloud-connected devices—as long as you have everything set up on your computer as well as on your iPod.

If you haven't signed up for an iCloud account, stop off at *www.icloud.com* and click Sign Up. If you have an Apple ID, enter your user name and password to log in.

Windows users must download a setup program for iCloud's control panel from the site first. Once you install the Apple iCloud software on your computer, go to Start→Control Panel→Network and Internet→iCloud and log in with your user name and password.

In the window that pops up (shown above), turn on the checkboxes for the stuff you want to sync from your computer, including mail, contacts, calendars, and bookmarks. Windows users need Microsoft Outlook 2007 or later to sync their mail, contacts, and calendars over iCloud. You can also turn on Photo Stream here; page 212 has more on that.

Mac OS X 10.7 (Lion) users just need to visit →System Preferences→iCloud to get to the options for syncing Mail accounts, Mac OS X Address Book contacts, iCal calendars, and Safari bookmarks.

Once you have iCloud configured on both your iPod (described on the previous two pages) and your computer, you're syncing. Want to know where else you can see your iCloud info in a pinch if your computer or iPod isn't within reach? The Web, of course, as the next page explains.

Use iCloud on the Web

YOU CAN GET TO your iCloud mail, calendars, contacts, and more through just about any Internet-connected computer. Being able to get to your iCloud data through the Web is great for those times when you don't have access to it through your home computer or iPod Touch—like when you're on your office PC, or on the road without electronics.

To see your iCloud mail, for example, just grab a web browser and go to *www. icloud.com*. Type in your iCloud user name and password to see your In box on the Web. (If you had an old MobileMe or .Mac account, you can see your messages from those, too, providing you converted your old account to an iCloud account at Apple's persistent prompting.)

As shown below, the main dashboard on the iCloud site also offers clickable icons for your contacts and calendars—both of which you can update here and have those changes show up on your Touch and computer back home. And although it's called Find My iPhone on the site, click the radar-screen icon to log in and locate the whereabouts of a missing Touch (see page 255).

Do you use Apple's iWork suite of productivity programs on, say, both on your iPad and iPod Touch to keep your documents up to date? Click the iWork icon here to see (and transfer) copies of those files from your online iWork file cabinet, where the latest version is always on file. It's also probably one of the most tidy file cabinets you'll see online.

Print From Your iPod Touch

YOU PRETTY MUCH HAVE two ways to wirelessly print messages, photos, and other documents from your Touch: apps or AirPrint.

The App Store (page 166) offers dozens of utility programs that let you print files from your Touch. Some may be more elegant than others, but odds are you can find something for less than $10. Just jump to the store, hit the search box, and type in *print* or *printing* to see your options.

The other way to print uses Apple's AirPrint technology. This approach can be more expensive, but ultimately easier to use, because the technology is built into your Touch—you're not at the mercy of a third-party app.

The AirPrint option works with only about 30 printer models—most of them made by HP, with a few Canon Pixma printers playing along. So if you don't already have an AirPrint printer in the house, you have to buy one, which can be expensive (at least $90). To see a list of AirPrint-compatible HP printer models, point your browser to *http://support.apple.com/kb/ht4356*.

AirPrint will hopefully become more widespread soon, but if you do have a compatible printer, here's how it works:

❶ If you just bought your AirPrint-ready printer, follow the printer's setup instructions for adding it to your wireless network. (You may have to upgrade certain models, like the HP Photosmart D110a, with a firmware update from the manufacturer; check the manufacturer's website for the steps.)

❷ Pick a file on your Touch that you want to print. AirPrint works with Mail, Safari, iBooks, and pictures from Photos. Other apps from the App Store, like iWork and the note-organizing Evernote app, also offer the Print option. With the file, web page, or picture you want to print open onscreen, tap ✉ and choose Print. In the Mail app, open the message you want to print and tap ↰ to get to the Print command.

❸ Tap Select Printer. The iPod searches the network for all the AirPrint machines it can locate and presents a list of the ones it finds. Tap the name of your printer to select it.

❹ With your printer now selected, tap the Printer Options arrow to go back to the main Print box. Tap Range to choose the pages you want to print. By default, you get All Pages, but if it's a long web page or file, you can change that. Tap the - and + buttons to decrease or increase the number of copies you print.

❺ Tap the Print button and listen for the sound of your printer whirring into action.

After you configure AirPrint the first time, the iPod remembers your printer and offers it as the default choice the next time you need to make paper.

Managing Print Jobs

Like computers 10 times its size, the iPod Touch shows you how many print jobs you have lined up in the Print Center area of its system software. This can be helpful if, say, you sent a few slow-printing photos to the printer upstairs and want to go pick them all up at once.

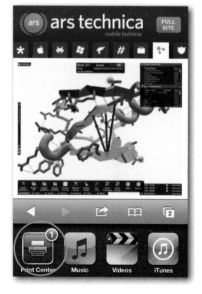

Checking the Print Center also gives you the chance to cancel a print job if you change your mind—or realize you just told the iPod to print 12 copies instead of two.

To see what jobs you have in the print queue, double-click the Home button and swipe through the app panel until you see the Print Center icon (circled). Tap it to see a summary of your print job (or jobs). Tap the Cancel Printing button to stop a job and save that ink and paper for another time.

TIP Have no plans to get an AirPrint-friendly printer and don't want to deal with apps? The Web has its own collection of creative workarounds. One is Netputing's AirPrint Activator for Mac OS X (*netputing.com/airprintactivator*), which lets iOS devices see and use a shared printer on a network; you can find a Windows version with a quick Web search. These shareware solutions often require some trust and technical fiddling, but they usually get the job done just fine.

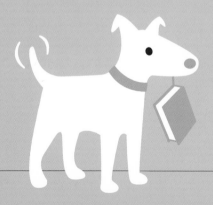

iPod and iTunes Out Loud

NOW THAT YOU'VE GOTTEN YOUR IPOD FULLY LOADED WITH COOL entertainment, you probably want to listen to your playlists, albums, audio books, and podcasts on a booming stereo setup wherever you happen to be—your car, living room, bathroom, wherever. If you can load it onto your iPod, you can channel it through most any sound system—and at a pretty reasonable cost, too. This chapter explains the simple procedures you follow to play your 'Pod through the woofers and tweeters in your life.

Got a second-generation Apple TV, an iPod Touch running iOS 5, and a zippy WiFi network? If so, you can stream video, photo slideshows, and more between iPod and big-screen TV without getting tangled up in cables and jacks. (If you have a different iPod, no Apple TV, or no WiFi network, flip back to page 196 to learn how to play video on your TV.)

One note of caution before you plunk down your hard-earned cash on a fancy audio gizmo: Apple has made a lot of iPod models over the years, and not every add-on or accessory works with all iPods. To be safe (especially if you recently bought your 'Pod), check the product's fine print to make sure your add-on and iPod will be happy together.

Take Your iPod on the Road

SINCE THE GLORIOUS DAYS of crackly AM radio, music and driving have gone hand in hand. These days, a stereo system with an AM/FM radio and a CD player is the bare minimum for most cars, and late-model vehicles now cruise around with all sorts of high-end equipment, from multi-disc CD players to satellite radio. (Whether the music played on them has improved over the years is subject to debate.)

If having your playlists with you is your idea of paradise by the dashboard light, there are several ways to integrate your 'Pod with your car's stereo. Whatever method you choose, you have to consider two factors:

- **How to connect your iPod to your existing audio system**. You have your pick of a wired or wireless connection.

- **How to power your iPod**. Of course, your iPod can run fine on its battery for everyday trips, but if you're retracing historic Route 66, you probably want to invest in an adapter that can power your 'Pod from your car's electrical system.

You can choose from four main ways to get your iPod's sounds piping through your car speakers, some of them more satisfying (and expensive) than others. Here are the typical options (you can get most of the gear discussed here from sites listed at the end of this chapter):

❶ **Via an FM transmitter**. These inexpensive devices let you borrow an empty FM frequency from your car's radio and play the iPod's music over the airwaves—with no cables snaking across the dashboard (though some transmitters include iPod charger cords for the car's 12-volt port). Setup is easy: Scan your FM dial for an unused channel, connect the transmitter to your iPod, and push Play.

Advantages: Convenience; everybody's got an FM radio.
Disadvantages: Long road-trippers constantly have to search for new frequencies. It may be tough for urban dwellers to find available signals.
Audio quality: Fair.

If it involves getting the iPod to play in the car, odds are Griffin Technology has a product for it. From the left: $50 iTrip FM Transmitter, the $15 DirectDeck wired cassette adapter, and the $10 auxiliary audio cable. You can find all these items (and more iPod-related goodies) at www.griffintechnology.com.

Using a wired adapter. Another option—if your car still has a cassette player—is one of those cassette-shaped gadgets that slip into your tape deck and offer a 3.5 mm miniplug for the iPod's headphones port. Griffin Technology, Belkin, and Monster all make 'em.

Advantages: Simplicity; insert cassette and you're good to go.
Disadvantages: Not everyone has a cassette deck anymore.
Audio quality: Fair.

Using the auxiliary jack. If your car's stereo console has a 3.5 mm jack as an auxiliary input, you can use a simple male-to-male miniplug audio cable to connect your iPod to the stereo. Radio Shack, Griffin Technology, and Monster Cable can help you out for less than $10.

Advantages: High-quality sound.
Disadvantages: You still have to run your iPod using its controls.
Audio quality: Great.

Using a special iPod aftermarket kit or custom installation. If you *really* want fine sound and have the budget for it, several companies offer kits that add an iPod-friendly cable to your existing in-dash stereo system. Apple lists your options by car manufacturer at *www.apple.com/ipod/car-integration*. Equipment-wise, Alpine stereo fans may be able to use the $30 iPod Interface KCE-422i cable (*www.alpine-usa.com*), while Pioneer Electronics owners can find compatible iPod cables, adapter boxes, and accessories at *www.pioneerelectronics.com*.

Advantages: Great sound, integrates controls into existing audio system.
Disadvantages: None, aside from price.
Audio quality: Great.

Making sure your new car has an iPod jack. Many automakers now integrate iPod playback capability in their cars. If you're in the market for new wheels anyway, why not ask about iPod compatibility?

Advantages: Great sound, integrates controls into existing audio system.
Disadvantages: None, though may add to cost of car.
Audio quality: Great.

You can connect your iPod to several Pioneer car stereo systems with the Pioneer CD-IB100ii iPod Interface Adapter. The dashboard display even shows the track titles and lets you shuffle songs. Check it out at www.pioneerelectronics.com.

Connect Your iPod to a Home Entertainment System

CD PLAYERS THAT CAN play discs full of MP3 files cost less than $100. But if you have an iPod, you already have a state-of-the-art MP3 player that can connect to your existing stereo for under $20—or spend a little more and get the full iPod AV Club experience.

Connecting with an Audio Cable

To link your iPod to your stereo, you need the right kind of cable and a set of input jacks on the back of your receiver. Most audio systems come with at least one extra set of inputs (after accounting for the CD player, cassette deck, and other common components), so look for an empty jack labeled "AUX."

The cable you need is a Y-shaped cord with a 3.5 mm (1/8-inch) male stereo miniplug on one end and two bigger male RCA plugs on the other end. The stereo miniplug is the standard jack for headphones, microphones, and some speakers; RCA plugs are the standard red-and-white audio connectors for stereo components.

Plug the miniplug into the iPod's headphone jack and the RCA plugs into the left and right speaker jacks on the back of your stereo. Most online iPod superstores, like XtremeMac, Griffin Technology, DLO, and Belkin, sell their own versions of the Y-shaped cable. (See the list of sites that sell helpful iPod stuff at the end of this chapter.)

Connecting with an iPod Dock

Investing in an iPod dock is another way to link your player to your permanent home-entertainment system. A typical dock provides a notch for your iPod to sit upright, with cable jacks on the back for tethering the dock to your stereo or receiver. As a bonus, you usually get a remote to control the iPod from across the room. Apple sells its $50 iPod docks and $50 AV cables at *www.apple.com/ipodstore*. You can find even fancier gear from other manufacturers. For example, Sony Electronics (*www.sonystyle.com*) sells docks that pipe audio through integrated hi-fi systems and clock radios.

iPod Speaker Systems

YOU CAN HOOK UP your iPod to a home audio system to share your sounds, but sometimes it's more convenient to get the iPod a set of speakers to call its own. Some speakers connect to the iPod's headphone jack with a stereo mini-plug cable, while others connect via an iPod dock.

The price and quality of iPod speakers can range from $15 cheap plastic things sold at the grocery store to $300 systems from high-end audio companies like Bose, Altec Lansing, Sony, Tivoli, and others. Wireless speaker systems range in price from about $200 to $700. Here are a few to sample:

- **Altec Lansing iMT630 Sport**. Available in red or teal, the iMT630 is one of the more colorful members of the inMotion family of iPod speakers. The unit comes with its own remote control and works with all dock-connecting iPods—and with the iPhone as well. You can find the $150 inMotion speakers (along with other models) at *www.alteclansing.com*.

- **Bose Sound Dock**. Bose is known for superior acoustics in its speakers and headphones, and the Sound Dock line for iPod continues that tradition with a large, imposing speaker that looms behind its integrated iPod cradle. Sound Dock prices range from $300 to $600; you can see all the models at *www.bose.com*.

- **Etón Soulra**. This portable speaker system looks like a no-nonsense black boombox, but it's secretly "green" thanks to a flip-up solar panel that lets you draw power from the sun. It can also charge itself the traditional way with its AC adapter. You can pick up the Soulra for around $200 at online stores like Amazon, and find technical details at *www.etoncorp.com*.

- **Eos Wireless**. For $300, you get an iPod base station with its own set of speakers, plus an extra wireless speaker. To spread the sound around, you can scatter up to four additional wireless speakers—in either black or white to match your decor—in other rooms for about $150 each, all on the system's own wireless network (*www.eoswireless.com*).

Stream Music and Video from iTunes

THERE ARE A COUPLE of ways to stream entertainment from your 'Pod to the portals around your house. AirPort Express (Apple's portable wireless base station) handles music, while Apple TV lets you stream sounds, video, and photos.

Make AirPort Express Sing

What do you get when you mix an existing home WiFi network with iTunes and AirPort Express? Music anywhere you want it, thanks to the AirPlay feature. Just plug in one of these white boxes anywhere in the house you've got a stereo or powered speakers. If you don't have an AirPort Express, you can buy one for $99 at *http://store.apple.com* and other places. Here's how to get started:

❶ **Plug the AirPort Express into an electrical outlet near your stereo (or near a pair of powered speakers)**. Repeat this step in any other room where you want to beam music.

❷ **Connect your stereo system or powered speakers to the AirPort Express**. After you plug the AirPort Express into the wall, buy a Y-shaped cable (the one with the two RCA plugs on one end and the miniplug on the other, mentioned on page 264) to connect the AirPort Express to your stereo system or to a pair of powered speakers. If your system has a digital TOSLINK port, you can use a digital fiber-optic cable to connect the two for better sound. (Speakers that use a USB connection don't work here.)

❸ **Install the AirPort Utility software from the CD in the box**. The Utility program (Start→All Programs→AirPort [Applications→Utilities→AirPort]) walks you through the setup process, automatically picking up your WiFi settings and prompting you to name the AirPort Express. Naming it something like "Living Room Stereo" is helpful when it comes to using iTunes, as you'll see in the next step.

❹ **Open iTunes and look for a pop-up menu that lists your AirPort Express**. Once you launch iTunes with the Express running, you'll see a pop-up menu at the bottom-right of the iTunes window

(circled). If you installed multiple Expresses, each one is listed. (If you don't see the pop-up menu icon, choose Edit [iTunes]→Preferences→Devices and make sure you have "Look for remote speakers with AirPlay" selected.)

❺ **Press Play**. With everything connected and turned on, select the AirPort Express base station in the iTunes pop-up menu and click the Play button on your iPod to blast your playlists across your home. To play music through more than one set of speakers, choose Multiple Speakers and then put a checkmark next to the name of each base station you want to use.

View Video and Photos with Apple TV

In addition to streaming music through connected speakers, you can stream iTunes music, video, and photos over a wireless network to an Apple TV. On the latest Apple TV (the little black one released in September 2010), you stream using iTunes' Home Sharing feature (page 110). If you haven't turned it on, choose Advanced→Turn On Home Sharing and type in your iTunes account name and password so Apple TV can see your library and pull in the stream to your TV.

You can also stream videos, photo slideshows, and music directly from your iPod Touch to your television with the AirPlay technology built into it and the Apple TV. On your iPod, call up the file you want to play, tap the AirPlay icon (⟎), and then tap the name of the screen you want to watch on. It may take a minute or two to buffer up, but then your video or

slideshow magically appears on the big TV. When you're done watching, tap the AirPlay icon and choose iPod Touch to return the picture to the small screen.

Using the iPod Touch as a Remote

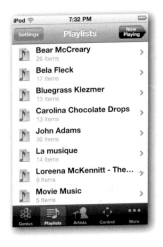

If you have a Touch and you don't want to be tied to your computer to manage your media, the iTunes App Store offers a cool program called Remote. It detects your WiFi network so you can control your media from anywhere in the house. Even better, it's free.

Install the Remote app from the iTunes Store (Chapter 7) and connect your 'Pod to iTunes. Tap the Remote icon and, on the next screen, tap Add Library. An icon for Remote appears in iTunes' Devices list. Click it and type in the four-digit code displayed on your Touch. Click OK, and your iTunes library and playlists appear on the Touch. You can now play, pause, skip, and jump through your music library to your heart's content. You can also control an Apple TV with it.

Find a Power Source for Your iPod

YOUR CAR'S CIGARETTE LIGHTER can serve a far healthier role than its original purpose: It can breathe life into an iPod battery. You won't ever again have to worry about the iPod conking out in the middle of your favorite song when you're on the road. Several companies make travel-worthy chargers, including four well-known iPod accessory shops:

- **PowerDuo**. This $40 set of chargers from Griffin Technology powers 'Pods on the road and at home. It includes the PowerJolt 12-volt car charger for mobile juicing and the PowerBlock AC charger (with a folding set of prongs) for wall outlets. You just need to supply the USB cable to go from the charger to your iPod. The set works with most modern dock-connecting iPods, including the Touch, Nano, and Classic; you can find it at *www.griffintechnology.com*.

- **XtremeMac InCharge Home USB**. If you don't want to drag around a charger for each device in your iOS arsenal, this $30 flat, black 10-watt charger powers up iPods and has the electrical oomph to handle iPhone and iPad charging as well. XtremeMac also sells the $80 InCharge Home BT model that does two jobs: It charges your iPod over a USB connection and also works as a wireless audio receiver to pump out tunes to the stereo or speakers over a Bluetooth connection. The company sells a $30 USB syncing and charging dock, too; all models are at *www.xtrememac.com*.

- **Belkin Mini Surge Protector**. Ever been in an airport or hotel room with minimal electrical outlets and no room to plug in your laptop, phone charger, and most importantly, iPod? Stick the travel-sized Belkin Mini Surge Protector into the wall and make three outlets out of one. It also has two powered USB ports just waiting for you to plug in your iPod's USB cable for charging alongside your various power-hungry devices. It sells for $25 in the iPod accessories area at *www.belkin.com*.

Where to Find Cool iPod Stuff

SINCE THE IPOD'S ARRIVAL in 2001, its accessories market has been growing by leaps and bounds. There are several online iPod superstores with a huge selection of merchandise, from stylish cases to cleaning kits to travel speakers. If you want to see what's out there without having to leave your desk, the bigger 'Pod-focused web shops include these:

- **The Apple Store** (*www.apple.com/ipodstore*). Apple has pages and pages of products for all its iPod offspring. You can shop the store based on the model of iPod you have—which should help ease any compatibility worries.

- **The iStore** (*www.theistore.com*). Jam-packed with a collection of cases, docks, car chargers, earphones, speakers, and more for iPods, this site also sells quite a bit of iPad and iPhone gear for all your iNeeds. The iStore features products from several manufacturers, so along with Apple's iPod store, it's a good place to see a wide selection of goods.

- **Belkin** (*www.belkin.com*). With fashionable cases, chargers, and a spider-like attachment called the Rockstar that lets you attach five sets of head-phones to one iPod, Belkin sells a variety of fun—and functional—iPod extras. There's even a case that doubles as a stand so you can watch your iPod Touch video comfortably on a table or desktop.

- **XtremeMac** (*www.xtrememac.com*). XtremeMac has a good amount of iPod merchandise. It's notable for its colorful cases for active iPod lovers, creative charging solutions, and portable travel speakers so you can blast your music wherever you happen to be.

- **Griffin Technology** (*www.griffintechnology.com*). With its iTrip line of FM transmitters and its DirectDeck, Griffin's forte is products that get your iPod thumping through car and home stereo speakers. The company also sells a handful of cases and items like iFM, which is designed to add FM broadcast radio to the iPod Touch.

Other companies like Kensington (*www.kensington.com*) and Monster Cable (*www.monstercable.com*) have healthy iPod accessory sections on their sites, especially if you're looking for cables, docks, FM transmitters, and similar after-market products.

Computer and electronics stores like Fry's and Best Buy usually have a section devoted to iPod cases and speakers. And, in a sign of just how mainstream iPods have become, even all-purpose suburban bazaars like Kmart and Target include a rack or two of iPod stuff for sale.

CHAPTER 13

What to Do When Your iPod Isn't Working Right

IT'S BOUND TO HAPPEN SOMETIME: YOUR IPOD LOCKS UP, FREAKS out, or just isn't its usual cheerful self. Luckily, you can solve many iPod problems with a button-tap here or a battery charge there. Then your portable 'Pod is back to normal.

But your iPod is a mini-computer in its own right, and getting it back in working order might involve more than a button press or two—and maybe even the attention of a technical expert. This chapter explains what to do if your iPod starts acting weird—and where to go if you can't fix it yourself.

But iPod triage isn't all about magnifying glasses and tiny screwdrivers. Yes, the iPod is a nice piece of hardware, but where there's hardware, there's software. In this chapter, you'll also learn how to keep your iPod up to date with the latest software from Apple so you have the latest bug fixes and new features right in your pocket.

The Five "Rs" of iPod Repair

YOU NEVER KNOW WHEN disaster (or annoyance) will strike, but when you encounter trouble with a Nano, Shuffle, or Classic, Apple suggests its easy-to-remember "Five Rs" approach to troubleshooting:

- **Reset** your iPod, as explained on the next page.

- **Retry** your iPod connection by plugging it into a different USB port on your computer.

- **Restart** your computer and check for iPod software updates (page 276).

- **Reinstall** your iPod and iTunes software at *www.apple.com/ itunes*.

- **Restore** your iPod's software (also explained later in this chapter).

If you have an iPod Touch, try this set of "Rs:"

- **Recharge**. Make sure your Touch has gas in its battery tank.

- **Restart**. Press the Sleep/Wake button until the red Off/On slider appears. Slide the Touch off, and then press Sleep/Wake to turn it on again. If that doesn't do much, try resetting the Touch as described on the next page.

- **Remove**. Synced content may be sinking your Touch. Connect your iPod to iTunes, remove any recently added stuff (since they may have triggered the problem), and resync.

- **Reset Settings**. Tap Settings→General→Reset→Reset All Settings. The option to erase all your content and settings may solve the problem, but it's a drastic move. (If you're just having trouble connecting to the Internet, try the Reset Network Settings button first.)

- **Restore**. Connect your Touch to iTunes and click Restore to reformat it.

The next few pages cover these steps and more, so you can avoid that sixth, painful "R": *Ramming* your head into the wall when your iPod won't work.

NOTE No matter which iPod model you have, when you're having trouble and don't know where to start to fix a problem, take a browser ride to Apple's iPod help guides (pictured above) at *www.apple. com/support/ipod*.

Reset Your iPod

IF YOUR IPOD SEEMS frozen, confused, or otherwise unresponsive, you can *reset* it without losing your music and data files. You might not be able to save some settings, like bookmarks in long audiobooks or unsynced playlists, but you can get things running again with this quick, easy fix—after you check to make sure the issue isn't simply an out-of-juice battery.

Here's the reset sequence for all four 2011 iPod models:

- **iPod Touch**. If restarting the Touch (see the previous page) does nothing for you, go for the Reset. Simultaneously hold down the Sleep/Wake and Home buttons. Let go when you see the shimmering Apple logo.

- **iPod Nano**. Press the Volume Down and the Sleep/Wake buttons (the two outer ones on the Nano's edge) for about 6 seconds, and let go when you see the Apple logo pop up onscreen.

- **iPod Shuffle**. The tiniest iPod may also need a good, firm reset from time to time, but like the Shuffle itself, resetting it is a bit simpler than wrestling with the other iPods: Turn the On/Off switch to the Off position, wait 10 seconds or so, and then flip it back to the On position.

- **iPod Classic**. Slide the Hold switch on and off. Press and hold down the Menu and center Select buttons simultaneously until you see the Apple logo appear on the screen. This could take up to 10 seconds, and you may have to do it twice, but keep at it until you see the logo.

If the technology gods are smiling at you, your iPod will go through its start-up sequence and return you to the main menu.

Download and Reinstall iTunes and iTunes Updates

IF ITUNES IS ACTING up, you may need to download and install a fresh version of the program. The latest version is always waiting at *www.apple.com/itunes/download*. Your iTunes program itself may alert you to a new version—or you can make sure it does so in the future:

- If you installed iTunes on a Windows PC and installed the Apple Software Update utility at the same time, iTunes displays an alert box when an update is ready; it also offers to install the new version for you. If you skipped installing the utility, choose Edit→Preferences→General and turn on "Check for updates automatically." If you prefer to check manually, choose Help→Check for Updates. In either case, your iPod prompts you to snag any available updates.

- The Mac's Software Update program is designed to alert you, via a pop-up dialog box, about new iTunes updates. If you turned Software Update off (in System Preferences), you can run it manually by choosing →Software Update.

As with any update, once you download the software, click the Install button or double-click the installer file's icon and follow along as the program takes you through the upgrade excitement. If the iTunes version you're installing is newer than the one you've got, you get Upgrade as a button option when you run the installer—and an upgrade usually takes less time than a full reinstallation.

If you're installing the same version of the program, the iTunes installer may politely ask if you want to either *Repair* or even *Remove* the software. Choosing Repair can often fix damaged files or data that iTunes needs to run properly. It can also be a quicker fix than fully removing and reinstalling the program.

Use the Diagnostics Tools in iTunes for Windows

WITH DIFFERENT WINDOWS PC hardware manufacturers out there and multiple versions of Windows in the mix, the PC side of the iTunes/iPod fence can be a little unpredictable. To help sort things out, iTunes for Windows includes a feature called Diagnostics, which helps trouble-shoot four categories of woes. These are your choices:

- **Network Connectivity**. These tests check your computer's Internet connection and its ability to access the iTunes Store.

- **DVD/CD Drive**. If you're having trouble importing music to iTunes from a CD—or if you can't burn your own discs—these tests inspect your PC's disc drive for problems and incompatibilities.

- **Device Connectivity**. These diagnostics don't actually test the iPod's hardware or software; they examine the way your PC connects to your iPod.

- **Device Sync**. These programs actually *do* test the Touch's hardware and software to make sure it can transport the data you're trying to sync.

To run this battery of tests, choose Help→Run Diagnostics, select a category, and then follow the onscreen directions. Each diagnostic program runs tests and then displays a red, yellow, or green light. Click the Help button next to a red or yellow light to get troubleshooting help from Apple's website. (Green means groovy.) Once you finish the tests, you can copy the results to the Clipboard and save them to a text file so you can share them with support techies.

Update the iPod's Software

UPDATING THE IPOD'S INTERNAL software—which Apple does occasionally to fix bugs and add features—is much easier than it used to be, thanks to iTunes. No matter which iPod model you have, iTunes 10 and later handles all software update chores for you.

If you formatted your iPod Nano or Classic for Windows, then update it on a Windows PC; update a Mac-formatted iPod on a Macintosh. You can tell which system you formatted your iPod for by choosing Settings→About. On the Nano, flick down to Version to get to the format info. On the Classic, press the Select button twice.

You can update a Touch from either a Windows PC or Mac. (If you have an iPod set to auto-sync with a particular computer, update it on that computer to avoid erasing your iPod.) In fact, if you have iOS 5 installed on your WiFi-connected Touch, you don't even need a computer. Just tap Home→Settings→General→ Software Update to check for new software. And with iOS 5, the updates are much smaller because you're just getting the new code, not the whole iPod operating system.

To make sure you have the latest version of the iPod software, follow these steps:

❶ Connect your iPod to your computer, and then select it in the Source list.

❷ On the Summary tab, click the Check for Update button in the Version area. If your iPod is up to date, iTunes tells you so.

❸ If iTunes finds new iPod software, you'll be prompted to download it. Click the Downloading icon in the Source pane to monitor your progress (shown below). Sometimes iTunes will have already downloaded the new software. In that case, just click the Update button in iTunes' main window.

❹ Follow the onscreen instructions.

Older iPod models may require the use of an AC adapter to finish the update, but newer iPods mainly just sit there quietly with a progress bar and an Apple logo onscreen. Once all that goes away, your iPod screen returns to normal and iTunes displays a message letting you know the update is complete.

If you're updating your iPod Shuffle, play close attention to the progress bar on the iTunes screen and follow any instructions given. Since the Shuffle has no screen, iTunes is the place to monitor your update. You'll know when iTunes finishes because it returns the Shuffle's icon to the Source list.

NOTE As mentioned earlier in this chapter, the iPod support section on Apple's website (*www.apple.com/support/ipod*) has grown tremendously since Apple introduced the first iPod in 2001. It includes knowledge-based articles and user forums for troubleshooting. But if you need to dig deeper or want to attempt your own hardware repairs, check out the iPod forums and repair guides at the do-it-yourself site *www.ifixit.com/Browse/iPod*. If it's an out-of-warranty hardware problem that's too daunting for your taste, try a specialized iPod repair shop like *www.iresq.com* or *www.techrestore.com/ipod*. And when it does come time to upgrade or replace your 'Pod, you can learn about Apple's recycling policy at *www.apple.com/recycling*.

Start Over: Restoring Your iPod's Software

JUST LIKE THE OPERATING system that runs your computer, your iPod has its own system software to control everything it does. *Restoring* the iPod software isn't the same thing as updating it. Restoring is a much more drastic procedure, like reformatting the hard drive on your computer. For one thing, restoring the software *erases everything on your iPod* (unless you're restoring your Touch from a previous backup; see the note below.)

So restore with caution, and do so only after you try all the other troubleshooting measures in this chapter. If you decide to take the plunge, first make sure you have the most recent version of iTunes (flip back a page for information on that), and then proceed as follows:

❶ Start iTunes, and connect your iPod to your computer with its cable. (You can't wirelessly restore your Touch, so go find that USB cable.)

❷ When your iPod appears in the iTunes Source list, click its icon to see the Summary information (in the main area of the iTunes window).

❸ In the Summary area, click the Restore button.

NOTE As with any computer, it's a great idea to back up your data regularly, and the Touch is no exception. In fact, it's such a good idea that iTunes does it automatically as you sync your Touch. When disaster strikes and your Touch is a zombie—or worse, stolen—you can restore your contacts, calendars, notes, and settings without having to start from scratch. Just connect the Touch (old or new replacement) and right-click (Control-click) on its icon. Choose "Restore from Backup" and click Restore in the box that pops up. You can also restore the Touch from an iCloud backup when prompted during the iPod setup.

④ If you have an iPod Touch, iTunes gives you the chance to back up your settings—like your contacts and calendar syncing preferences and other personal data. This means much less work getting your Touch all re-personalized if you have to reinstall its software. If you want to wipe every trace of your existence from the Touch, then skip the backup.

⑤ Because restoring erases everything on your iPod, you get a warning message. If you're sure you want to continue, click Restore again. If you use a Mac, enter an administrator password; a progress bar appears on your iPod's screen.

⑥ Leave the iPod connected to your computer to complete the restoration. You may also see an Apple logo appear onscreen.

After iTunes restores your iPod, its Setup Assistant window appears, asking you to name your iPod and choose your syncing preferences—just like when you connected your iPod for the first time. In fact, if you have everything that was originally on your iPod in your iTunes library, let iTunes autosync it all back to where it was before you started the restore session. You can also add back your songs, photos, apps, and videos manually and see if this little procedure has fixed the iPod's ailment.

TIP If you manually manage your music and you restore your iPod's software, you'll lose any songs not stored in your iTunes library (if you copied a song from a friend's computer to your iPod, for example, but didn't sync the 'Pod back to iTunes). If you manually update, you may want to get a program that lets you harvest songs off the iPod (*www.ilounge.com* lists several, and so does Chapter 5) and back up your music to iTunes regularly.

Understanding the iPod's
Battery Messages

REMEMBER HOW YOU WERE taught that certain kinds of batteries (in laptops and camcorders, say) worked better if you occasionally fully drained and then recharged them? Forget it. You want to keep the iPod's lithium-ion battery *always* charged, or else you'll lose your clock, date, and other settings.

The color screens on the Touch, Nano, and Classic display a green battery that virtually runs out of juice as you use the player. When the battery turns red, it's time to recharge, because you have less than 20 percent of your iPod's power left. The screenless Shuffle communicates its battery needs through a small colored light: green for a good charge (between 100 and 50 percent), amber for 25 percent of the charge left, and red for a battery that needs juice pronto.

Some imperiled iPods display a dull gray charging icon and won't turn on. This means the poor thing doesn't even have enough energy left to show its battery-charging icon in color. On other iPod models, you may see a yellow triangle next to a colorless battery graphic and the stern message, "Connect to Power."

Plug your iPod into your computer or an optional AC adapter, and give it about half an hour of power to get back to its regular screen graphic. (When the battery gets this depleted, you may have to charge it up for a while before it even shows up in iTunes.)

NOTE If you leave your iPod plugged into your computer all night and it still barely shows a charge, it's probably because something went to sleep besides you: your computer. An iPod won't charge properly when your machine goes into Sleep, Hibernate, or Standby modes, so adjust your computer's power-saving settings to make sure it doesn't conk out before your iPod gets juiced up. An AC adapter, available at most iPod accessory shops (Chapter 12), lets you skip the whole computer-charging thing.

Apple's Tips for Longer iPod Battery Life

APPLE HAS POSTED VARIOUS recommendations on its website for how to treat an iPod battery to ensure a long life:

- Don't expose your iPod to extreme hot or cold temperatures. (In other words, don't leave it in a hot, parked car, and don't expect it to operate on Mount Everest.)

- Use your iPod regularly (not that you wouldn't). And be sure to charge it at least once a month to keep that battery chemistry peppy.

- Put the iPod to sleep to conserve battery power. (Press the Play/Pause button until the iPod display goes blank, settling into slumber; on the Touch, click the Sleep/Wake button on top.)

- Take the iPod out of any heat-trapping cases before you charge it up.

- On the Classic, use the Hold switch when you're not actively fiddling with the iPod's controls. This keeps it from getting turned on accidentally.

- When you see the Low Battery icon or message, plug your iPod into a computer or an electrical outlet using its AC adapter.

- iPod features like the backlight and the equalizer—or jumping around within your media library—can make the battery drain faster, as can using big, uncompressed song-file formats, like AIFF.

- That wireless chip inside the iPod Touch saps power even if you're not trawling the Web. Save energy by turning it off when you don't need it at Settings→WiFi. Lowering the frequency with which your Touch checks email or has data pushed to it from the Internet can save some energy as well—you can make those adjustments by choosing Settings→Mail, Contacts, Calendars.

- Background Touch apps (page 91) may be draining power. To quit these vampires, double-click the Home button to reveal the apps panel. Press an app's icon until the ⊖ appears, and tap those ⊖ icons to close those apps.

Replace Your iPod's Battery

THE IPOD USES A rechargeable lithium-ion battery. Unlike players that run on Duracells, you can't easily pop out an old battery and replace it when the cell wears out after repeated charge-and-use cycles.

But that doesn't mean you *can't* replace the iPod's battery; it just takes a little time and effort. If your battery is too pooped to power your 'Pod, here are some options:

- You get a full one-year warranty on your iPod battery (two years with the optional AppleCare Protection Plan; see the opposite page). But Apple itself offers an out-of-warranty battery replacement service for $49 to $79, depending on the iPod model, at *www.apple.com/support/ipod/service/battery*.

- Milliamp (*www.ipodjuice.com*), offers do-it-yourself iPod battery replacement kits for most iPod models, with prices starting at around $20.

- PDASmart.com will replace your iPod's ailing battery for $50 (parts and labor included). Learn more at *www.pdasmart.com/ipodpartscenter.htm*. The company can also fix broken screens and hard drives.

- Other World Computing sells high-capacity NewerTech iPod batteries for all models of iPod. The company has do-it-yourself instructional videos on its site, but will also replace the battery if you send in your iPod (*http://eshop.macsales.com/shop/ipod*).

AppleCare—What It Is and Whether You Need It

YOU PROBABLY HAVE AN insurance policy on your house and car, so why not get one for your iPod? That's the logic behind the AppleCare Protection Plan. The price for this peace of mind? For the iPod Classic and Touch, it's $59, and coverage for the Nano and Shuffle is $39.

When you buy a brand-new iPod, you automatically get free telephone support to fix one problem within your first 90 days of iPod ownership, plus a year-long warranty on the hardware. The latter means that if the iPod starts acting up or stops working altogether, Apple will fix it for free or send you a replacement 'Pod.

If you buy the AppleCare Protection Plan (available in many places where you buy iPods or at *www.apple.com/support/products/ipod.html*), you get the following:

- Two full years of free telephone support from the date of your iPod purchase

- Two full years of hardware protection from the date of your iPod purchase

If you need an iPod repair or replacement, you're covered, and the plan covers your iPod's earphones, battery, and cables, too. Paying an extra $39 or $59 for the extended warranty may not appeal to everyone, but if you want a little peace of mind with your new iPod, it's a small price to pay.

Index

Have it your way.